Play-
from the

Play-by-Play from the Minors

Profiles of Baseball Broadcasters from Scranton to Yakima

John Kocsis, Jr.

Foreword by Benjamin Hill

McFarland & Company, Inc., Publishers
Jefferson, North Carolina

LIBRARY OF CONGRESS CATALOGUING-IN-PUBLICATION DATA

Names: Kocsis, John, 1994– author.
Title: Play-by-play from the minors : profiles of baseball broadcasters from Scranton to Yakima / John Kocsis, Jr. ; foreword by Benjamin Hill.
Description: Jefferson, North Carolina : McFarland & Company, Inc., Publishers, 2023 | Includes index.
Identifiers: LCCN 2023036364 | ISBN 9781476691442 (print) ∞
ISBN 9781476649450 (ebook)
Subjects: LCSH: Baseball announcers—United States—Biography. | Sportscasters—United States—Biography. | Minor league baseball— United States.
Classification: LCC GV742.4 .K63 2023 | DDC 070.4/497960922 [B]— dc23/eng/20230819
LC record available at https://lccn.loc.gov/2023036364

BRITISH LIBRARY CATALOGUING DATA ARE AVAILABLE

ISBN (print) 978-1-4766-9144-2
ISBN (ebook) 978-1-4766-4945-0

Front cover images © 2023 Shutterstock

Printed in the United States of America

McFarland & Company, Inc., Publishers
Box 611, Jefferson, North Carolina 28640
www.mcfarlandpub.com

Mom, you've always encouraged creativity
and taught me to reach for the moon.
Twenty years ago you helped me write stories
about our puppy in a notebook.
I hope you enjoy this book bound by a publisher.
Thanks for teaching me to embrace telling stories.

Contents

Acknowledgments

The journey of typing out these pages taught me a lot about our industry. It allowed me the opportunity to talk to a few broadcasters I already knew and to network with a handful who I had never met prior to writing this book. We're currently in one of the biggest transition periods in Minor League Baseball history. After the pandemic struck in 2020 and all the MiLB Leagues were restructured, a lot of people's jobs were changed or even eliminated.

Some of the memories shared in these pages will become the stuff of the past, stories from a time we no longer recognize—one with overnight bus trips or wacky promotions in the days before the pandemic restrained budgets. There's one thing that won't change, though. The broadcasters mentioned throughout this book are going to keep doing their thing and telling stories just like the ones encapsulated here. Support them! Listen to these broadcasters in action over the course of the summer. For Joe Block and Robert Ford, you'll have to look into a package for MLB.TV or listen through TuneIn Radio if you don't live in Pittsburgh or Houston. The vast majority of broadcasters in this book, though, have links through their team's website, where you can listen to them for free regardless of where you are in the country. You can also watch video streams of their broadcasts on MiLB.TV and listen to the yarn that they spin over 100 nights a year.

I think it goes without saying that I couldn't have gathered all the stories within this book and I couldn't have researched many of these moments without the help of the people highlighted throughout, but there are also a lot of unnamed people who helped me finish this project. I had peers sift through and edit the book, friends and family members who listened to a retelling of the stories within before they were etched into a digital document and colleagues who pointed me in the right direction of where to look for many of the older promotions. All the help was paramount to finishing this project. Thank you. There were

Acknowledgments

also many industry professionals in the publishing world and beyond who guided me through the process of finding a publisher and who read through sample chapters to see if the book was fit to print. I couldn't have persevered and honed the pages into what they are now without their assistance. Finally, McFarland helped this book find a home and make its way onto physical paper. As a first-time author, I can't say how much it means to be able to have the opportunity to read my name in print and have it distributed so people can read these stories and confirm some tales they may have heard about their favorite teams across America.

As long as there is professional baseball and fans can stop by to hear the crack of the bat or the pop of the glove, there will be people who describe—maybe *narrate* is the better term—these scenes to those who are listening from afar.

Foreword

by Benjamin Hill

Not that anyone asked, and not that I'm qualified to give it, but here's a piece of advice for aspiring baseball broadcasters: it's a long way to the top if you wanna rock 'n' roll.

This sentiment, lifted from the bagpipe-drenched AC/DC song of the same name, has echoed through my mind over the course of a career spent traveling the Minor League Baseball landscape. In my capacity as a writer for MiLB.com, I've visited 182 ballparks and met untold hundreds of strivers doing their best to make their way to The Show. This includes the players, of course, but also the umpires, groundskeepers, statisticians, front office salespeople, food and beverage directors and, of course, the broadcasters. Always, the broadcasters.

Among those who've set course on this hopeful professional baseball journey—which, when you're on it, often seems like a thankless slog—it is the broadcasters that I have always related to the most. Perhaps this is because of how much they contributed to my own love of baseball. Growing up, I idolized Philadelphia Phillies play-by-play icon Harry Kalas to the extent that I would often tape the post-game highlights show just so I could hear his calls again (and again and again). Because of this totally normal tendency, certain thrilling moments from otherwise forgotten games are burned in my memory forever ("Hayes scores, Thon scores, holding at third.... No! Dykstra runs through the stop sign, he scores!"). Traveling through the minor leagues gives me the chance to meet broadcasters in their natural habitats, honing a seemingly simple but deceptively difficult skill, nine innings at a time. Via talent, hard work and luck, that time-honored yet nebulous combination, they might one day make it to the major leagues. To young fans today, they'll be what Harry Kalas was for me and what your favorite broadcaster was for you. To achieve this is to truly live the dream.

But until that day comes, if it ever comes: the minors. In *Play-by-*

Foreword by Benjamin Hill

Play from the Minors, Columbia Fireflies broadcaster John Kocsis, Jr., offers a revealing glimpse into the lives of 13 individuals (including himself) who make a living on the mic. Some have reached the majors, some are still trying to take it to the next level, some have found contentment right where they are and some have pivoted to other professional opportunities that developed along the way. You'll learn who these broadcasters are, what motivates them, how they approach their craft and the myriad ways in which the industry cliché "other duties as assigned" can rear its unpredictable head. (Want to work in baseball? Get ready to pull tarp.)

There are all sorts of small joys within the profession as well, many of them applicable to my own job: the opportunity to explore America, visiting off-the-beaten-path tourist destinations and locally beloved restaurants along the way. This book is full of such anecdotes. Let them serve as a reminder: While the broadcasters might not know all, they know more than just about anyone else you might cross paths with at a ballpark. The lonely rigors of game prep combined with the incidental knowledge accumulated from evening to evening, bus ride to bus ride, season to season, make them consummate autodidacts. Some of them might even drop such $10 words on the air from time to time, just to see who's paying attention.

The last time I crossed paths with Kocsis, it was inside a cramped rooftop press box at Hagerstown's Municipal Stadium, accessible only via a nausea-inducing spiral staircase. On the way back down I nearly ran into the visiting broadcaster, Greg Giombarrese of the Lakewood BlueClaws, as he prepared to lug his equipment up this long and winding vertical pathway. But that's the minor leagues for you, where broadcaster accommodations aren't exactly a front-of-mind concern. A dispiriting trend in ballpark design is to locate the broadcast booths down the base lines, so that the area directly behind home plate can be utilized as revenue-generating group seats. But still the broadcasters persist, because persist they must, devotedly bringing the game to a devoted but not always particularly sizable audience.

You—yes, you!—can easily be a part of this audience. Via internet radio and MiLB.TV, every evening of the season offers a smorgasbord of game broadcasts to tune into. Listen to those profiled in this book, if you haven't already, or tune into a broadcast featuring an affiliate of your favorite team. You'll soon have a cadre of favorite voices, opening up a new facet of baseball fandom. And if you enjoy a broadcaster's work, reach out and let them know. It can be lonely talking to oneself for

2

three hours a night. They're all on Twitter (now X), and they'll be happy to hear from you.

A final point in this pre-game show, before turning it over to Kocsis and company: While the term "minor league" often has negative connotations in society at large, please know that those currently honing their broadcasting skills in the minors are already some of the best in the country. Just to be in the industry is to be a success, and, given the sacrifices involved, it is to no small extent a labor of love. To listen to these broadcasters work is to feel that love, even if it's subtle, under a layer of road-weary cynicism. After all, competition is fierce and opportunities for advancement are few. It's a long way to the top if you wanna rock 'n' roll.

Benjamin Hill covers the business and culture of Minor League Baseball for MiLB.com, a job he has held since making it up in 2005. He has visited 186 ballparks, highlighting unique characteristics and memorable characters at every stop along the way. Career highlights including curating his own Topps insert set, getting endorsed by Bill Murray and dominating every between-inning contest in which he has ever participated.

Preface

The life of a broadcaster is interesting, to say the least. Nights on the road in different cities across the country, endless hours spent mastering a craft, meeting an eclectic group of people and telling their stories—that's just the start of the job. Pair it with an incredibly unique industry—Minor League Baseball (MiLB)—and one finds a whole new set of responsibilities.

I can assure you that the broadcasters profiled in this book have all worked endless hours. Of course, the hours aren't always spent writing or in a radio booth; a lot of times, broadcasters cut their teeth and get their hands dirty helping around the stadium. Some folks will regale you with tales about painting stairs yellow or power-washing concourses a few nights before Opening Day, and others can recall the legwork behind zany promotional nights (where Minor League Baseball is second to none) such as Redneck Night or Bob Ross Night and even fireworks shows and on-field concerts.

Yes, you'll still hear plenty about traveling and a diverse group of people, but this book isn't about flights on private jets to the Big Apple or Los Angeles. Rather, it's about 10-hour bus rides to towns you've never heard of. It's about trips to Great Falls, Montana, on a bus winding along a two-lane highway, it's about stopping for barbecue on the side of the road at a shop with a tin roof near Jackson, Tennessee, and it's about seeing a young 18-year-old in Myrtle Beach see his dreams come true at Wrigley Field a few years down the line. Regardless of whether you have experienced these feats before or you're an MiLB novice, this book is here to provide you with a fresh perspective on the stories and culture of Minor League Baseball through the voices that have called the games and have experienced all the unique aspects this industry has to offer.

So what's the best thing about this book? It makes it all the more relatable to you, the average fan, a fellow broadcaster or a bookworm looking for a good story. We've all had days at the office that just haven't

5

Preface

gone right, but when has that day involved a 1,500-pound tarp? How about a bus that has broken down in the middle of nowhere? Or a rogue fan who sabotaged an otherwise flawless promotional night?

While this book doesn't contain any government secrets or describe any calamitous tragedies, it will open your mind to one of the largest communities in the United States. A community that welcomed more than 41.5 million fans through its gates in 160 towns across the country in 2019. A community that gives tens of millions of dollars annually in charity, according to Big Brothers Big Sisters of America. In fact, in 2018, MiLB reported that teams contributed $45 million in cash and in-kind donations to various charities around the country.

I'll save you the time of reading about the money and jobs that minor league teams generate for local communities. I've worked with high schoolers and college kids just looking for a summer job so they can go to the movies or bars with their friends. I've also worked with retirees who want a fun and active way to make a few bucks and even people coming straight from their day job to buoy their income with a part-time gig that offers some flexibility. In short, the microcosm that is Minor League Baseball isn't so "minor" or "micro" after all. It's a huge part of small-town America.

My working title for the book was "Through the Eyes of Your Ears." As technology has expanded, we have all seen vastly more visual media available via streams or even television deals. While media deals in Major League Baseball (MLB) greatly changed after the emergence and success of Turner Sports and WGN, many minor league teams broadcast solely on radio or have a video stream with sound that is ripped directly from a radio or an audio stream. What the majority of my colleagues and I have done—some for decades, some for a few years—is describe to the listener exactly what is happening in front of them. While it could be as simple as "driving the 0–1 pitch to the right field wall to plate a run and give the home team a 3–1 lead," what truly makes a broadcast riveting is the extra color added to it.

Whether that means sprinkling in physical attributes of the players, like talking about a burly first baseman trying to muscle a homer, or of the park, like describing puffball clouds moving across an otherwise crystal-clear sky, these professionals have found ways to bring the listener right next to the action. So, in a way, as you're listening to the words coming through your headphones or speakers, you're also mentally drawing a picture of the scene happening right in front of these broadcasters.

6

Preface

Biologically, the eyes and ears are connected. When you glance left to right, your eyes roll in your sockets and your eardrums actually move with them. In the same vein, you need your ears to listen to the words these broadcasters are saying so your mind can paint a picture for your eyes to see. As fans, we trust broadcasters to be our eyes, like when a blindfolded contestant is being led to a mascot during an in-game promotion between innings.

The greatest thing any broadcaster has to offer is their stories, of which this book has plenty. We'll dance from stellar players to long bus rides and even cover a few fun games. The intrigue of this industry can provide a unique look behind the scenes of a baseball game regardless of whether you're a season ticket holder, a casual fan, or someone who has never even seen a baseball diamond. We'll cover plenty of engaging tales throughout these pages that give a new vision of what happens outside the lines of the diamond. Besides, if there's one thing all of us can agree on, there isn't a much better setting for a good story than a ballgame.

Before we dive headfirst into this world, I want to thank all my friends and, quite frankly, family in Minor League Baseball. I've had the pleasure of "living the dream" among some of the greatest individuals imaginable for nearly a decade now, and I certainly wouldn't change any of it. I've learned some great life lessons from a number of people in this industry and I hope that this book can make you crack a smile, offer a laugh or, heck, even help you start a conversation at the next ballgame you attend.

Obviously, this endeavor wouldn't be possible without the many talented broadcasters who generously donated their time and stories. Just remember, the story doesn't end here. Listen to these individuals in action. Most of them call more than 100 baseball games a year, and all of them spin yarns in unique and enjoyable ways. Who knows? Maybe you'll tune in for the next great minor league saga. Let's play ball!

1

John Kocsis, Jr.

Currently with the Columbia Fireflies
Previously with the West Virginia Power
and Hagerstown Suns

I would be remiss if I didn't lead off this book with my own experience in Minor League Baseball. I grew up in Cleveland, Ohio, in the 1990s amid the rebuilding of a powerhouse Cleveland Indians team that would sell out 455 consecutive games at Jacobs Field. The grind-it-out, blue-collar grit of the city certainly rubbed off on me along the way. The passion that "The Land" demonstrated toward its three major sports teams, the Browns, Cavaliers, and Indians (now the Guardians) is something that has always resonated with me.

Jacobs Field was part of one of the most successful urban revitalization projects in the United States in recent memory. The Gateway Project was completed in 1994 and helped rejuvenate a rundown portion of downtown Cleveland. Now that area, just south of Tower City and near Playhouse Square, has a crop of bars and restaurants nearby and is one of the most exciting parts of downtown. Because the city felt a lot of pride in the success of that area, I believe it increased the enthusiasm of the fan base of the Indians, a team that struggled for decades prior to the 1990s.

Growing up in Cleveland and being a fan of the Indians, I listened to Tom Hamilton on the radio while driving around on summer days. One attribute that makes Hamilton an award-winning broadcaster is his passion for the game. Most of his broadcast is slow and deliberate. His orotund tone cuts through the AM buzzing on WTAM 1100, and you can always tell when the ball is headed for the left-field bleachers because you'll hear Hamilton's iconic "A SWING AND A DRIVE ... A-WAY BACK ... GONE!" While Cleveland has had many incredible broadcasters over the years such as Joe Tait, Fred McLeod and former player Herb Score, none are quite as revered as Tom Hamilton. The

Play-by-Play from the Minors

Waterloo, Wisconsin, native's ability to captivate his listeners separates him from any other broadcaster for Tribe fans.

As I grew into a sports consumer, I also began to listen to Bob Uecker, Vin Scully and Bob Costas. Each of these national icons has made a living off their unique style of calling a game. Uecker made his mediocre career as a player famous by seamlessly sliding some self-referential humor into each broadcast. While his jokes are not as abundant as those given to the character he played in the *Major League* movies, one doesn't have to listen long to start chuckling along with him on air. If you need a good example, I highly recommend listening to his Ford C. Frick Award acceptance speech in 2003. As a former player, he certainly can spin a yarn, and he'll have the whole family laughing like he's in the living room or car with you.

John Kocsis, Jr., joined the ranks of Minor League broadcasters in 2018 as an intern with the West Virginia Power. Since then he has led the broadcast efforts for the Hagerstown Suns and most recently the Columbia Fireflies. John has called nearly 500 Minor League baseball games and has had the pleasure of recording tape at a 2019 Washington Nationals game (photograph provided by the author).

Vin Scully is pointed to as one of the greatest, if not *the* greatest, baseball broadcasters of all time, and I would say that his delivery and method of storytelling were second to none. Scully let a broadcast breathe in a way that allowed you to feel the emotion of the moment, from the roar of the crowd to the silence or collective gasp at a setback on the field. If you need a way to visualize what that means, watch a clip of Hank Aaron's record-breaking 715th home run with Scully on the mic. After that, listen to Milo Hamilton calling the same moment. Hamilton did a great job, but what Scully did is why he is considered one of the best ever.

1. John Kocsis, Jr.

Finally, while Bob Costas made his mark broadcasting several sports on NBC, calling significant football and basketball games, his love of baseball shines brightest. Costas has a quick pace and packs in stats and information until the broadcast seems filled to the brim. When I finish listening to Costas, I've typically learned quite a bit.

Now, how did I move from a sports consumer into a career as a broadcaster in Minor League Baseball? Admittedly, somewhat by accident. I attended Ohio University to study journalism, knowing that I wanted to get involved with sports broadcasting in some capacity. Early on, I covered a lot of football, basketball and hockey, but after an internship as the play-by-play voice of a summer league team, the Southern Ohio Copperheads, I was absolutely hooked on calling baseball games. Still, that experience turned out to be drastically different from my first experience in MiLB. Affiliated ball is special.

You get to see extremely young, talented players while they're still incredibly raw. Sure, you witness more mistakes than you would at the major league level, but to first watch Derek Jeter commit 56 errors for the Greensboro Hornets in 1993—a South Atlantic League record—and then see him throwing off his back foot to get a tough out at first in The Show is indescribable. The work put in to get from A to B is incredible, and as a broadcaster you get a front row seat to this development. Besides seeing remarkable star power and getting paid to watch the sport I love on nearly a nightly basis, Minor League Baseball has a number of additional benefits.

One often wears multiple hats on the same day, and no two days are the same. Planning a promotional night from start to finish and watching it come to fruition with an excited group of fans is super rewarding (more on that later). Giving a helping hand to the grounds crew, distributing pocket schedules or getting into a mascot suit, while not the most exciting gigs, breaks up the longer days and allows you to see the impact you have on the community or on the final product the fans see when the gates open up. Truthfully, I have never walked through the doors of the front office on a game day and been able to predict everything that would happen. The unforeseeable nature of working in the sports industry is arguably the most exciting part of my job.

Once all that work is finished and it's time for first pitch, your actual job title of baseball broadcaster can be fulfilled. Reading this, you now know my four biggest broadcasting influences growing up and my mindset about what it means to be in Minor League Baseball, but to me, broadcasting a game, by itself, is something that a lot of people can do well. The basic description of the job is simply narrating the events unfolding in front of you, but there is a massive difference between doing the job well and being great at it.

The most important part of taking the step from good to great is the broadcaster's ability to tell a story. By describing a game well, you can give the listener the excitement of a player scoring a run or pitching a big strikeout, and that's good, but to be able to bring that player into the listener's household or car and make him feel like a familiar presence is on an entirely different level.

I've told stories about players who had off-season jobs feeding cattle or as substitute teachers in French or math to help fans see how down to earth a lot of players are. I've delved into tales of guys beating the odds after growing up in poverty or abusive situations by earning scholarships, gaining incredible educations, and ultimately realizing their childhood dreams. I've even worked in anecdotes of players who moved overseas by themselves at 18 years old and learned new languages to adapt to and navigate an increasingly diverse America, as well as communicate with their teammates from various countries. The humanization of players, in my opinion, is what makes the game beautiful to so many people. Impeccable storytelling can elevate a broadcast like nothing else.

I've been able to tell players' stories for three different teams now, all in the South Atlantic League (SAL): the West Virginia Power (now the Charleston Dirty Birds), Hagerstown Suns and Columbia Fireflies. In the SAL circuit, we're fortunate to have plenty of great towns to travel to. Columbia, South Carolina, hosts a Southeastern Conference school, as does Lexington, Kentucky. Charleston, South Carolina, is one of the larger Class-A markets you'll travel to, and the history of the city is fascinating to take in. Asheville, North Carolina, has a great brewery scene—so it's no surprise that they are the "inventors" of the Thirsty Thursday ballpark special. Despite all of that, my favorite ballpark to travel to is the home of the Jersey Shore BlueClaws, Lakewood, New Jersey.

Not only does Lakewood have a welcoming downtown area with good food, but you're also only about a 15- to 20-minute Uber from the Jersey Shore. If you've finished your work the night before a game, you can head out to the beach in the morning to take a stroll along the boardwalk for an hour or two. Nothing beats grabbing an ice cream cone on a hot summer day and listening to the waves crash against the sand while you mentally prepare to call a game. On top of the beach, the

12

ballpark itself is beautiful. FirstEnergy Park has a mini golf course fans can play just beyond right field, and, typically on bigger nights, a live band performs along the third base line. Near the band, there are a couple of bars serving drinks. These are for fans, of course—although I was able to partake once, which allowed me to view the ballpark from a different vantage point. The 360-degree concourse has games and plenty of food options, and the press box, located on the suite level above the walkaround, has a fantastic view of home plate.

The night I was able to have a couple beverages from the bars at FirstEnergy Park was set up by an internet outage. This outage was a bit larger than one where resetting a router would fix the issue. There was a construction crew outside the stadium that cut into the fiber that brought service to FirstEnergy Park. At the time, I was with the Hagerstown Suns, who ran an internet-only stream of the broadcast, so I was at a stadium for a game with no way to bring the sights and sounds of what was occurring to my audience. In the spirit of Margaritaville Night, I decided to head down to the concourse and sip a few drinks. Fortunately, the problem was fixed before the Suns left town, and I was able to broadcast a few games.

While the many unique locations in small-town America make Minor League Baseball special, what determines success for these teams is their marketing and promotional prowess. While MiLB certainly cannot compete with the star power or skill level of the average major league team (although remember, most of those players started in MiLB before they became "the stars of today"), it puts out some of the most creative and attention-grabbing theme nights in any setting. Just ask the Asheville Tourists, who brought Thirsty Thursday and cheap alcoholic beverages to the MiLB circuit, or ask any of the teams who have pulled off *SpongeBob SquarePants*, *Paw Patrol* or Princess and Pirates nights. The promotions in Minor League Baseball are simply the best.

The most memorable promotional evening I have ever been a part of was Mugshot Monday, which the West Virginia Power launched in 2017. Our weekly Monday night promotion was Family Buck Night, where fans could buy $1 general admission tickets or $3 box seats to the game. They could also purchase a soda, popcorn or hot dog for just a buck. It was a nice way to get fans through the door on a traditionally slower night. Then ... enter Joshua Hanshaw.

Hanshaw was a 35-year-old ... well, criminal from West Virginia who decided to break into the locker room at the Power's stadium, Appalachian Power Park (now GoMart Ballpark). He got away with some

13

valuables, but was caught and detained by police officers not far from the ballpark. Of course, the story didn't end there. When the police booked him and took his mugshot, they kept him in his stolen West Virginia Power jersey for the photo, which—thanks in part to some articles from the sports sites Deadspin and Yardbarker—went viral. As a team, we *had* to lean into it. We advertised that if fans brought a mugshot—their own or someone else's—on the next Monday, they would receive a free ticket to the game. We decorated the concourse, using a clothesline to pin up famous mugshots of everyone from Tim Allen and O.J. to Lindsay Lohan and Martha Stewart. On the video board, we showed more celebrity mugshots and put prison bars in front of Power players' photographs. We played plenty of theme music such as "Jailhouse Rock" and "Prison Song" to add depth to the experience. We even rolled out a "Which Celebrity Went to Jail?" trivia contest between innings. While I don't remember the exact figure, I believe around 30 people brought mugshots for free tickets and about 10 of those were their own mugshots.

That's one example of a great MiLB theme night that you won't see at a big league game or other venues. Another example that caught my eye while I've been in the industry came from the Jacksonville Jumbo Shrimp. I didn't play a part in their July 2019 "Florida Man" Night, but the idea was tremendous. No doubt the front office was making fun of the articles everyone sees that are headlined "Local Florida Man [does something absolutely ridiculous]." In addition to naming the promo "Florida Man" Night, the team gave out 1,000 Florida Man bobbleheads and attempted to break a weird and obscure local law each inning. I don't know how that night could be considered anything other than a complete and total success. Promotions are the most noticeable and marketable difference between a major league and minor league team's operations, but behind the scenes, there are plenty of differences between how major league and minor league teams are run.

One of the differences is travel. The Washington Nationals take a plane to pretty much every road destination they travel to, but the Hagerstown Suns, who were a farm team of the Nationals through 2020, rode a charter bus to their road games. While most trips weren't terrible, it does take a while to get to Georgia from upstate Maryland. For example, Rome, Georgia, is about 650 miles away, or a 10-hour bus ride. Yes, some trips are done on off days, but a lot of the time a team will hop on the bus directly after a game and start pushing toward the next destination with their next game less than a day away.

Considering that each team plays more than 15 series on the road

1. John Kocsis, Jr.

each season, it's hard to find a broadcaster who doesn't have a story about a time a bus has broken down, how they were trapped in a terrible traffic jam or how the bus's AC stopped working on a hot summer day. My personal best "wacky road trip story" happened in August 2019. It was one of those fortunate non–game day travel opportunities for the Suns. The team finished up a home loss against the Columbia Fireflies on a Tuesday afternoon, received the remainder of the day off and reported to the bus Wednesday at 10 a.m. to drive to Lexington, Kentucky. For context, the ride from Municipal Stadium in Hagerstown to Whitaker Bank Ballpark in Lexington was 465 miles or, without traffic, roughly seven hours and 15 minutes.

The plan was to drive straight through to Charleston, West Virginia, stop at the big mall downtown for an hour or so to grab some food and then check into a hotel in Lexington at around 6–7 p.m. This schedule would have given the players and staff time to get settled in the hotel, grab a bite to eat in Lexington and then wind down and relax for the remainder of the evening. Fate had other plans, though.

The first abnormality of the trip came near Morgantown, West Virginia, about two-and-a-half hours into the journey. The bus stopped at a large gas station for 30 minutes to perform, as the driver, Terry, said, "routine maintenance." For those who have never taken a charter bus, there is almost no circumstance where the bus needs "routine maintenance" less than 200 miles out of the gate. Some guys stayed on the bus, but most wandered into the gas station to grab snacks or use the restroom before continuing our journey. We assumed this pit stop would be a minor inconvenience nobody would remember by the end of the evening. Boy, were we wrong.

Seventy-five miles later, in a rural part of the "Wild and Wonderful" state of West Virginia, along I-79, Terry once again had to stop the bus, on the side of the highway in Burnsville. This time when the bus stopped, it did not want to go any further. After sitting beside the highway for about 25 minutes, Terry concluded that we needed to wait for a new bus, one that was coming from Roanoke, Virginia. So we slowly made our way to the next exit, where we parked the bus for good in front of a GoMart gas station with an extension store called Guns, Guns, Guns, Ammo, Ammo, Ammo. Outside of gas and guns, there was a bank and a couple of houses scattered around the hilly, forest-covered countryside. Initially, most of us stayed on the bus. After some time passed, however, we learned that the new bus wouldn't make it to Burnsville until at least 7 p.m.

15

Play-by-Play from the Minors

Now the search for food began. There was no Uber or Lyft in the area and the closest people that any of us knew were in Charleston, which was still over an hour's drive away. The nearest food option we saw on the map was a Mo's Barbecue a few miles down the road, so a group of us left the bus and started walking along the main street by the highway to go toward town. After walking about a mile, we found a shack on 5th Street that wasn't marked on Google Maps. It was next to a gas station and had an outdoor walk-up window with a few picnic tables set up under an overhang. The group texted some people on the bus, and soon enough, the majority of the team walked over to the stand. While it seemed that the store was primarily a place to sell ice cream, they also had pizza, chicken, subs and some other food options. Naturally, having a whole baseball team show up overwhelmed the staff a bit, but one of them walked to a nearby house and came back with "Grandpa," who hopped right on the grill to cook the grub.

The Hagerstown Suns were fed and we sat around telling stories at those picnic tables for a few hours. We eventually got a phone call alerting us that the bus coming to rescue us had also broken down and we would be stuck in Burnsville until midnight. We stayed at those picnic tables until it got dark, and then we returned to the GoMart parking lot, stocked up on drinks and snacks and waited for the bus to pick us up. We didn't get to Lexington until around 5:30 in the morning and reported to the ballpark around 2 p.m. later that day. Despite being tired and thrown off our routine a bit, the team was still able to eke out a 3–1 victory over the Lexington Legends (now the Lexington Counter Clocks).

Obviously, this job is more than just promotional nights and long bus rides. The real perks of the gig come from having the opportunity to see the show before The Show. Throughout this book, you'll hear the names of guys who have made it or who will be coming up next and are extremely talented. You'll read about incredibly big moments that never found the national spotlight, but that players and fans of that team will remember forever. Finally, you'll hear about learning moments, because, as simple as the game of baseball is, there's always plenty you can learn, regardless of your level of knowledge about the game.

I'll start with the best prospect I've ever seen play. This player comes with a bit of his own mystique. In 2017, Oneil Cruz was a 6'6" 18-year-old shortstop out of the Dominican Republic. He played for the Great Lakes Loons of the Midwest League in the Los Angeles Dodgers farm system until the trade deadline. At the proverbial buzzer, the

1. John Kocsis, Jr.

Dodgers were looking for strong relievers and pulled the trigger on Pittsburgh Pirates closer Tony Watson. The Buccos received Cruz and Angel German in return. German was a pitcher who could touch 100 mph on the gun, but had trouble keeping the ball in the strike zone. Cruz, on the other hand, was rumored to have some of the best natural power that scouts had ever seen. (That rumor was true.) The 18-year-old was tall, but he weighed just 160 pounds (according to MiLB.com). When Cruz reported to West Virginia a day or two later, he certainly stuck out. Not only was he tall, but he also had dreadlocks that nearly reached his shoulders. His hair made Cruz very easy to spot because the Pirates required their minor leaguers, which included the West Virginia Power at the time, to be clean-shaven (outside of allowing them to grow a mustache, if they'd like to) and keep their hair inside their ball cap until they received major league service time. Cruz was able to dodge those requirements in 2017 because the Pirates elected to send him straight to West Virginia rather than have him report first to the Bradenton Spring Training facility. When he reported in 2018, his hair was cut to the Pirates' standard. Those who follow the Pirates will know, that since he made his Major League debut October 2, 2021, he has started to grow his signature hair out again.

If you were a Pirates fan, Cruz's dreadlocks were a welcome sight, as they might have reminded you of All-Star and MVP Andrew McCutchen. But his build and the power he generated from his bat were more reminiscent of Giancarlo Stanton or Gregory Polanco.

On Cruz's first day with the Power, he was pretty quiet. He fielded a few ground balls and milled around a bit until batting practice. Then a group of people gathered around, waiting to see the rumored power that *Baseball America* and MLB Pipeline had been raving about. He watched a couple of pitches go by before his first swing, but once the bat moved through the zone and collided with the baseball, the ball flew through right field, not only beyond the fence at Appalachian Power Park, but over the concourse, across Morris Street and a couple of rows deep into a CVS parking lot across the street. He then proceeded to knock the next two balls out of the park as well, showing that the first wasn't an accident.

I had the pleasure of watching Cruz for two years in West Virginia, and he was always considered a top-five prospect for the Pirates. He certainly had the most pop of any minor leaguer I've gotten to watch.

Anyone can say that they saw a top prospect contribute to a team, but one of the most rewarding parts of working in Minor League

Play-by-Play from the Minors

Baseball is seeing an unsung hero succeed. Think of some of the biggest names, now Hall of Famers, you grew up watching and loving. Jim Thome was picked in the 13th round, Mike Piazza was selected in the 62nd round and even Albert Pujols was a 13th rounder. None of them were considered top prospects right out of the draft, but eventually they developed into the star players we all know and love. One of the unsung heroes I've had a chance to watch grow and develop is Francys Peguero. Signed by the Nationals as an infielder in 2013 (at 17 years old, which is very common in baseball), Peguero had moved to the mound by the time I saw him in Hagerstown.

The righty sported a three-pitch mix and, due to a lack of offensive support, had an ugly 2–8 record that went along with a 2.95 ERA in 17 games. He tossed nearly 100 innings in a Suns uniform before getting the call-up to the Advanced-A Potomac Nationals down the stretch. He fanned 80 batters while walking only 19 hitters in that time. Did he have the best stuff on the team? No, but Peguero was a strike thrower, who understood his role in the rotation in his first year of "full-season" baseball. He routinely got ahead in counts so he could go deep in games and limited runs, despite having a high WHIP and opposing batting average.

Talent is what gets a lot of fans to notice who you are, but the community and the people who work in the front office tend to choose their favorite players based on character and personality. Which player has the greatest personality or is the best locker room presence is something a lot of broadcasters talk about, providing a behind-the-scenes look for a lot of fans, but it is probably the hardest question to answer for someone assessing a team from the outside. The reality is, there are a lot of great guys playing in the minors, and I'm sure I'll feel bad for omitting about 20 names, but if someone were to ask me, "Which player have you met that you think has the best personality?" I would have to go with Cody Bolton.

A top-tier righty drafted out of high school in California, Bolton has never lost touch with who he is. The son of a preacher, Bolton understands service and what being present in the community can do to benefit others. He would always volunteer to catch first pitches or go to schools to read to kids or do literally anything in the community. Once there, he always went above and beyond expectations and legitimately enjoyed helping others.

When it's time for business, though, Bolton is one of the hardest workers out there. He quietly attacks bullpen sessions, stretching exercises and the weight room, and enthusiastically has back-and-forths

1. John Kocsis, Jr.

about pitching strategy and development with his coaching staff and catchers. In the offseason, he helps raise cattle, loading bags of feed into large troughs and even bottle-feeding a few babies. Bolton is no stranger to hard work and, of course, finding a delicate balance in his craft. I remember going down to the Power's clubhouse to interview Bolton after a string of strong starts to begin his professional career and finding him going through a lifting session after the team had finished workouts. I told him I would come back later to chat, but he was adamant about fitting the interview in between sets so he wouldn't create a time crunch for me. Bolton always puts others first.

The players on each team are like the pistons in an engine. They're an integral part of the machine in Minor League Baseball, and by themselves can stand out, make or break an individual game or even propel a team into a championship. Where it gets really interesting is when those pistons pump together and create awe-inspiring moments for the fans in attendance.

I've had the good fortune of calling a lot of cool moments during my time in Minor League Baseball. Choosing among them is probably the hardest thing to do for a broadcaster, because it is so hard to compare a walk-off with a championship win, or a no-hitter with a milestone homer. For me, the best moment came at Segra Park, on one of the biggest games of the year in 2021. Although they couldn't have a traditional Fourth of July game, the Fireflies hosted the Myrtle Beach Pelicans for an Independence Day Celebration on June 26, as teams were being held to a tight schedule, playing six games against an opposing team and utilizing an off day for COVID testing before moving to the next location so as to try to slow the spread if there was an outbreak among the players. With a fireworks show planned, thousands of fans stuck around in the waning moments as the Fireflies battled the Pelicans. Myrtle Beach jumped out quickly, scoring a pair of runs in the first inning. After that, the Fireflies' pitching was lights out. Juan Carlos Negret smashed a homer to left-center field to tie the game 2–2 in the eighth, which set the stage for the two teams to play on into extra innings.

After Patrick Smith stranded the placed runner on second base in the top of the 10th, Jared Wright was tasked with shutting down the Columbia bats in the home half. Matt Smith led off the 10th, with Gage Hughes placed on second base since it was an extra innings minor league game. The Fireflies' first baseman charged the ball deep enough to center field that Hughes moved to third base, so Buddy Bailey, the Pelicans' skipper, opted to intentionally walk Maikel Garcia and Herard

19

Play-by-Play from the Minors

Gonzalez to load the bases and create a force-out at home and a potential double-play situation at the plate. After a mound visit, Darryl Collins stepped into the batter's box and did not waste a second of time. He pulled the first pitch he saw over the right field wall to hit a walk-off grand slam. I knew right off the bat that the ball was gone and the team just needed a sacrifice fly to win. After hearing the pop, the stadium went berserk and the team was bouncing with excitement. The outfielder from the Netherlands hit the first walk-off home run in Columbia Fireflies history, giving the fans some fireworks before the Independence Day Celebration fireworks. The grand slam was Collins's fourth and final home run in 86 games that season, and it's one that season ticket holders still mention every time they talk about the outfielder.

Those types of moments are scattered among the teams playing each night across America. They are rare, like winning a championship, but the players who make up these moments more often than not become the guys who fill out major league rosters.

In my short time in Minor League Baseball, I haven't called games for a championship-winning team. I also haven't had the opportunity to call games for a playoff-clinching team, but the amount of talent hidden away within teams that don't make the playoffs is incredible. Despite the fact that I have yet to call a game for a team that has made the playoffs, I have called games for teams with a handful of top organizational prospects and I have called games that involved future major leaguers. If I were to pick the most-talented team I have called from 2017 to 2020, I would choose the 2018 West Virginia Power roster. The Class-A affiliate for the Pittsburgh Pirates was loaded with pitching prospects and had a couple of strong bats that were acquired from trades at the deadline in back-to-back seasons.

The 2018 crop of players included the aforementioned Oneil Cruz, a top-100 overall prospect according to both MLB.com and *Baseball America*. It also held a top-10 Pirates prospect at backstop, Deon Stafford. Stafford grew up in Harrisburg, Pennsylvania, and became a star for his bat while he was at Saint Joseph's. When he was in West Virginia, he was able to become an all-around star because of his growth defensively behind the plate. Though he always had the arm strength and mental fortitude to call a great game, he really honed in on blocking the plate well and making the throw down to second quicker. That, combined with a plus bat ("plus" means above-average in baseball scouting reports), made him fun to watch in the middle of the Power order that year.

1. John Kocsis, Jr.

The real highlight of the roster, as I said earlier, came from the pitching staff. This team struggled with injuries, but, at different times, the rotation was able to boast second-round pick Travis MacGregor; top-lefty prospect Braeden Ogle, whose slider was vicious for the few games he pitched in; and highly touted high school draftees Max Kranick and Cody Bolton. Domingo Robles, an org pitcher (another "inside baseball" term), had a standout year, earning a 2.97 ERA across 21 games to help blend the staff together. The bullpen had some filthy stuff, too. Matt Seelinger struck out 52 batters in just 32.2 frames. Blake Weiman, a tall lefty closer, had a 1.29 ERA while slamming the door, and the Dartmouth product Beau Sulser shocked the baseball world in 2018.

Sulser was picked in the 10th round and struggled with a 5.31 ERA in the New York–Penn League in 2017. He worked with his brother, Cole, who played in AAA, over the offseason, and the 2018 results spoke for themselves. He held onto a 0.82 WHIP and walked only four batters the whole season. Most impressively, he didn't walk a single batter in his first 30 appearances. He finished the campaign with a 2.35 ERA and eight saves, but stats don't do his impact justice. He entered a game on the road in Columbia with the bases loaded and no one out, rung up one batter and then got the next man to pop out into an inning-ending double play (after a play at the plate from shallow left field resulting in a 6–2 putout). Sulser was Mr. Clutch when he hopped on the bump 60'6" away from home plate. It's unfortunate that the season came to an end with him on the mound.

The Power had a magic number of one to clinch a playoff berth with two games remaining in the regular season. All that was left to do was get one win against the Charleston RiverDogs at Joseph P. Riley Jr. Park or back their way in via a loss by the Kannapolis Intimidators (now the Cannon Ballers). Kannapolis won out, and in the bottom of the ninth on the final day of the season, Dermis Garcia hit a three-run homer off Sulser with one out in the frame. John Pomeroy had allowed a pair of hits before manager Wyatt Toregas opted to throw in Sulser to see if he could pull another Houdini act—this time to put the Power in the playoffs.

Sulser wasn't able to bail out the Power and send them to the postseason, but he learned a ton about preparation from his brother in the offseason and how it would pay dividends for him during his future in baseball. That's what this level of the game is all about: learning and development. The players on the field aren't the only people learning at your typical baseball game, though.

Play-by-Play from the Minors

While I certainly knew a lot about baseball heading into this career path, there are things that you can only learn through experience and by attending over 100 baseball games a year. Because of how much time a broadcaster spends at the ballpark, you're bound to see a few unbelievable plays you've never seen before pop up each season. One of those moments came in a wonky game in Lakewood in 2019. Hagerstown Suns catcher Nic Perkins bunted a ball up the first-base line. The runner on first moved to second, the catcher elected to take the inside track on the throw to first, and the ball glanced off Perkins and rolled to the tarp near the right-field corner. Perkins was called out for runner's interference—the umpire claimed he had run out of the baseline, but that wasn't the surprising thing about this situation. The man on first, who during the play advanced to third, had to go all the way back to where he began the play. I was certainly bewildered at the time as to why the runner wasn't able to stay at second, where he would have been had the ball not gone off Perkins, but hey, that's baseball.

We've made it close to the end of the first chapter. I've introduced you to my background, the industry of Minor League Baseball and we've talked a little bit about what hard-core fans really appreciate—what happens on the field. Before I start introducing you to some of the long-time and influential broadcasters in this book, I want to turn to another fun topic. Let's go over a few things that broadcasters love talking about to other broadcasters when they have a chance to catch up over a drink or have some time to kill in a rain delay.

We'll start off with something that will satisfy the wanderlust crowd and the people racking up their frequent flyer miles. Broadcasters love to compare the top restaurants they have visited while on the road. This selection is a tough one, and it requires people to go off the beaten path. It's easy to go to the Cracker Barrel right next to the hotel or to hit up a Mellow Mushroom near the stadium. They're everywhere, you know they will have good food and food that you have had before, so your expectations are set. Despite that, whenever I travel, I try to go to at least one mom-and-pop shop per town.

There are many great places I can name, but I think my favorite one is Johnny's New York Style Pizza in Rome, Georgia. Located right across Broad Street from another good eatery, the Jamwich food truck, Johnny's is right in the middle of downtown and near a bunch of little shops for you to peruse after filling up. It may be cheating to call Johnny's a mom-and-pop shop, as it's part of a franchise that started in Louisiana and has 38 locations, primarily located in the Southeast, but just stay with me here. Despite its popularity in the South, it is certainly a place that an Ohio native such as myself would probably never have heard of. I walked into a traditional bar and grill setting and was greeted with good service. I ordered one of the best meat lover's calzones I've ever had. The crust was flaky and there was just enough sauce in the cheese-loaded missile, speckled with pepperoni, sausage and bacon. The meal absolutely filled me up and exceeded expectations, but Johnny's has a couple of other attractions if you visit town and have a free evening. They have live music a few nights a week, and if you're into trivia, they host that as well. It's certainly a worthwhile experience if you're ever passing through northwest Georgia.

Another topic I think you may be interested to hear about from a broadcaster is: If you could call one moment in baseball history that has already transpired, what would it be? For mine, I have no doubt. The greatest baseball moment I have ever witnessed was Rajai Davis's two-run homer off Aroldis Chapman to tie Game 7 of the 2016 World Series with two outs in the bottom of the eighth.

The Cubs were leading 6–4, Davis was certainly not known for his power and Chapman was the most formidable reliever in all of baseball. The crowd at Progressive Field was on its feet, many running their hands through their hair or clapping them together. In other words, there was a tremendous amount of tension on the corner of Carnegie and Ontario. After falling behind, Davis faced a 2–2 count, and his hands choked up significantly on the bat. After fouling off a couple pitches, he roped a ball down the left-field line that looked like it would never leave the park, but when it did, it was pure pandemonium. The teams with the two longest World Series droughts in baseball history were knotted up heading into the ninth in a winner-take-all ballgame.

I think I've talked enough about myself for now. In the coming chapters, you'll hear from guys who have many years of experience in a variety of different leagues telling you about their favorite stories, nights at the ballpark, players and towns they have visited during their careers. Together we'll explore stories from the past three decades for 39 different teams and 12 different broadcasters who have made their living relaying these stories to you.

2

Adam Marco

Currently with the Scranton/Wilkes-Barre RailRiders
Previously with the West Virginia Power,
Oklahoma City RedHawks and Williamsport Crosscutters

After introducing you to who I am, it's only fair that the first broad-caster I write about is Adam Marco, who helped me break into the industry and pushed me toward accepting a video production intern-ship with the West Virginia Power in 2017. Eventually that internship, which stemmed from networking via a mutual connection at the MLB Winter Meetings, led to the career I have today.

Marco didn't start too far away from where he is right now, work-ing as the director of communications/broadcaster for the Scranton/Wilkes-Barre RailRiders, the Triple-A affiliate of the New York Yankees. Marco hails from Leechburg, Pennsylvania, which is about a four-hour drive from Scranton. A suburb northeast of Pittsburgh, Leechburg sits along the meandering Kiskiminetas River. The Kiskiminetas is a tribu-tary of the Allegheny River, which flows right into the heart of down-town Pittsburgh, meeting with the Ohio River and the Monongahela River near where PNC Park and Heinz Field currently sit, and where, in Marco's childhood, Three Rivers Stadium was. The Pennsylvanian watched many Steelers and Penguins games not too far from where those rivers meet, and he certainly found himself at his fair share of Pirates baseball games as well—although his fan allegiance shifted throughout his childhood.

"When I was a kid, all of my friends were Pirates fans. Early on, I might have been. There are pictures of the Pirates Parrot holding me," Marco relays. "I read *Boys' Life* magazine because I was a Boy Scout in the late '80s and early '90s, and they had a story on Orel Hershiser in it. This was pre–88, but right around then I kind of jumped on their [the Los Angeles Dodgers] bandwagon. I was a Dodger fan for their World

2. Adam Marco

Series run in 1988, and I read Hershiser's book, *Out of the Blue*, and wrote book reports on it I think every year from 1989 to 1992."

While he certainly was not a fan of the Pirates, he lived and died by both the Steelers and the Penguins, and in Pittsburgh during that time, you could get away with that. From 1984 to 1990, the Pirates finished the season a minimum of 15 games out of the playoffs each year, and spent two years more than 40 games away from the post-season. Naturally, the intensity of the fans who watched three World Series wins from 1960 to 1979 had wavered during Adam's most formative years of baseball fandom. If you pair that with Adam's family's interests while he was growing up, he'd surprise most with his eventual career in sports. His mother was a music teacher and, while his sister did play softball, everyone was certainly more involved with choir and band

Adam, the 2022 *Ballpark Digest* Broadcaster of the Year, used to run a blog that detailed the best places to eat in the South Atlantic League. While the blog isn't active anymore, people can still follow him on Twitter to see some of the best cuisine he finds while he's traveling (photograph courtesy Adam Marco).

than they were in athletics. Marco also participated in choir and played tuba and percussion in the school band, so he stuck with his family's musical background and then added sports to that.

As far as his Dodgers fandom was concerned, he fell off that train when Hershiser left to sign with the Cleveland Indians in 1995. "I was kind of a Cleveland fan in the mid–90s for a little bit in that era with Albert Belle, Carlos Baerga and Hershiser. Those teams that you just wanted to beat the Braves to get over the hump."

Play-by-Play from the Minors

When Hershiser left the Indians prior to the 1998 season, as a 39-year-old, to play for the Giants, he lost Marco's team-hopping support. It was at that point that he grew into loving the Pittsburgh Pirates. "It was at the tail end of Three Rivers Stadium during the 1998 home run chase, and we could get into McGwire and Sosa games for like eight bucks," Marco remembers.

Adam attended Mercyhurst College in Erie, Pennsylvania; he remembers interning in Pittsburgh around then and being excited about the unveiling of the new ballpark, which many still consider to be one of the most beautiful parks in the senior circuit today. From that excitement, he grew into being a Pirates fan, and, for the last 20 years, Adam would say, he is more a fan of the Pirates than of any other team in Major League Baseball.

Marco didn't have much of a chance to listen to Vin Scully—unless the Dodgers were on a nationally broadcast game. In that era of Pittsburgh sports, that means he grew up listening to a different broadcaster, Lanny Frattare. Lanny, a 2008 Ford C. Frick Award nominee, spent over 30 years calling Pirates games, but right before he was in Pittsburgh, in 1974–75, he was the play-by-play voice of the Charleston Charlies, the Pirates' Triple-A affiliate.

Marco was strongly influenced by Mike Lange, who used to broadcast Pittsburgh Penguins games. "Mike Lange was one of the kings. Everyone loves Doc Emrick, but Mike Lange was synonymous with hockey for me in the '90s. Maybe that's the Pittsburgh influence, but Mike Lange and Myron Cope were both onboard with the ESPN catchphrases when I was growing up." Marco continues, "Mike Lange was [saying things like] 'Elvis has left the building' and 'Scratch my back with a hacksaw.' Lange was always able to turn a phrase."

Lange *could* turn a phrase, and that was part of a big trend in broadcasting while Adam was growing up. Nationally, he loved listening to Jack Buck, who coined the catchphrase "We will see you tomorrow night." He also fell under the influence of the Braves' broadcasts on TBS when Ted Turner brought national attention to a team in Georgia that would build one of the best rotations in baseball history during the '90s. More than anything, though, Adam looked up to the superstars of broadcasting at that time, the anchors of *SportsCenter*.

"How they utilized language to show excitement had a tremendous influence, not only on me, but a lot of broadcasters. I think, for the longest time, you didn't necessarily want to be a play-by-play guy, you wanted to be on *SportsCenter*, and that's because of them," Marco said.

26

2. Adam Marco

Through all of that, though, Adam's motto is to try to emulate, not replicate, the great broadcasters that he has seen or listened to. "There's already one Mike Lange, so do we really need another guy that says, 'Elvis has left the building'?" Marco continued. "Emulation is an homage, but you have to find your own unique way to make your voice your own."

That authenticity is what Marco believes is the most important thing for a broadcaster. He says it may be an acquired taste, like oysters, but authenticity and the conversational tone you bring to your commentary is what people appreciate when they listen to your show.

One part of that authenticity for Marco is his love of exploration, as well as the food scene, across small-town America. He started a blog during his time in West Virginia titled *Minor League Kerouac* where he shared stories of his travels and his favorite places to grab a bite to eat in the South Atlantic League. Going on the road is part of the fun of being a broadcaster, and all broadcasters are always searching for more content to push out to ravenous fans, who consume everything that you can offer about your team.

"We write game stories constantly. We write pages and pages of game notes daily. I wanted that blog to be some of the things that I wasn't necessarily talking about, but how it plays out. What does a road trip really consist of?" Adam explained. "The early stories ended up being game stories that weren't explicitly about games. Then, it started to become more about life off the diamond for the team and the broadcaster. It eventually morphed into what I was eating on any particular day."

The idea for the blog was essentially that the team was headed to all these smaller towns across the Eastern Seaboard. So, while he was exploring those towns, Adam would look for something that would be interesting to somebody listening in Charleston, West Virginia, or maybe to a family member of one of the players who was listening from California. What would they enjoy about Kannapolis, North Carolina? The blog was a way for the people who would probably never visit those places to experience them.

As the blog grew in age, it adapted. There were years where Adam would try to find the best restaurants in different leagues. Initially, he would look for the cuisine the area was known for and then look for restaurants or things to do that he may never have the opportunity to go to again. For example, he really enjoys running around the Indiana Central Canal system when Scranton/Wilkes-Barre visits the Indianapolis

Play-by-Play from the Minors

Indians. Indianapolis also plays host to the NCAA Headquarters and the NCAA Hall of Champions, which is a unique place to visit, filled with sports history.

If you'd like to check out the blog, you can certainly visit *Minor League Kerouac*, which is still on the Medium platform and has plenty of great travel stories through 2015, but, since you're already here, I'll let you in on some of Marco's top picks from the South Atlantic League. One year, he embarked upon a quest to find the top sandwich in the league's territory. Eventually, he came up with Zunzi's in Savannah, Georgia. While Savannah hasn't been in Minor League Baseball since 2015, the South Africa–influenced restaurant still holds its spot along East York Street, sharing a building with a psychic, a legal office and a tattoo parlor. The restaurant was recommended to Adam by the Power's groundskeeper, and he tried The Conquistador. Simplicity is the name of the game with this sandwich, which is made with lettuce, tomato and special sauce on French bread, according to Adam's blog post. He still feels the impact of the sandwich eight years later.

"It was amazing. It was so simple and yet done so well," Marco remembered.

He found the best barbecue on the other side of the South Atlantic League territory, in Lexington, Kentucky. Willie's Locally Known was Adam's choice for best barbecue in 2014, and he discovered it when it resided just a few blocks from Whitaker Bank Ballpark, the home of the Legends. Then the barbecue joint moved to Southland and was a big reason why, in his last few years in the league, the Power radio guy liked to drive to Lexington. To quote the blog, "When visiting Willie's, you have to order the burnt ends. They aren't even on the menu anymore because the restaurant runs out of them daily, but they melt like butter and should be the first cuisine on your mind when you make it to Lexington." Unfortunately, Willie's has closed its doors permanently.

One final favorite of Adam's is Greenville, South Carolina's Smoke on the Water. Just down the street from Fluor Field in the West End, fans have an opportunity to be adventurous and try Smoke on the Water or visit a few chains like Mellow Mushroom and Eggs Up Grill. Marco will tell you to be bold. *Minor League Kerouac* will also tell you to make sure that you get your pulled pork sandwich at Smoke on the Water pre-sauced—so the meat has time to soak it in. When Adam visited Smoke on the Water in 2014, he ranked it third out of four barbecue joints he had been to in the South Atlantic League territory, but in 2020 he recalled that he really enjoyed visiting it each time his team made the trek to Greenville.

2. Adam Marco

"Those are some of my favorite spots that year after year I would go back to," Adam says. The blog's influence even reached the famous "Toast Section" fan group of West Virginia. Lexington isn't far from Charleston, and the Power would travel three or four times a season to visit the Legends. Because of the close proximity, the dedicated cheering section would try to venture to a road game in Lexington each year. One year, they decided to check out the Windy Corner Market because it was mentioned in the blog. Word travels quickly and effectively when good food is involved.

The word on food may travel fast, but the word on talented broadcasters sometimes takes time to reach the right ears. The job search process is arduous to say the least, and it took a while for Adam to find his way into a minor league booth. He graduated from Mercyhurst in 2001, but didn't work for the New York–Penn League's Williamsport Crosscutters until 2007. That's because, if Adam is being honest, play-by-play in Minor League Baseball wasn't always his plan.

"I went to school thinking I was going to be a serious journalist, and 20 years later, I broadcast baseball," Marco reflects.

He loves it, but he isn't the guy who breaks the news and tells the hard-hitting stories that he envisioned he would become when he was taking journalism and communications classes in Erie as a 19-year-old.

Adam got his start right out of college as a country radio DJ working part-time and manning the overnight shift. It wasn't his end goal, but he just needed something to get by at the time. After about three months with the station, they offered him a full-time gig and they also needed someone to broadcast high school football games. The guy who had been broadcasting those games was a Minor League Baseball broadcaster, and he ended up not coming back to the station, which opened the door for Marco. Though Marco wasn't very experienced with football—at Mercyhurst he primarily called basketball and baseball games—he decided to give it a shot.

"It was basically: Have voice; will travel, in western Pennsylvania and northeast Ohio," Marco relays, and that was the process from 2001 to 2007. He would broadcast a bunch of games for high school and small collegiate teams, sometimes up to four a week, and meanwhile he would continue to DJ at his local station. After laboring for seven years in talk radio, learning the back end and audio editing, he had an experience that changed his career outlook.

Marco moved to North Carolina for a brief time for a job that he didn't stay at long, but while he was there, he was the board operator

29

Play-by-Play from the Minors

for Kinston Indians games. While working in this position, Adam realized that broadcasting Minor League Baseball games could be a potential career for him. Then, in 2005, he packed his bags and went to Dallas for his first Winter Meetings. He wasn't able to lock down anything, but in 2006 he decided he would give it another shot. This time, the trip was to Bay Lake, Florida, where, after getting a couple of interviews, the young broadcaster eventually earned a job with the Williamsport Crosscutters.

"I left a full-time job with benefits and I became a 27-year-old intern making $500 a month," Scranton's call-man remembers.

His family was supportive of the move, but the sacrifice meant that he wouldn't have a job after the three-month season was up. However, Marco believed he needed to make the leap and give it a shot. After all, he knew he wasn't getting any younger, and that career changes wouldn't get any easier in the future.

Marco called 38 road games in Williamsport, and at home he managed the press box and promotions. After that, he saw an opening in Triple-A for the number two position in Oklahoma City. He didn't think he had much of a shot at landing the gig, but he decided to try anyway. He ended up getting the opportunity, which allowed him to grow and learn under Jim Byers, who started his broadcasting career in 1988 and had spent nearly a decade with the RedHawks by the time Adam found himself there. He spent two years in Oklahoma City before he moved back closer to home.

Prior to his second season in Oklahoma, Adam's then-girlfriend and now wife, Brienne, moved to Charleston to work for a federal judge. So, Adam eventually followed and found a job as a traffic reporter with a local West Virginia Radio Corporation station.

"Charleston is a small city with the convergence of three highways, and I was stunned that they had traffic reports, but I did morning and afternoon traffic for six months," Marco said.

While working at the station, he met a couple of people who worked in the Power's front office, including Kristen Call, the team's promotions manager; Dan Helm, who was in charge of video production; and general manager Andy Milovich. Andy's girlfriend, Cher, worked at West Virginia Radio Corporation with Marco, which proved to be a valuable connection.

Adam was able to meet the media department of the Power through Cher, earning his first experience with the Power by making playlists for their fireworks shows at Appalachian Power Park. Cher also worked with Marco on remote broadcasts at local car dealerships and the like, which allowed them to build a relationship that eventually led to his job with the Power.

Then 2010 came around, and Adam had expected to return to Oklahoma City that summer. But by this point, Brienne had moved to Richmond, Virginia, to work at a different federal job. It was a transitional time for Adam. He was no longer doing traffic reports or working at West Virginia Radio Corporation. Instead, he moved to Virginia and tried his hand at selling used cars. Knowing he would go back to baseball, he knew he had limited time to work a job, and most potential employers balked at the short-term commitment that a seasonal baseball worker could offer. Marco only sold cars for three months before a surprise came his way.

"I got an email from Andy Milovich asking if I wanted to interview for the West Virginia Power job. I [had] never applied, never sent him a demo or a resume, but he knew my work from West Virginia Radio, so I had my 'in' there," Marco remembers. "We interviewed for 15–20 minutes, he asked me about my time selling used cars and then he made me the offer to become the broadcaster for the West Virginia Power."

Adam and Brienne moved back to Charleston in 2010 and would spend the next eight years at a place that they still consider home to this day. The initial goal was to stay in Charleston for at least five years. If Brienne practiced law in Charleston for five years, she would gain reciprocity and could move to over 40 different states without having to retake the bar exam. However, after the loss of her mother, they decided to wait a few extra years to make their move while they helped take care of Brienne's teenage sister.

He shot a few applications to some places, like the Pittsburgh Pirates when they had an opening, but didn't seriously start looking until the winter of 2016. He sent his resume to the two people in Minor League Baseball who had hired him, Andy Milovich and Gabe Sinicropi of the Crosscutters. Because baseball is such a small industry, the general managers and presidents of organizations you've been a part of typically hear a lot about the job market and what is opening up across Minor League Baseball.

"I said, 'I think it's time,'" Marco explains, "The timing was right, and it was going to work."

He started talking with the RailRiders' general manager and president, Josh Olerud, in December 2016, and Olerud thought that both of his broadcasters might be leaving Scranton/Wilkes-Barre. In 2017,

Marco stayed with West Virginia, but he heard some news shortly after the season ended.

"I got an email from Josh asking me what my future plans were, and it turns out that it was working with the Scranton/Wilkes-Barre Railriders."

Today, after almost 15 years in Minor League Baseball, working with four different teams, Marco wouldn't change the path that he chose. Minor League Baseball is special to him. It's more than just hopping on-air to chat about baseball every night. For Adam, the promotions and marketing that bring out adoring fans really help make the job more of a lifestyle than a mundane work experience.

In Charleston, he learned about the passion of fan bases across America. He learned firsthand through observing Rod Blackstone, the former deputy mayor of Charleston and, more famously, the Toastman. The Toastman is a superfan in the Toast Section who slings stats and jests at opposing players who enter Appalachian Power Park and tosses toast into the stands for each strikeout a Power pitcher records, while yelling, "You. Are. Toast!" at the opposing player as he slowly walks back into the third base dugout.

One of Adam's favorite memories of West Virginia, and one of his all-time favorite promotions that he's gotten the opportunity to be a part of, is the Power's annual Redneck Night. This theme night has seen many variations over the years, but it won a Golden Bobblehead—the industry's Emmy equivalent—in its first go-round in May of 2012. The promotion has had longevity, too. The team skipped it for a few years before revitalizing it in 2019, and it is now nationally known.

"It's meant to be tongue-in-cheek and [we] have some fun with it," Marco explains. "When people realize you're not making fun of them, but instead having fun with them, it pans out. No one makes fun of *Paw Patrol* or *Back to the Future*, you're paying tribute to it."

Every year, the Power staff has a handful of meetings to discuss the upcoming promotional calendar and what they want to fill it with, and one idea that came up often was Redneck Night. Yes, it was toeing the line and edgy, but the idea the front office had was to do something so over-the-top that it could land and be a major success.

The date was May 26, 2012, at Appalachian Power Park. The stage was set. The first 1,000 fans who attended received camo hats with the Power's logo on it. Steve McGranahan, known as "The World's Strongest Redneck," was at the game and helped with promotions between innings. The General Lee muscle car from *The Dukes of Hazzard* was at the gates for fans to see. Following the game, Cowboy Monkey Rodeo, featuring a monkey that rides the back of a dog like a cowboy would a horse, performed their act for the fans and finally, last but certainly not least, two visiting fans, Christina Frye and Jamie Campbell of Spencer, Washington, had a redneck wedding.

The wedding was part of a contest organized with West Virginia Radio, which was a big partner of the Power at the time. The local country music station advertised the opportunity to have a wedding at the ballpark, and people called in to try to win that experience. After West Virginia Radio Corporation had their contestants, they put the couples' bios and stories on their website for fans to choose from. Fans of the team and listeners of the station had a few weeks to vote for their favorite couple, and the winners got hitched on the dugout.

"It was a shotgun wedding on the top of the dugout where your ballpark emcee gets ordained as a minister," Marco remembers. "It was fun. It was innovative. It is one of those things in our industry that everyone tries to do." Despite having had multiple redneck weddings at Appalachian Power Park, the Power keeps the promotion fresh with new twists each year.

In 2014 for the third annual event, the bride wore a white dress and the groom and groomsmen donned camo T-shirts and jeans. NASCAR legend Bobby Allison made an appearance and one of the portable food stands became a redneck sushi shack. In 2017, a local Ford dealer brought in a handful of pickup trucks that the front office lined with tarps and filled with water to make redneck hot tubs. On top of that, in between innings they had a redneck *Bachelor* contest where five contestants tried to earn a date with the redneck bachelor who won a radio contest. Everything culminated with a post-game concert by the country rock band Adairs Run and a ceremony for the winning couple. All of these successful promotions take a ton of effort to pull off, but when done correctly they gain a national spotlight, and that makes all the extra hours of work worthwhile to those in the front office.

It's a grind, but the effort that goes into each of the games is worth it for that sense of community that you feel as fans come together to cheer. Many broadcasters do a lot of extra tasks during the day to get to do what they love to do, and Adam is no different. It's necessary to get on the phone and try to sell tickets to groups, or to pull the tarp when it rains. Broadcasters find themselves putting together marketing and social media plans and editing the website so fans can keep up with what is going on at the ballpark. But all that work is worth it when Adam gets to put on the headset.

Play-by-Play from the Minors

"The best part of every day for a broadcaster is 7:05 for first pitch. It's why we do everything else between 8 a.m., or on a school day 6 a.m., and the start of the game," Marco says. "For three hours, I get to push everything out of my mind, talk about baseball, talk about my team and what's going on in the league or around the world in some cases. That's the best part of every day."

What happens after first pitch is typically up to the players on the field and the creative minds in the front office. However, success or failure between the chalk generally isn't what a lot of fans remember after attending minor league games. One day that was certainly about more than baseball to the average fan was August 21, 2017. That was the day a total solar eclipse went coast-to-coast across America, and fortunately for Adam Marco, he was calling a game in Greenville, South Carolina, which was along the path of totality. A total of 6,636 people gathered for a day game on a Monday—a few thousand more than the Greenville Drive's average Monday crowd in 2017—and when the eclipse started, the team stopped the game for 34 minutes with one out in the bottom of the fifth.

"People were on the field and they passed out glasses so that the fans could view the eclipse properly," Marco remembers. "I know a lot of teams along the path of totality did something similar, but I thought that was a great use of something going on that they could have avoided, because they could have played that night and been done with it. Instead, they adapted to what was going on in the world and made an event out of it."

That's what Minor League Baseball oozes at its best. It's where you can watch a baseball game, grab some food or cheap drinks and have a unique experience. The more than 6,000 fans who attended that game in 2017 were treated to an incredible contest, and the Drive walked it off in the 10th inning. Odds are, if you were to ask someone who was there to describe the game, they'd say they remember watching the eclipse at the ballpark ... oh, and the home team won the game in extra innings. Sure, someone who watches every Pirates or Dodgers game on television may be watching for a different reason than the fans buying tickets to MiLB games, but that's the beauty of baseball.

"[Big league] baseball people won't understand that. Minor League Baseball people do get it," Marco explains. Although, when he thinks back to the night of the eclipse, he may not necessarily be thinking about baseball or the rare event where the Moon blocks the Sun. That's because in all his time in West Virginia, he hadn't been on a trip where the bus had broken down ... that is, until that August night of his final season with the Power when they were leaving Greenville following the eclipse game. Because they had played a day game, the team was fortunate to be on the road and traveling by 5 or 6 p.m. back to West Virginia. Typically, this drive takes under six hours and clocks in at a hair over 350 miles. Of course, because everyone along the way was out and watching the eclipse, traffic did not make it that easy. In fact, the relatively short journey over to Charlotte to get back to I-77 had already cost the team a few hours because of the number of people on the road.

Normally, Marco is a quiet guy on the bus. The team had a backup bus driver, though, and Marco mentioned that if the team went through Asheville, it was supposed to save some serious time. Unfortunately, the driver said he wouldn't change the route, and it cost the team. The broadcaster remembers it took four hours to get to Charlotte, when it should have taken just an hour and a half. Then, the team started driving north and things went from bad to worse.

"The bus started going up this hill and just died. We pulled off to the side of the road and all the lights went out," Marco says.

This incident happened at 11 p.m., and after letting the bus sit on the side of the road for some time, they were able to get it started. That only lasted about a mile before the bus died again.

"Eventually, we eke our way into an exit, and at two in the morning, I'm buying hotel rooms for the team on my team card. We stayed at a Super 8 for the night," Marco continues.

The bus needed a technician to come out to fix an error in its computer, and they couldn't get someone to do that at night. So, the team camped out in a motel just two hours away from Appalachian Power Park until the morning. What should have been a six-hour bus trip turned into a 17-hour ride. Marco surely won't be forgetting that trip anytime soon, just like the fans in attendance won't forget the eclipse they saw that day.

While most local fans will be drawn to a minor league game because there's a special on beer or a fun promotion, some national fans follow around top prospects to have the opportunity to see them play before they make it to The Show. They also enjoy being in a smaller park with the players, and having an increased chance of meeting one of them and getting an autograph. Even for broadcasters, having the opportunity to see those players and cover them on a daily basis adds an extra level of excitement to the daily regimen.

When Marco is asked to name the top prospect he's seen, he

immediately thinks of Bryce Harper when he was a Hagerstown Sun in 2011.

"He was the next big thing. He was the LeBron or the Jordan of baseball," Marco remembers. The year that Harper was picked first overall and went through the South Atlantic League, the Power had the second overall pick in Jameson Taillon and the Delmarva Shorebirds had the third pick, Manny Machado. All three would make the All-Star Game for the Northern Division that year. Harper came to West Virginia at the end of April for a five-game series, and Adam had the opportunity to see him smash five extra-base hits, including two homers. In the second game he played at Appalachian Power Park, Harper hit a homer that still sticks out to the Pennsylvanian to this day.

"He hit an absolute bomb, across the street, into the parking lot behind that plaza beyond right field," Marco recaps. "People were talking about that home run for a long time. That's one of the most famous home runs in West Virginia Power history."

Of course, it's not every day that Bryce Harper walks into a ballpark and attracts fans from all over the state to see him smash his raw skill. Sometimes, you have under-the-radar players who grind away and make a name for themselves in the organization or among the fans. One of those guys was a backup catcher for the Pirates out of Punta Cardón, Venezuela, Francisco "Frankie" Diaz. Diaz spent parts of four seasons playing for the Power, and, ironically enough, in Adam's first year in Scranton/Wilkes-Barre, he spent 34 games with the team after being signed by the Yankees in November 2015. He was a perennial backup for every organization he had been with, but came with a positive attitude and did his job well. In 2012, during his first season with West Virginia, he hit .302 in 45 games, and in 2015 he only played 26 games for the Power, but he averaged .353.

Now, where Frankie Diaz made his fame was in a matchup with Hunter Harvey, a 2013 first-round pick of the Baltimore Orioles and a top-100 consensus prospect when the Power faced the Delmarva Shorebirds on May 18, 2014. The Power were up 1–0 in the fifth with a pair of outs, a runner on second and a 2–2 count on the backstop when Marco's favorite memory of Diaz occurred.

"He hit a home run off Hunter Harvey on a Sunday afternoon, and you just don't pitch to Frankie Diaz on a Sunday," Marco states. The homer knocked Harvey out of the game and contributed to the Power's 7–0 win.

Diaz is just one of a long line of great guys that Marco came across in the Pirates organization, but one first-round pick stands out above the rest. If you know Marco, you know how much he likes Cole Tucker, the curly-haired Arizona native who has been with the Pirates since the 2014 draft.

"When I met Cole, he was young, enthusiastic and genuinely one of the nicest people you would come across and not expect that he is a millionaire first-round pick," Adam remembers.

Tucker was with the Power in 2015, a difficult year for Marco. He didn't tell any players about what was going on, but some family health problems were weighing heavily on him. Meanwhile, Tucker was injured in late July. Marco would see him briefly to catch up at spring training, and, after more rehab games, he eventually made it back to West Virginia during the 2016 season for the Mother's Day game. Despite the fact that Tucker had gone through his own struggles, and plenty of time had passed since the two had talked, he still asked Marco about what he was going through. He came into the office the night prior to Mother's Day, saw Marco and asked how he was doing and how his family was adjusting to the changes that they were going through.

"That spoke volumes to me about the character that he has," Marco says. Then, for Adam's 40th birthday, his family traveled to Pittsburgh to see the Pirates play. There was a rain delay, but eventually, things were getting ready to start back up, and the players began stretching. Fans lined up near the field to get autographs, but Marco was just trying to get a glimpse of some of the players he had formerly worked with. Then, he saw Tucker taking grounders by second base and the young major leaguer made a beeline to the broadcaster.

"We [only] talked for like 30 seconds, but I haven't seen many players who have their feet on the ground like that considering the circumstances in the air around them," Marco says. "I really hope he figures everything out and becomes a star for the Pirates. I'm biased, I want him to succeed for the Pirates, but wherever he goes, I will be a fan of his."

Not only does Tucker have one of the best personalities of players that Marco knows, but he also played on one of the top teams that Marco has broadcast for, the 2015 Power. That team finished the regular season with an 87–52 record prior to dropping the divisional playoff series to the Hickory Crawdads.

Despite the harrowing end of the season, Marco still remembers that team fondly, and many of the players have gone on to have a significant impact in the majors. The team included future major leaguers Kevin Kramer, Jordan Luplow, Dovydas Neverauskas, Kevin Newman,

Play-by-Play from the Minors

Stephen Tarpley and Tucker. That year was special to Adam for many reasons: it was one of the most talented teams that he broadcast for, it was a fun year with Brian Esposito as the Power's manager, and the team commemorated the 55th anniversary of Bill Mazeroski's famous 1960 walk-off home run in the World Series. The Power wore retro jerseys at home games and striped socks, which was noticeable because Pittsburgh required that their farmhands wear their socks high at that point. To add to the aesthetic, the team had many promotions memorializing one of the greatest sports moments in Pittsburgh history. The Power didn't take home the championship that year, but it is still one of the most talented teams that Marco has been able to spend time with day in and day out.

That team also played through the most incredible moment Marco can remember calling. It was April 15, 2015, and the Power were playing the Hagerstown Suns at Appalachian Power Park. There was supposed to be a doubleheader that day, but after the first game went to seven innings, there wasn't enough of a window to play the second. None of the 1,862 people arriving at Appalachian Power Park that day knew it yet, but they were about to experience a historic game.

In the first frame, Jake Burnette walked the bases loaded while only retiring a single Suns batter. He fanned one more hitter before being pulled in favor of Jose Regalado, who issued a free pass to Jeff Gardner that scored Narciso Mesa, to put the Suns up 1–0. That seems like your average lackluster inning of Class-A baseball, but it's what happened next that made the day special. Regalado and Eric Dorsch didn't allow another hitter to reach base safely for the remainder of the game. Because the only batters to reach base were either hit by a pitch or walked, the West Virginia Power had a no-hitter.

What makes this story even more wild is that the offense couldn't put anything together that day. They had four hits scattered throughout the game and lost 1–0. So, the Power threw a no-hitter, but lost the game. While this had happened just two years earlier in the Gulf Coast League, a rookie-level baseball league, it is still an incredibly rare feat. To put it in perspective, only two major league teams have tossed a no-hitter and lost the game: the 1964 Houston Colt .45s and the 1967 Baltimore Orioles, according to a *Sports Illustrated* article published the following day.

Marco will tell you that he can't remember many moments on the field that meant a lot to him.

"It's like rounders and poker players. You remember the losses more

38

than the wins. For me, I remember the players more than the moments," Marco says.

Along the same wavelength, what Scranton/Wilkes-Barre's call-man considers his greatest lesson in baseball doesn't have to do with a singular moment on the field; rather, it's learning how to navigate the industry.

Marco calls it a series of moments in learning how to become a better broadcaster, and then reflects on whether that matters in the grand scheme of becoming a better Minor League Baseball employee. The thought hit him for the first time at his first Winter Meetings.

"There are hundreds or thousands of us and there are so few jobs," Marco recalls. "There were like 300 broadcasters for maybe nine jobs. This industry is so competitive, and you have to pay your dues and do your time. It was about learning whatever skills I could to develop myself."

Fast forward to today, and Adam has navigated this industry at every level possible, ranging from short-season baseball to Triple-A with the New York Yankees. He has stepped up and become a mentor to many young broadcasters, helping guide them to that same realization themselves. From networking and molding youngsters into successful broadcasters to calling games in the booth in Scranton/Wilkes-Barre, Adam still enjoys the game as much as that young boy who opened *Boys' Life* magazine to read about Orel Hershiser.

That's why, if Adam could go back and call any moment, he'd go back to his heritage—his heritage of being a Dodgers fan in his youth. He thinks of Kirk Gibson's home run off Dennis Eckersley in the 1988 World Series, when Marco was just nine years old. Everyone can remember CBS's broadcaster Jack Buck and his call about the Dodger star who had injured his hamstring and knee earlier, in the playoffs, and had to sit out the remainder of the World Series after his infamous home run.

"Jack Buck, his call 'Unbelievable!' You're right, it absolutely was. Here's a guy who could barely walk to the plate. He could barely stand. He told his manager he had one good swing and got it on a backdoor slider. It was the only at-bat for Kirk Gibson in the World Series that year," Marco states. "I just hope that I could do it enough justice as what was done at the time."

3

Joe Block

Currently with the Pittsburgh Pirates
Previously with the Milwaukee Brewers,
Billings Mustangs, Great Falls Voyagers,
Jacksonville Suns, St. Paul Saints and
Charleston RiverDogs

Adam Marco isn't the only broadcaster who has always considered Pittsburgh home. When the average fan thinks of Joe Block, it's as the play-by-play voice of the Pittsburgh Pirates. After accepting the job in Pittsburgh, he considered it a homecoming after traveling all around the country to get there.

Block has worked with seven teams in his 18-year broadcasting career, and for the last nine seasons he has occupied a major league press box. After sharing a broadcast booth in Milwaukee with the legendary Bob Uecker for his first five seasons as a major league play-by-play broadcaster, Block was able to find a job in Pittsburgh, about a 15-minute drive north of his wife's hometown. While Block grew up in Michigan, in a Detroit suburb, his grandparents lived in Wheeling, just south of Pittsburgh in West Virginia's Northern Panhandle, and Byesville, which is about 50 miles west of Wheeling in southeastern Ohio. So, after nearly 15 years of living in the western plains of Montana and the southern swamps of Jacksonville and Charleston, South Carolina, with a stint in the Midwest in Milwaukee and Minnesota, Block was able to return to his roots.

Block is a family man, no doubt about it. The narrative doesn't change when talking about his fandom, either. Growing up in Detroit in the '80s, he experienced the Tigers' fourth World Series win when he was just six years old. Admittedly, he didn't know much about what was going on at the time, but he knew there was something good brewing in Detroit in the mid–'80s. Of course, it helps to have a united front of baseball fans around you as you grow up.

3. Joe Block

"My great-grandparents, three different families of great-grandparents, really loved baseball, and they all talked to me about it. I watched them watch it and listen to it, so those were the early influences for me to get me into baseball," Block says.

Although Joe remembers his great-grandfather listening to Tigers games on the radio and watching them on television at the same time when he was younger, his earliest memory of an actual major league stadium is from near the end of the regular season for the Tigers. His great-grandmother, who had played baseball and softball in the sandlots of New York in the mid- to late '30s, got a young Joe out of

Joe Block has been a part of Pittsburgh's broadcast team since 2016. He entered the Pirates' booth after spending four years working with legendary broadcaster Bob Uecker (photograph courtesy Joe Block).

school to attend his first-ever Tigers game at the old Tiger Stadium, a September 1985 showcase against the Boston Red Sox.

"It's the typical story, especially at those older ballparks where the concourse was underneath the seats, so you look up and you look out and see the green. There's the old adage that you'd never seen grass that green and uniforms that white, and that definitely applied to me," Block reminisces about the stadium he has seen a hundred games at. "That was what sold me. Because it was one of the last games of the season, that next season I was hooked. I was following the whole offseason."

Growing up a fan of the Detroit Tigers, Block listened to a Hall of Fame broadcaster on the radio and watched two more on television. Because of that immersion, the young fan learned a lot about how to broadcast a game.

On the radio, Block heard Ernie Harwell, a Hall of Famer, who spent 55 years broadcasting baseball games—42 of which were in the booth for the Detroit Tigers—and Paul Carey, who some in Detroit referred to as "the voice of God." The nickname came from his slow cadence and

41

deep voice to pair with it. Harwell was a special broadcaster who earned accolades and recognition both inside and outside of the Motor City, but a lot of people don't know that there was a unique quirk about his career. Famed general manager Branch Rickey, who signed Jackie Robinson to the Brooklyn Dodgers, traded a young player, Cliff Dapper, who caught for the Dodgers, to the unaffiliated Atlanta Crackers for Ernie Harwell, making Harwell the only broadcaster ever traded for a player. Harwell filled in for Red Barber that season, as Barber started to fall ill near the end of his famed career.

The television team was composed of George Kell and Al Kaline. These two were both Hall of Famers as well, but they were inducted for their playing careers. Kell may be most famous as being the player who won the 1949 batting crown over Ted Williams by two ten-thousandths of a point. The 10-time All-Star was in the booth from 1959 to 1996 for Detroit. Kaline was known as "Mr. Tiger." He played in Motown for 22 seasons and has his number six hanging in the rafters at Comerica Park. The 1980 first-ballot Hall of Fame inductee was an 18-time All-Star and won 10 Gold Gloves and the 1955 batting title as a player.

"Whether I'm watching or listening, I have a Hall of Famer there. George and Al's style was talking about the game and their experiences relating to the experiences of the players out there. So, I learned a lot about how the game is played through those two," Joe explains. "Ernie and Paul taught me descriptions and how to bring the game to life through that aspect. Through those four guys, every Michigander was treated to the game in the best possible way."

Ernie Harwell was known as a mentor to many young broadcasters, and before he passed, Joe and the Hall of Famer became good friends. Because of this friendship, every once in a while, you'll hear Joe offer "baseball greetings" at the top of his broadcast when he's thinking about the late Tigers play-by-play man. He'll also use the phrase "he kicks and deals" Harwell was famous for when a pitcher entered a wind-up. Of course, Harwell wasn't the only broadcaster Block grew up listening to that influenced him. Thinking of George Kell, Block remembers his childhood.

"When I was a young kid, I would talk into a tape recorder. George Kell was from Arkansas, and so I would try to imitate that drawl and do a game into my tape recorder as if I was George Kell when I was eight or nine years old," Block remembers.

The one Kell phrase he'll still use is "donnybrook." It's a little old-school and may sound out of place, but that matches the instance it's used in during a ballgame. Whenever the benches clear and there is a brawl, rather than referring to it with a commonplace term, Block will call it a "donnybrook," which means a scene of uproar and disorder or a heated argument, according to Oxford Languages.

Of course, there was a lot of time between the young Joe Block imitating George Kell into his tape recorder and his becoming the voice of the Pittsburgh Pirates. The first stepping stone came in 1999 when he graduated from Michigan State, where he had done the typical sort of work at student radio stations and other on-campus activities to pair with some internships. After working at a few newspapers, including *The State* in Jackson, Michigan, Block took it upon himself to write to some of his favorite *SportsCenter* broadcasters. Broadcasting in baseball had been a dream of his for a long time, but he had thought he would be able to make a lot more money—at least initially—writing for newspapers.

Jack Edwards, who worked for ESPN from 1991 to 2003 anchoring *SportsCenter* and doing play-by-play, took an interest in Joe's career. Edwards recommended that Block attend the Winter Meetings that year to see what was available. Through the 1999 Winter Meetings in Nashville, Block met a member of the Goldklang Group who eventually gave him a job as the play-by-play voice of the Charleston RiverDogs. Most entry-level play-by-play jobs in baseball are seasonal, or single-year contracts, but this gig turned into much more than a one-year deal, as the ownership group moved him to St. Paul, Minnesota, where he became the voice of the St. Paul Saints. After a two-year stint up north, he traded in his gloves and boots for some swim trunks and sunglasses as he moved to Jacksonville, Florida, to work for the Double-A Suns.

He found a sports talk radio gig to pair with the job for the Suns, which he retained for four years before heading out west to the Pioneer League. He only spent a single season in Great Falls, Montana, before he was able to find a job working for his first MLB team, the Los Angeles Dodgers. He did pre- and post-game hosting while managing the audio for the radio broadcast during the game. His next, and final, non-play-by-play stop was occupying a similar role for the Charlotte Hornets in the NBA before he was able to find his footing in Milwaukee.

In his first major league play-by-play gig, Block had the opportunity to learn from one of the industry's most-revered figures, Bob Uecker. The 2003 Ford C. Frick Award winner, National Sportscasters and Sportswriters Association Hall of Famer, National Radio Hall of Famer and Milwaukee Brewers Ring of Honor member has left a mark on the sport that will never be forgotten. Block had the opportunity to work with and learn from Uecker for the better part of four seasons. His sentiments regarding what he learned from Uecker are very similar to what Adam Marco said about finding your own voice through the emulation of other broadcasters.

"He taught me how to entertain. What I mean by that is: I'm not trying to be him, but I can be me. I can use not only my sense of humor, but my charm and wit," Block explains. "For example, my style is that I like plays on words and subtle references. Maybe it's a double entendre or maybe it's a movie quote or rap lyric ... where if you're not aware of it, it does flow, but if you are aware of it, you go, 'oh wow!' It's a way to entertain yourself too, because you spend about 500 hours on-air a year."

Uecker's influence can't be overstated in making Block comfortable in his first big league job. He taught the young announcer to be comfortable on air, so that he wasn't just worried about the nuts and bolts of the job. Uecker educated Block on the game of baseball from the vantage point of someone who had played at the highest level and had broadcast from a major league booth for 50 years. All of those lessons from Uecker allowed Block to get to where he is today with the Pittsburgh Pirates.

"This opportunity is the one place we [Block, his wife and children] would have left Milwaukee for. Our kids were born here, we got married here. We finally bought a house, and it has been pretty great," Block explains.

With nearly 20 years of experience behind the mic, Block has a pretty good idea of what it takes to be a good broadcaster. In fact, for over six years, Block ran the website CalloftheGame.com, which countless broadcasters, including some mentioned in this book, utilized when they first tried to break into the industry. The website essentially connected young broadcasters to job openings in sports broadcasting, and, at its peak, attracted more than 2,000 unique visitors a day.

Despite his mentorship to many young broadcasters and his seat at the table in the MLB circuit, Block will tell you that he is not finished.

"It's something that I'm striving to do. I think I'm good, but I would like to be great and there are days that I think everybody can be great, I just want more of them."

First, he emphasizes you have to have the basics down, relaying all the information available correctly. When you get good, it's a lot about repetition, according to Block, but to get to the next level, the broadcast veteran says, you need to be a wordsmith. He goes on to explain that a lot of your ability to do that comes from your preparation and your understanding of what is going on beyond just the numbers. Sometimes it's relaying what you hear from both teams in the clubhouse before and after each game. If you hear a few guys joking around while playing cards in the clubhouse before the game and notice that all of them look good during the game, maybe you talk about how the team has gelled and has good locker room chemistry. Another thing to maybe toss out there is if a player mentions to you that they love playing in a certain ballpark or if they have family or friends in the area, and again, if they play well, it may be worth mentioning that they enjoy playing for those people. Gathering all of that perspective helps a broadcaster to be great.

"A broadcaster's job is to augment and explain what the people are watching. All of the work that one does [before the game] makes it that much easier to sew up or encapsulate a moment the way that you want to. That's because you know what is happening and how everyone is feeling and thinking down on the field in that moment, live," Block emphasizes. "That is what really separates the great from the good. It's having the command of the language and doing the work to know what is happening and what people are thinking about to relay it to the audience."

So, when you listen to a Pirates broadcast, yes, the stats are important, but know that all the preparation Block has done helps him to fine-tune his diction and what he will deliver to the audience.

Block has traveled in some of the biggest markets in America during his time in the majors, and the Michigander has spent time in four different MiLB leagues. Despite going through all of the big markets of major league, Double-A and independent ball teams, his favorite town to visit is Missoula, Montana, home to the PaddleHeads of the Pioneer League. Like most cities in the short-season circuit, Missoula is small—with a population around 70,000, according to the most recent census data. Despite that, there are a lot of great things to do in Missoula. It plays host to the University of Montana and it is part of the absolutely breathtaking northwest corner of the United States. The mountains can clearly be seen beyond the outfield fence at Ogren Park at Allegiance Field, which was built in 2004. Even Missoula's previous field, Lindborg-Cregg Field, which was a dilapidated, old park by the time it was phased out, still was breathtaking because it had beautiful mountains all around it.

Missoula was built up around the Clark Fork River and, situated right in the heart of the town, along West Broadway, was a small

Mexican restaurant called La Parrilla. Certainly a trendy spot in a college town, it advertised on its website that they had the best fat burritos that you could get your hands on, but the Michigander had a different favorite on their menu.

"I probably had this every time I went to Missoula the two years I was in the league. They had this buffalo meat salad with gorgonzola and some other stuff and I would get it every single day. I still think about it," Block says.

Another one of Block's favorite cities is Winnipeg. Growing up not far from Windsor, Ontario, the broadcaster jokes that he loves Canada. That's because to get to Windsor from Detroit, all you have to do is take a short trip south along the Gordie Howe International Bridge. Living "north" of the border, he has a soft spot for his country's neighbor. That soft spot includes the city of Winnipeg, which he visited a handful of times when he called games for the St. Paul Saints. He was a 23- to 24-year-old when he made those treks, and the party scene was great for him and the rest of the (younger) team. After going out to the bars at night, Block enjoyed a nice cheap meal in the morning or afternoon the following day.

"My favorite restaurant there was Tim Hortons," Block laughs. "I would get a chicken salad sandwich, a maple doughnut and a peach pop and I was in heaven, because it was basically $2 and there was a 15 percent exchange rate at the time, so it really helped stretch out the meal money that was granted to us."

As Joe reminisces about some of the old stops he would go to while in minor league ball, he mentions that he would love to visit Missoula and Winnipeg again to see how the cities have developed.

One of the great fortunes of Joe's career is that he has worked for a bunch of teams that not only traveled to interesting towns on the road, but were also located in scenic and fun hometowns. One aspect of a hometown that broadcasters tend to weigh heavily is the quality of its ballpark. Of course, a nice stadium doesn't mean much if the team can't sell tickets consistently. Some of us tend to overlook small problems with a press box or stadium if a team draws particularly well, and one thing that really affects how a team draws is fun promotions. In Block's time with the Goldklang Group, particularly in Charleston right after Joseph P. Riley, Jr. Park was built in 1997, he had the opportunity to see a lot of unique promotions. In addition to recycling old, successful promotions routinely, the team was widely encouraged to push new ideas—regardless of how unusual they may seem.

46

3. Joe Block

In 2000, one of the owners of the Goldklang Group, Mike Veeck, had an idea that was certainly outlandish, but that's his style. Veeck has a long history of wild promotions. No doubt a flair for the zany runs in the family genes. Remember the infamous Disco Demolition Night at old Comiskey Park in 1979? The one where fans were given admission for under a dollar if they brought a disco record, with all the records to be blown up in center field by a local DJ in between games of a doubleheader? That was the idea of Bill Veeck, Mike's father. Our Veeck, Mike, was the business and promotions manager of the White Sox at that time, learning from his dad. (Unfortunately, the explosion led thousands of fans to storm the field and the White Sox ended up forfeiting the second game.) Fast forward a few decades and travel to South Carolina, where Mike became the brains behind the first "Nobody Night," where gates were closed to fans to get an attendance of zero for the evening, thereby setting a record. (Fans were eventually let in for the final inning.) He even came up with "Vasectomy Night"—which just so happened to get canceled at the last minute in the early 2000s. While Block was in Charleston, the most famous promotion the RiverDogs held came right after one of the biggest scandals in U.S. Olympic Figure Skating history.

In January 1994, two days prior to a pre–Olympic trial in Detroit, Olympic hopeful Nancy Kerrigan was attacked by a man with a club while she was leaving the practice arena. According to *History.com*, the man hit her in the back of the knee, injuring her and forcing her to withdraw from the U.S. championships. This ensured that fellow Olympic hopeful Tonya Harding would qualify for the Olympics. After a few weeks, Harding's ex-husband came forward and confessed to arranging the crime. Eventually, Harding, too, was implicated in the conspiracy. She was also involved in a separate situation where she got into a confrontation with a fellow motorist and law enforcement found her with a bat in her hands.

Fast forward to the year 2000: The scandal was still fresh in everyone's memory and Veeck invited Harding to the ballpark to sign autographs. Meanwhile, fans were told that it was mini-bat giveaway night at The Joe, the RiverDogs' stadium. Enter the perfect storm. Harding was set up at a table near the gates to autograph whatever fans gave her, and fans were being handed mini baseball bats.

"The Tonya Harding mini-bat night was hilarious. She obviously was not keen on it once she figured it out and she walked out eventually, but she was there for a while. When people started walking in asking

47

her to sign mini-bats and there were four or five of us by her, she eventually left, but it got people's attention initially, so it was good," Block recalls.

That was a typical Veeck-inspired night, but, as mentioned earlier, in that ownership group all sorts of ideas are on the table.

"A few years ago, I was digging through a bunch of notes and folders of things that I had, and one of the things I proposed was Pride Night—and this was in 2000. We ended up not doing it that year, but I was proud that we were at least talking about it in 2000," Joe explains.

Of course, today Pride Night is an event that is held at nearly every MiLB ballpark across America, but this group was certainly ahead of their time in trying to make the stadium an open environment to everyone interested in attending a game.

While it is always the goal of teams to become more inclusive and to get more people to the ballpark, sometimes it's difficult just to get the *team* to the yard. When Block was broadcasting in Jacksonville with the Suns, they had a tough road schedule by anybody's standards. After the Orlando Rays left the league, the closest opponent was a six-hour trip from Jacksonville. Though traveling to any game was a trek, one trip in particular stands out in Block's mind as the longest. The Suns had just finished a game against the Birmingham Barons. Normally, the journey through Talladega National Forest and down the Eastern Seaboard is a lengthy one, but it isn't terrible, clocking in at about seven hours to drive 492 miles, but on this trip, things were a little different.

"It was about a 24-hour bus drive from Birmingham to Jacksonville. And you say, 'Well, why was it 24 hours, Joe?'" Block begins the story. The bus broke down in a small town called Pell City, Alabama, about an hour into the drive back home. It was around midnight, and the team was sitting in an Exxon parking lot in the stifling 90-degree heat of a Southern summer night. After some time, the manager spoke with the owners of the team and they decided to send a bus from Jacksonville. Now, it seems like it would make more sense to get a bus from Birmingham, which the team was only an hour away from, but the Suns ownership group owned a busing company in Jacksonville. This key detail meant it was much cheaper for them to send a bus from their fleet in Florida than to try to work something out with an Alabama company. In other words, the team would have to wait at least five or six hours for a bus to come to their rescue.

"I remember Joel Hanrahan had spread out cardboard on the cement and tried to get some sleep there. Our starter the next day was

3. Joe Block

Eric Stults, and the manager said, 'You need to get some rest, so you should go on the bus and try to get some sleep,'" Block recalls. "I remember going on the bus and looking at him trying to sleep and the sweat was dripping into his eyes. He just kept wiping his eyes every two or three minutes and he just could not fall asleep."

The team slept in the parking lot until the sun rose, and when the sun came up and the small Exxon convenience store opened, the team got what they could there.

The bus finally arrived to rescue the team at noon, nearly 12 hours after their bus had broken down. It had taken the bus company some time to find a driver who could pick up the route, as this was in the era prior to cell phones.

Initially, the organization wanted them to hurry back without stopping so they could play their home game that evening in front of what would surely be a large Saturday night crowd, but, later that day, the Los Angeles Dodgers' farm director, Bill Bavasi, called the front office and said they were canceling the game that night. He instructed the team to stop in Atlanta before finishing the homeward journey and told them they were going to have a real meal.

"We all went to the Applebee's right off the exit and the Dodgers were paying for it all. It felt like we had never eaten a meal before and we had this hot food in front of us. We didn't end up getting back until around 10:15 after that meal, and Stults was finally able to sleep without the sweat stinging his eyes," Block finishes.

Joe, like many other broadcasters and players, looks back at memories of long bus rides and says that they sucked at the time, but now they're all funny stories. Those are the times when the guys really banded together and built a feeling of comradery. It's true that although 25 guys get drafted and put on a team, they are still individuals, and if they want to have any success as a team, they have to come together. A lot of that happens playing Pluck on the bus or sharing a pizza after a game.

At the same time, while teamwork is important, individual talent is something that helps good teams win consistently, and the most talented guy Block saw while broadcasting in the minors was Miguel Cabrera. It seems obvious now to say that the 11-time All-Star and member of the 500 Home Run Club would have been outstanding to see at such a young age. But Joe will tell you that although there was hype for Cabrera, he certainly wasn't at the level some guys today are at, like Vladimir Guerrero, Jr.

49

Play-by-Play from the Minors

Block had the opportunity to see Cabrera in 2003 when he was in Jacksonville, and the slugger left a very favorable impression. "It was a four-game series in early May and his batting average was .400 entering the series and still went up every single night. He was hitting three, four, five rockets every night and playing Gold Glove third base. When you saw Miguel Cabrera, it was very easy to know that he was going to be a very, very good player," Block states matter-of-factly.

It wasn't just one moment that sealed the deal for Block in that four-game series; rather, it was the collective play of Cabrera. Imagine: to increase your batting average when you're hitting .400, you have to go at least 2-for-4 every evening, and Cabrera was doing it with power. He was phenomenal in 69 games in the Southern League, playing for the Carolina Mudcats before he got the call up to The Show and helped the Florida Marlins win a World Series that same year. He ended up hitting .365 with a .429 on-base percentage, blasted 10 homers and drove in 59 runs in only 266 at-bats. To go further, 43 percent of Miggy's hits that season were extra-base knocks. To put that into perspective, the National League average extra-base hit percentage in 2003 was 33.93 percent, or 10 percent lower than what Miggy hit.

Just as Cabrera's career is winding down, Block believes that the role of the organizational player is coming to a halt, too. We're already seeing it at the major league level, but after the MiLB consolidation took place, the reality is that there are fewer roster spots available for guys who are mentors to younger players on the team. According to their broadcaster, a big reason why the 2005 Jacksonville team was so successful is because of the organizational-role guys who were there to teach character and values to the young future All-Stars.

Block views that championship-winning team as the top group he got to call in the minors, and a lot of the credit goes to the future All-Stars on that roster. Joel Hanrahan, Edwin Jackson and Russell Martin were all able to earn that elite tag while playing in the bigs, but longtime major leaguers like Delwyn Young, Eric Stults, James Loney and Andy LaRoche also populated the team that won 79 games in the 140-game regular season.

Joe doesn't think they could have won it without the outfield the Dodgers decided to place in Double-A that year. Tydus Meadows, Todd Donovan and Jon Weber were the three guys who manned the outfield grass. Not one of them went on to play Major League Baseball. However, all three were able to hold their own weight, hitting around .275 with a little bit of power, and all three were in their late 20s, right at the prime of their playing careers.

What they added to the team was their veteran presence and mentorship to all the young prospects that anchored that squad. Their impact in keeping those guys loose and ready to play was immeasurable to the team, according to Block.

"Jon Weber and Delwyn Young were the prankster-type, animated guys in the clubhouse to fuel all of that for the team," Block recalls. "While Donovan and Meadows were the workman-type pros that show you how to go about it and are important to have as well. It's probably my favorite team I've been around because of the personality, the talent and the everyday vibe of being around that group."

Those types of players, the high-character players, are a big part of what makes coming to the ballpark every day so enjoyable. While Block says that each team has at least one or two individuals that are incredible locker room guys, such as Weber, Donovan and Meadows, there's one guy who really stood out in the 2005 squad. Block met Tim Dillard while the 16-year veteran was in Milwaukee. It was right around that point that Dillard started making funny social media videos. His last season in the majors was way back in 2012, but he played in Triple-A from 2013 to 2019, and while there was no Minor League Baseball in 2020, he signed a contract with the Milwaukee Milkmen to return to Wisconsin and continue his playing career. Because the Milkmen are an Independent League team, they had a season in 2020, which allowed Dillard to play one more season before he announced his retirement in March 2021.

Dillard continued to play baseball not for another shot at The Show, but rather because he enjoyed the atmosphere and thought he could still contribute to a team. Block considers him "a fun, positive person to be around." If you're looking for an example of his entertaining personality, check out some of his social media pages; he's typically @DimTillard. In his last year with the Milkmen, he came out with a Create-A-Player video and a dub of *Anchorman* that inspired a lot of fan interaction.

During his time with the Brewers, some of his top YouTube videos were "Brewers Night Live," which took the iconic saxophone riff from *Saturday Night Live* and introduced different players, executives and even Bob Uecker instead of comedians from the actual show, and "The Rules of Wiffle Ball," where Dillard used some effects to make an old-timey video about how to play the common backyard game.

Although baseball is typically a welcome distraction from harsh, real-world problems that people come across on a day-to-day basis, Block's proudest moment as a broadcaster came when real-world issues coincided with baseball at the start of the 2020 season. In March, the morning after the NBA suspended its season due to Covid, Block showed up at the ballpark, thankful for baseball, but ready to make an announcement. With some studying and guidance from Block's wife, a nurse practitioner, the broadcast team learned as much as they could about the pandemic prior to going on-air. Block and his producers created graphics, so when they went on air, he was able to help educate his audience about the novel virus and what medical officials were doing to limit the outbreak.

The Michigander and self-proclaimed news junkie figured that the severity of the virus would cause all professional sports to be postponed or canceled when he went to work that morning and was happy the team decided to take that day's broadcast to educate their audience about the pandemic.

"It was probably a lot of people's first indoctrination to 'what is this coronavirus?' Does it come with a lime? What is this? We were trying to be a little educational while still having a little fun, but there was definitely a tenor of what the gravity of the situation was," Block remembers. "I was really proud of taking that approach, because when we signed off for the day, we were the last North American professional sports television broadcast for around four months."

Although baseball isn't as dire or grave as educating the public about a major pandemic, the truth is, broadcasters are always scouring websites and other resources to learn more information about everything they can to relate to fans. When it comes to the game of baseball, Block is a stickler for the rules and will tell you that broadcasters should have a good feel for the rulebook. It's important that they understand what is going on, and that they can explain those things to fans. He'll also tell you that if you don't know the answer, it is okay to not say anything and to wait until you can get the correct answer. With that being said, he will also tell you that most fans are typically forgiving if you get a rule or an interpretation of a rule wrong.

"Where I really feel like I can fail is when it comes down to people. I try to always get the story right, which is why I always talk to the player. I don't just rely on a Wikipedia article or newspaper story. I go to the player and make sure I get it right and in the right context," Block says.

He double-checks the details because a small detail from an outdated newspaper story can lead to a huge error in the story you are currently telling. For example, what if a player's mom has passed away in the two years since an article was published? Another error you could be led into is misstating the correct number of children someone has because they had a baby in the offseason, or calling a player's wife his girlfriend on-air because you were quoting an old article rather than asking the player. That's the biggest lesson that Block has taken away from his time in broadcasting—the importance of the human element and accurate storytelling that supplement your broadcast.

Joe has done a lot working in baseball. He's called future All-Stars, he's discussed an international health crisis and he's mentored young broadcasters. But one thing he hasn't been able to do is broadcast for a World Series–winning team. He got to work with that Jacksonville Suns team in 2005 that won a Double-A championship, but he hasn't been able to call one at the big-league level. One of Block's career goals is to broadcast a World Series, so it's fitting that if he could call one moment in baseball history that has already happened, he would go back to a time when the Pirates won a championship. More specifically, October 13, 1960, when the underdog Pirates beat the New York Yankees.

Block thrillingly described the theatrics that went into the moment. In the eighth and ninth frames, the game went back and forth, but Hal Smith put the Pirates ahead 9–7 in the eighth with a three-run homer on a 2–2 count with two outs. Then, the Pirates' most reliable reliever, Bob Friend, came in to clean up the game in the top of the ninth, but didn't record an out. The Yankees scored a pair of runs after Friend was pulled off the hill and tied the game at 9–9. When it was Pittsburgh's turn at the plate, Bill Mazeroski led off the bottom of the ninth.

"Maz should have been sacrificing because he was such a light hitter, and he's the one who hits a home run? In that cavernous Forbes Field? It's an afternoon game, and I love day baseball, especially in the fall in the old park at Pittsburgh. That's the era of baseball I probably enjoy the most and it's for my team," Block explains.

Of course, that game was broadcast by the Yankees' Mel Allen and Pittsburgh's Bob Prince—two excellent call-men. Our broadcast veteran has a lot of respect for them and simply says:

"I don't know how I would call it any differently. I know how I would prepare for the game, but I don't know what I would say in the moment with the great surprise of anyone hitting a home run in Game 7 of a World Series. Especially in that back-and-forward type affair. I don't think people realize still to this day, outside of Pittsburgh maybe, how much of an underdog the Pirates were. It's all the things you want in a game and it's won on a home run; so improbable, and it's David vs. Goliath."

What's interesting about the tape of that particular game, a game that is viewed as maybe the best game ever played, is that it was lost for years. For the longest time, no one could find the complete broadcast that NBC produced that day. That is, until 2010, when an entire copy of the game footage was found on 16 mm tape in the wine cellar of Bing Crosby's former home. Crosby was part owner of the Pirates from 1946 until his death in 1977. When the tape was found, it was such a big deal that MLB Network created an event to view it, and Bob Costas interviewed many of the surviving members of the 1960 World Series–winning Pirates. Now that the film has been discovered, fans everywhere can watch one of the greatest moments in baseball history as though they are listening to Joe broadcasting today's Pirates games. If you watch the tape, you can ponder, just as Joe did, what you would say during the moment of Mazeroski's famous feat.

4

Jesse Goldberg-Strassler

Currently with the Lansing Lugnuts
Previously with the Windy City ThunderBolts,
Montgomery Biscuits and Brockton Rox

Joe Block has always made sure to pass along the mentorship he received from broadcasters he has shared the booth with. One way he did that was through his old website, Call of the Game. One broadcaster who went from searching job listings on Call of the Game to being a call man in professional baseball is Jesse Goldberg-Strassler. The Maryland native went as far as awarding the website a "chef's kiss." After all, Call of the Game helped Jesse land his first job in baseball, and that job has led to a successful career lasting nearly two decades describing the action between the chalk.

Goldberg-Strassler is a mainstay broadcaster of the Midwest League. Serving as the broadcaster for the Lansing Lugnuts since 2009, he has called nearly 1,500 Lugnuts games and has experienced some of the top plays in the Midwest League over the last decade. Not only has the Ithaca College graduate called Championship-caliber teams, but he also broadcast the 2018 Midwest League All-Star Game and has seen top prospects such as Mike Trout, Fernando Tatís, Jr., Byron Buxton and Vladimir Guerrero, Jr. He has certainly seen his fair share of interesting things at the ballpark, but he keeps enthusiastically charging toward his ultimate career goal, calling MLB games.

In addition to working in MiLB, Goldberg-Strassler has been the play-by-play voice of the Central Michigan Chippewas women's basketball team since 2014, is a curator at the Michigan Baseball Hall of Fame and is a writer for *Ballpark Digest*. Furthermore, Jesse has written two books, *The Baseball Thesaurus* and *The Football Thesaurus*. To say that the winner of *Ballpark Digest's* 2019 Minor League Broadcaster of the Year award likes to stay busy in the industry would be an understatement, and a lot of his work ethic comes from finding himself lost in books while growing up in Greenbelt, Maryland, in the 1980s. Jesse recalls frequent trips to the local library growing up, rereading picture books until it was time to peruse chapter books and then consuming everything obtainable at his grade school library.

"I was always reading. I think that led to the *Thesaurus*. I read the Matt Christopher baseball books—and all his different sports books. There was also the Baseball Hall of Shame books and books of great World Series games and NFL games," Goldberg-Strassler relays. "They were all so vivid in how they described the action. That captured my imagination more than anything else. For example, the batter never 'hit' the ball, the batter would 'launch' the ball. I loved being able to see that on paper."

While a thirst for knowledge helped guide him to broadcasting, his love for sports was built-in because of the way his father raised him and his two siblings. He grew up collecting baseball cards and hitting a baseball off a tee as soon as he was able to. However, the family's love of sports didn't stop with baseball. In the fall, they followed football and in the winter, basketball—along with a myriad of other sports. Yet, his young journey into sports began with Kirk Gibson hitting his famous homer off Dennis Eckersley in Game 1 of the 1988 World Series.

"My memory tells me I was scared of the A's, who were unstoppable and intimidating. You couldn't do a thing with Jose Canseco or Mark McGwire—you didn't even want to pitch to those guys," Jesse recalls. "There was no beating the Eck. And so, when Gibby hit the homer off the Eck, I remember just going nuts. I was dancing around and I was only six years old."

What started with watching one memorable game on a large stage grew into so much more. Jesse found something new to enjoy about each team and in each game he watched as he blossomed into a young baseball fan. Growing up in Maryland in the late '80s and watching Cal Ripken, Jr., become the Iron Man of baseball, Goldberg-Strassler tuned into quite a few Orioles games. Jon Miller broadcast for the Baltimore Orioles from 1983 to 1996, prior to his tenure with the San Francisco Giants, where he would eventually call Barry Bonds's record-breaking 756th homer in 2006 and win the Ford C. Frick Award in 2010. During that time, Goldberg-Strassler was forming his baseball fan allegiances. Miller was part of a broadcasting team (between television and radio) that included Joe Angel, who broadcast for nearly 20 years for the O's;

4. Jesse Goldberg-Strassler

Chuck Thompson, who had come out of retirement to cover for Miller when Miller picked up ESPN's *Sunday Night Baseball* in 1991; and Fred Manfra, who finished a 25-year career broadcasting Orioles baseball in 2017. These four certainly have storied careers, and the budding baseball fan tuned into many of their games, but what influenced Jesse the most from these four was a highlight VHS tape from the 1989 season. It was a special year in Baltimore. The 1988 Orioles were one of the worst teams in baseball history, finishing the season with a 54–107 record, good for seventh place in the AL East and 34.5 games back of the Boston Red Sox. No one in the lineup even managed to hit .300; right fielder Joe Orsulak's .288 average was the top mark. Outside of 30-year-old Mike Boddicker, no starting pitcher

Jesse Goldberg-Strassler has been a fixture in the Midwest League since 2009 and in the summer of 2022 got the chance to call his first Major League games, getting the call-up for the Oakland Athletics when they journeyed to Fenway Park. He filled in for Ken Korach in the booth (photograph courtesy Jesse Goldberg-Strassler).

had an ERA south of 4.00. But the 1989 season came to be branded as the "Why Not?" season in Baltimore.

The Orioles would make a playoff push in '89, finishing 87–75 and remaining in playoff contention until the final series of the season. Ripken and Mickey Tettleton both smacked more than 20 homers and Bob Milacki and Jeff Ballard anchored the rotation, both with ERAs in the mid–3s. The 1989 highlight video had a lot for Baltimore fans to be excited about, but what stood out most to Jesse was how the four broadcasters vividly described the game.

"All the words that Joe Angel and Jon Miller used to describe them, they just got imprinted on my subconscious," Goldberg-Strassler says. "The way I was influenced by the broadcasters I listened to while I was growing up was that the way that they described the game became the way that I would describe the game."

Following his graduation from Ithaca College, Jesse was unprepared to enter the industry, but found some unique ways to build his resume and figure out how to plant himself in the garden of Minor League Baseball. Due to the location of Ithaca, he was only able to call two baseball games while he was in college, despite the fact that he had entered the school wanting to become a sports broadcaster. Most games were snowed out or canceled due to bad weather.

His first step toward becoming a professional baseball broadcaster was securing an internship at WBAL in Baltimore, covering the Orioles. His primary duty was to gather sound while milling around the stadium in the summer and winter when he was home from college. After being shut out of the industry after college, Jesse turned to narrating theater performances for people who were visually impaired.

"I was now broadcasting performances. I did *Jesus Christ Superstar* in the Washington, D.C., area at [a] musical theater," Goldberg-Strassler recalls. "I did the 'play-by-play' for it. It was a lot of fun. The actors after one show said, 'You're talking way too loudly, you gotta stop that.'" Luckily, after attending Baseball's Winter Meetings across the country in Anaheim, California, in 2004, and landing a gig with the Brockton Rox, the future industry award-winner wouldn't have to worry about talking over a musical any longer.

Part of what makes Minor League Baseball so interesting is how unusual it can be. A lot of the creative promotional content that you see comes from people who think outside of the box regularly. To secure his first job, Jesse found out just how important this mindset was to executives seeking new hires.

In one of Jesse's first interviews, he spoke with a higher-up who asked him how he felt about working in a cubicle all day. The follow-up to that question was how he would react to a job that didn't involve baseball. After responding that his reaction to both would be negative, the interviewer asked Jesse which of the seven dwarfs from *Snow White* was his favorite and what movie he would like to be able to watch over and over again on DVD.

Despite his strange opening interview, because Goldberg-Strassler had answered honestly and well, he made it to future interviews and, eventually, earned his first job in baseball. After stints in local radio and detailing musical performances, Jesse had finally made it to broadcasting live baseball. Reflecting upon those early years and how his career has moved along so far, there's no doubt for Jesse about the most important duties of a broadcaster and what attributes make a good broadcaster great.

After focusing on the language of baseball early in his career, Goldberg-Strassler found another rung to reach on the ladder of diction in the game. It is important to understand and fully utilize the language one is working with. In a sense, that language can be both the English language and the language of baseball. Utilizing the language well is important to becoming a good broadcaster, but according to Goldberg-Strassler, the difference between a good broadcaster and a great broadcaster is being a good translator. In other words, a broadcaster who can relay what is going on is good, but to be great, you have to be able to say it in such a way that someone who may not understand baseball or have all the context about a game can understand what is truly great or poor about what is happening in an ordinary situation on the field.

"I see our job as [like] the person at the United Nations. If there is somebody up there speaking and somebody listening, two ambassadors, then we are the person in between translating. The person on the podium ... is the pitcher on the mound or the batter at the plate, and the person sitting in the seats with the earpiece in, that is all of our listeners," Jesse explains.

It is more than just saying what is happening in the moment. It is more than just regurgitating numbers. It is telling the story of the pitch, the at-bat, the game and the season, and giving full context to the stories happening both on and off the field.

Jesse's start in the industry was in 2004, following the goofy interview mentioned above. He worked as the number three broadcaster for the Brockton (Massachusetts) Rox—a job he accepted for a stipend of $500 per month. He became the studio host for a call-in show during the postgame broadcast. After the season, he was finished in Brockton, but following a broadcasting happy hour in Dallas at the Winter Meetings in 2005, where he met Jim Tocco, he interviewed for a job with the Montgomery Biscuits and eventually accepted their number two position.

After two years (2006–07) in the Southern League, Goldberg-Strassler's role was eliminated, and he was on the search again. Then, in his final stop prior to making it to Lansing, he spent the 2008 season back in independent baseball, working for the Windy City ThunderBolts in Crestwood, Illinois. The bouncing around did bear some personal fruit, however, as from 2006 to 2008, he had the good fortune to broadcast back-to-back Southern League Championship teams and then the 2008 Frontier League champions, the Windy City ThunderBolts.

So far, all of the Maryland native's jobs had been seasonal, meaning that each off-season, he was returning home to be a substitute teacher. He worked with any age group from elementary school to high school seniors, with a variety of different subjects. The broadcaster would receive a call at 6 a.m. giving him an assignment, and he would choose whether he wanted to accept the position or not. Goldberg-Strassler was a long-term substitute for a few classes, including as a music teacher and a third-grade and sixth-grade teach-all-subjects instructor. Despite being in the classroom for a few months each year, Jesse was closer than he knew to securing more permanent footing in baseball. In December 2008, he went to the Winter Meetings again and found his home in Lansing, where he has been since the 2009 season.

Jesse has lived in Michigan for a little over a decade now, but he still enjoys the thrills of traveling on the road. As the Lugnuts' call-man thinks about all the different places he's been to on road trips, he points to the Midwest League as his favorite for travel destinations. The league encompasses cities from Wisconsin to Kentucky, so there are towns to fit everyone's preference somewhere in that range. All in all, the East Coaster picks two Indiana road cities, South Bend and Fort Wayne, as his favorites. Both teams have hotels in excellent locations. They're both in busy areas where you can walk around and explore a bunch of nearby restaurants and shops. Both stadiums, Four Winds Field and Parkview Field, are beautifully built and located downtown near the bustle of everyday city life. Jesse particularly gravitates toward Fort Wayne, a city with a little over 265,000 people, according to 2021 census data. "The Summit City" was built along the Wabash and Erie Canal and is nicknamed as such because it is the highest point along the canal route.

One reason Jesse is so attracted to Fort Wayne is a local restaurant, Cindy's Diner, located just three blocks north of Parkview Field. Initially opened in 1952, this greasy spoon has the slogan "We serve the whole world, 15 at a time." From the street, you'll see a white building with green trim along the roof. It sits catty-corner to an intersection and has two picnic tables out front with umbrellas for outdoor eaters to stay cool on sunny days. The interior is dominated by a long red counter that contrasts with the black-and-white tiled floor.

Staying true to its roots, the '50s style diner offers a cup of joe for just two dollars and one can purchase the breakfast special for under six dollars. While the classic diner food and great prices are a drawing point, Jesse points to the atmosphere as the difference-maker for Cindy's Diner.

"It's the experience of being at this historic diner, where they know exactly who you are and the owner of the place, Angie, will see Fort Wayne TinCaps or Lansing Lugnuts players walk in and she gives it to them, because she knows everything about the team," the broadcaster professes. "So, let's say the starting pitcher from last night walks in with a girlfriend or with his parents. She'll be like, 'So what happened in the fourth inning?' It is so good. It's such a great experience."

The Maryland native is a Washington Commanders fan and the diner's owner supports the Philadelphia Eagles, so the two have long-standing bets on the results of games with mugs at stake. That type of experience, he says, is just one reason why Fort Wayne is such a great place to travel to.

Traveling through small-town America is special, and Goldberg-Strassler has had the opportunity to see some unique places, such as the Historic RailPark & Train Museum in Bowling Green, Kentucky; a stop on the Underground Railroad; the Devonian Fossil Gorge—the archeological remains of an ocean floor from 375 million years ago—in Iowa City, Iowa; and the College Football Hall of Fame in South Bend. These locations are all off the beaten path of the major megalopolises that many Americans frequent on vacations and trips across the United States, but are something most people who attend a minor league game can see on a day off from work. It's nice to be able to find the hidden gems of America while touring the countryside through baseball, but what Jesse finds most unique about Minor League Baseball are the promotions at the ballpark.

Through his 15 years in professional baseball, the play-by-play man has seen quite a few wild and wonky promotional nights at the yard. He's also been involved in planning some, ranging from Backyard Baseball Night in 2018, where the Lansing Lugnuts became the Mighty Wombats for an evening to celebrate the '90s PC game and fans who attended received a Pablo Sanchez bobblehead, to an evening in Brockton in 2005 where fans became the official scorers for the game. In the latter contest, a crowd of over 5,000 scored an error in the bottom of the sixth frame for their first decision of the evening. On what should have been a groundout to second base, the fans ruled an error on Keith Stegbauer, who fielded the ball cleanly but overthrew the first baseman.

61

Play-by-Play from the Minors

Jesse's favorite theme night that he has been a part of organizing came in 2019, though. The Lansing Lugnuts hosted Purge Night at Jackson Field. The promotion was loosely based on Universal Pictures' series of *Purge* films, in which a dystopian America celebrates a holiday each year called "The Purge," where for 12 hours all crime is legal. The Lugnuts' take on the holiday was a little different. Fans attended a seemingly normal baseball game, but after the top of the sixth, a siren played over the PA system to signal to the fans that all concessions (sans alcoholic beverages) would be free for the remainder of the inning.

Goldberg-Strassler recalls, "It went off and people hit the stands. That half inning, our guy [designated hitter Ryan Gold] hit a grand slam. The stands are empty and everyone is at the concession stands. It was the fewest amount of home fans to be able to cheer on a home grand slam. The guy was on his way to hit for the cycle for an incredible night, but everyone was gorging on food."

That home run was one of only two homers that Gold had in over 200 at-bats that season, but free food took precedence over the rare feat.

As if that wasn't wild enough, Goldberg-Strassler has seen his fair share of zany promotions on the road. One that jumps off the page dates back to 2008 in Ohio, where the Lake County Captains teamed up with Cleveland-based Monreal Funeral Home to give away a free funeral to a "lucky fan."

"They had a contest ... where they would put [famous] people's photos on the video board and they would ask, 'Are they dead?' If you got it right, you could get a discount off your funeral. I think the person [who played the contest when Lansing visited] won. I think their funeral is now discounted," Goldberg-Strassler relays.

The Bowie (Maryland) Baysox hosted an evening where members of the local theater would get up and sing between at-bats or innings to advertise an upcoming musical. The Great Lakes Loons held Pro Wrestling Night in 2018. The list could go on and on, but, as Jesse says, "Some of these are better as a memory than when they're actually going on, because sometimes you're just so embarrassed for everyone."

One team that seems to constantly turn out stellar promotional nights is the West Michigan Whitecaps. From Salute to Lumberjack Night to a pregame corgi racing tournament, Fifth Third Ballpark (now LMCU Ballpark) is known as a host to some of the wildest promotional evenings in America every season. One that stood out to the Lugnuts' radio guy was Australia Night, a theme night that took place on a Thursday evening in late August 2015. The Detroit Tigers system has had more ties to Australia than any organization in Major League Baseball, and they sent Sydney-born manager Andrew Graham to man the helm in Comstock Park in 2015. Longtime promotional manager Matt Hoffman decided to pay tribute to Australia for one of the final theme nights of the year. Nearly 7,000 fans in attendance were able to purchase Vegemite. After each score, "Australian" scorekeepers dressed like the late "Crocodile Hunter" Steve Irwin ran out into foul territory to add the runs up. Maybe the wildest part of the evening came right before the game, though.

"The night starts off with their on-field emcee, Bob Welsh, wrestling an inflatable croc," Goldberg-Strassler laughs. "A crocodile up there at home plate, and he just started wrestling it all over the place. If that doesn't get fans hyped up for a ballgame, I'm not sure what could."

Even with the excitement of seeing some of America's coveted small-town locales and fun theme nights at the ballpark, there have to be some setbacks to the gig. Every broadcaster has at least one story of a road trip from hell.

Jesse has had trips where the bus air conditioner broke down and everyone had to strip down to try to stay cool, as there are no windows that can open on a charter bus. He thinks back to a trip to Bowling Green, Kentucky, where funnel clouds were touching down all around the bus. After getting away from the storm, he remembers, the bus driver said, "I didn't think we were going to live through that." He's even had run-ins with bedbugs, but the memory that sticks out most to him is of his first season in Lansing, when the Lugnuts visited Clinton, Iowa.

The team arrived at the hotel around three in the morning. The athletic trainer called ahead, letting the hotel know that the team was on its way but would be arriving very late in the evening. The hotel responded, saying they were ready, but when the team arrived not one room was ready.

"It was decided that the staff and the starting battery [pitcher and catcher] for the next day would stay, and all the other players would get checked into a separate hotel," Jesse remembers.

After waiting around for an hour, Goldberg-Strassler finally made it to his room. He found that the breakfast buffet was not available that week, the bed was hard, the room had ants and the TV didn't work. While these are all things that frequent travelers deal with on separate trips, it seemed that everything was piling on for this venture to Iowa. The strangest part of the evening, though, came in the middle of the night, after Jesse had fallen asleep.

Play-by-Play from the Minors

"I get awoken by a phone ringing in my room. It's not the phone by my bed and it's not my phone. It's not coming from near the bed, so I walk over to try to find it," Goldberg-Strassler continues. "It is the front desk's phone and it is in my bathroom." The sleepy broadcaster answered the phone and the caller said he was looking for what room "Matt" was in. Jesse made a tired journey to the front desk, told them the situation and then returned to his room for the remainder of the evening. "I hope that person found Matt," Jesse chuckles.

Just as that person was searching for Matt, Minor League Baseball exists so that major league teams can search for their future players. They draft and then try to scrape the cream from the top crop of athletes. Many times, those players are first-round picks or highly touted international signees. It's easy for Goldberg-Strassler to say that Mike Trout is the top prospect he's ever seen. It's easy to look back and say that one of the best players in the history of the game was the best person he saw in Minor League Baseball. But Mike Trout wasn't a top-50 overall prospect in 2010. In fact, he wasn't even the top outfield prospect on the Angels' farm that year.

With that being said, he was the second-best outfield prospect for the Angels, and, according to *Baseball America*, the third-best prospect in the Angels system. The outfielder *Baseball America* had above Mike Trout? Peter Bourjos. Bourjos was probably ranked higher solely because he was more "MLB ready." He made his major league debut in 2010, but the career .237 hitter certainly isn't Mike Trout. The Angels' current center fielder only played 81 games in the Midwest League in 2010 before getting called up to the California League, but Goldberg-Strassler was lucky enough to see him for an entire series to lead off June. Through the course of his time in A-ball, Trout hit .362 with an OPS of .979. He had six homers and seven triples with Cedar Rapids, but finished the series where Jesse saw him 7 for 13. He scored seven runs, stole a pair of bags and hit a homer—all while striking out just once. What was most impressive about seeing the future AL MVP as a teenager?

"He beat you in any way that he wanted," Goldberg-Strassler explains. "Facing Mike Trout, if you challenge him, he homers. If he wanted to—and he did—he would drop down a bunt single and then steal bases. He's taking second and he's taking third, so if he gets on first base, you can't stop him. The way that he utilized his power and his speed and the way that he hauled it in from wherever it was hit in centerfield.... There was nobody like him. He was playing a different game."

4. Jesse Goldberg-Strassler

The Lugnuts' call-man also recalls Byron Buxton being very fun to watch, and gives an honorable mention to the trio of Bo Bichette, Fernando Tatís, Jr., and Vladimir Guerrero, Jr., all of whom played in the Midwest League in 2017 and participated in the All-Star Game.

While everyone has heard those names, there's another side to working in Minor League Baseball, and that is working with players that even some of the biggest baseball fans out there have never even heard of. Tim Locastro certainly fits that mold. The Syracuse, New York, native made his big-league debut in 2017 for the Los Angeles Dodgers. He has been traded three times and designated for assignment twice since being selected in the 13th round of the 2013 draft by the Toronto Blue Jays. But before all that, once Goldberg-Strassler saw a fellow Ithaca College graduate on the Lugnuts' 2015 roster, he was immediately intrigued.

"He joined us and the manager, Ken Huckaby, tells me, 'His nickname is the Magic Man, 'cause you watch, he's going to make magic happen.'"

The broadcaster recalls some traits of Lacastro: "He had a weak throwing arm that he had to put everything into to get the ball over to first base. He had a peculiar hitting style, where you weren't sure what he was trying to do with a baseball, but he made the pitcher's life a nightmare."

In 70 games in Michigan's capital, Lacastro hit .310 with only 25 strikeouts. He added 30 stolen bases and drew 21 free passes—which gave him an on-base percentage of .409. Goldberg-Strassler recalls a number of game-winning plays, including a bomb off future major leaguer Hunter Wood and a game-saving diving snag to rob a batter of a hit. "If he was involved late in a close game, we would win. If he was at the plate, if he was on the bases, if the ball was hit to him.... He was the Magic Man. He was a non-prospect who has made his way to the major leagues."

Behind the scenes, something that many fans may discount is player personalities and how some can really "steal the show" as the most-fun locker room presence. One guy who went above and beyond in that area in Jesse's mind was Jim Magrane of the 2006 Montgomery Biscuits.

"He had requested all the players' headshots after they were taken, and we didn't understand why," Goldberg-Strassler mentions. "Throughout the year, movie posters would pop up in the clubhouse. It was whatever movie was big in the theater at the time, with his teammates and the manager's headshots photoshopped in. It was entirely anonymous, so no one on the team knew who did it—and it was great!"

Play-by-Play from the Minors

While the broadcaster doesn't recall any of the movie posters used, he wishes he had taken some photos of them. Goldberg-Strassler says that type of player makes the year, and when the year ends, you miss that player and the impact he had on the locker room.

While players are dubbed "great" for a variety of reasons and some end up in the Hall of Fame, while others end up as managers or future broadcasters and personalities or coaches, most fans remember players because of singular moments in the game. Goldberg-Strassler has been fortunate enough to be behind the mic for some indelible occurrences. He's called championship-winning games, big comebacks and massive plays. What is his favorite moment, though?

He goes back to his second playoff game with the Lansing Lugnuts in 2011. After falling to the Dayton Dragons 7–3 in Game 1 of the quarterfinals, Lansing had their backs against the wall against the top team in the league in Game 2. After Dayton scored a pair of runs to begin the game in the first, Lansing got one back in the bottom of the frame, and that score held until the bottom of the ninth.

The Dragons sent out one of the top relievers in the league that season, Drew Hayes, to close out the frame. The Vanderbilt product finished the season with a 1.35 ERA, converted 22 saves in 23 opportunities and fanned 89 batters in just 60 innings of work. He would go on to make his big league debut in 2016 for the Cincinnati Reds—he was surely one of the most talented relievers in the Midwest League in 2011. After Marcus Knecht poked a single to right to lead off the inning, Carlos Perez bunted the game-tying run into scoring position for the first out. Then, K.C. Hobson got set down swinging on just three pitches to bring up the eight-hole hitter, Matt Nuzzo.

"We had resumed the game after a rain delay, but there was an enormous puddle in deep left field by the warning track and Nuzzo hits a ball deep to left," Goldberg-Strassler remembers. "Now, the left fielder is probably 5'6"–5'7" tall, but athletic. He jumps up as high as he can, but this ball skims over his glove for a walk-off two-run homer, as the player now lands into that puddle. We have shocked the Dayton Dragons. We go on to beat them the next day and knock them out of the playoffs. That home run was unforgettable for me as a broadcaster."

Another thing that makes that moment special is that Nuzzo, who beat the future major leaguer to win the game, was cut immediately after the season and turned to bartending—showing that anything can happen in baseball.

That 2011 team was great, but it doesn't make the cut for the most talented team that Goldberg-Strassler has called. He'll admit that he was spoiled in 2006–07 working for the Montgomery Biscuits when they had the talented crop of Tampa Bay prospects, including Evan Longoria and Wade Davis, who had remarkable major league careers, and Reid Brignac and Mitch Talbot, who were very highly regarded but never made a massive impact in The Show. He doesn't count out Lansing, though. There are two years where he thought that Lansing had unparalleled talent.

"In 2012, the Lansing Lugnuts with Noah Syndergaard, Aaron Sanchez, Anthony DeSclafani, Justin Nicolino, Kevin Pillar and John Berti were dominant. Also, in 2015, if Lansing had played for the Midwest League Championship in the first half with that starting lineup and the amount of major league–level players on that team, they would have won the whole thing," Jesse states.

That lineup had nine future major leaguers in it: Ryan McBroom, Richard Urena, Rowdy Tellez, Tim Locastro, Anthony Alford, Danny Jansen, Dawel Lugo, Jonathan Davis and Lane Thomas.

Broadcasters are experts in the field and know a lot about players and their background and the rules, but there are certainly a bunch of curveballs that come into play when you're watching 140 games a year that can surprise even the wiliest veteran.

"I'll give you a scenario. Vladimir Guerrero Jr. is at the plate, tying run is at third base, two outs, bottom of the ninth inning. It is a 3–2 pitch, it's in the dirt, Guerrero swings and misses. With his backswing, he hits the catcher on the head, catcher is knocked out, pitch goes all the way to the backstop. Guerrero takes off for first base and the runner from third rushes in. You make the call," Goldberg-Strassler explains. "It is a dead ball. The hitter is out and the ballgame is over."

He also recalls a situation where the New Hampshire Fisher Cats nearly had a Merkle's Boner, where a game ended because a runner didn't go to a base with a force out, despite the winning run scoring. The original Merkle's Boner resulted in the Cubs eventually winning their 1908 World Series—their last championship until 2016. Broadcasters see some zany things, and Goldberg-Strassler has been on the mic for over 1,000 games with a chance for that to happen. While not everyone dreams of those moments like a kid dreaming of batting in a tie game in the bottom of the ninth with the bases loaded and a 3–2 count, there are some that broadcasters yearn for.

Now that you know about Jesse's career and some of the amazing things he has seen, here's a look back at the one moment in baseball history he would have liked to call and how he would call it.

Play-by-Play from the Minors

"I would want to call a match-up from the East-West All-Star Game from the 1940s, when Satchel Paige faced Josh Gibson with the game on the line. I would have just wanted to be there for it, because I think one of our privileges as broadcasters is that we get this ability to enjoy the game and to share the game with anyone who can't be there. I would've loved to share that moment with anyone who couldn't have witnessed it. Satch struck him out and I think the heightening of tension with the at-bat would have been fantastic."

The aspect of the game that Goldberg-Strassler would have focused on was painting the picture visually.

"I would have described their movements and looks. After that, I'd let the crowd take over the rest. It would have been minimal, with brushstrokes of the looks, and then I'd just let the moment live."

Jesse Goldberg-Strassler has dreamt about peak baseball, calling the best against the best, and he would want to ride the wave into this 1940s All-Star Game matchup between one of the top pitchers and one of the top hitters of all time.

5

Terry Byrom

Currently with the Harrisburg Senators
Previously with the Ogden Raptors and
Fort Wayne Wizards

Like Jesse, Terry Byrom has spent an extended period of time with his current team, and both have a connection with Joe Block. Terry was also able to find his start in baseball after checking out the website Call of the Game. He has been able to move up in the ranks and now has his own major league aspirations.

Although Terry got a late start in broadcasting, he was able to quickly find a home in Harrisburg, Pennsylvania, where he has been since 2005. The California native started his career at age 39 with the Ogden (Utah) Raptors of the Pioneer League (now an independent league) in 2002. That was before a two-year stint in the Midwest League with the Fort Wayne Wizards. After year two in Fort Wayne, he was able to find his way to Harrisburg, which led to a professional dream coming true, as Terry was given the opportunity to call a series between the Washington Nationals and Atlanta Braves in 2018.

When Terry was growing up in Sacramento, California, his baseball fandom began with rooting for the San Francisco Giants. He lived with his mother and grandmother; his grandmother was born and raised in Oklahoma before moving west to California, and was an adamant baseball fan. Terry recalls sitting on the porch with his grandma in 1967, while his mom was working, and just listening to Giants games. It was the year before the Athletics moved from Kansas City to Oakland, so for that summer at least, it was all Giants. As he matured, though, Terry would listen to both the Giants and A's and watch the Saturday Game of the Week on television.

Because of his grandmother's passion for baseball, Terry grew into a big baseball, and Giants, fan. He was influenced early on by a few

Terry Byrom's path didn't start quite as soon as others featured in this book. Byrom was a personnel specialist for the United States Air Force and California Air National Guard before he worked his way into the radio booth of the Ogden Raptors to start his MiLB journey (photograph courtesy Terry Byrom).

broadcasters, but the name that sticks out the most for Terry is Lon Simmons. The former minor leaguer became the voice of the Giants when they moved from the Polo Grounds to Seals Stadium in the 1950s. He was also influenced a lot by Hank Greenwald, who broadcast for the Giants in the late '70s and early '80s. He grew up listening to Bill King for Warriors and Raiders games because he had quite a few relatives who were fans of those teams. Despite having all of these broadcasting influences from his childhood, it took a local broadcaster to make Byrom, just a few years into his radio career with the Senators, truly realize how much his roots impacted his professional development.

Gregg Mace was a local legend in Harrisburg. He started his career with WHTM, the local ABC affiliate, in 1979 as the station's first weekend sportscaster. During his career from 1979 to 2008, Mace covered everything from local high school sports to the Philadelphia Phillies' two World Series victories, one in 1980, the other in 2008. When Byrom joined WHTM, the two Harrisburg broadcasters worked out a plan where Mace would join Byrom in the booth for a doubleheader.

When Byrom had spent a few years in the booth in Harrisburg, Mace wanted to write a story about him. One of the first questions Mace had for Byrom was about his style of call. The previous few broadcasters for the Senators were big homers, so their enthusiasm for Harrisburg's team suffused the broadcast, while Terry is more even-keeled. That's when he reflected and saw the Bay Area's influence on himself.

"I think it's pretty obvious that I want the Senators to win, but if somebody does something good, they do something good, and if somebody does something bad, they do something bad. I think I really got that from Bill King and Lon Simmons. That's just the way that those guys are," the Californian said. "That's more of what I take from them. Ways to present a game when things aren't going well."

It took Terry a while to get into baseball. His career began in the National Guard while he was in California, but there was always a yearning to broadcast live sports. He just wasn't given an opportunity to do so initially. He had moved to Indiana right around the turn of the millennium. In Crawfordsville he moved from a rental house to a house that he and his now ex-wife owned, and they had three radio stations to listen to. While listening to one of the stations, he heard an ad for people who wanted to broadcast high school sports. With three high schools in the county and three radio stations, all the football and nearly all of the basketball in the county was broadcast over the airwaves. The next morning, Byrom called the station and said he was interested. After talking to the station director, he was told to go to a baseball sectional game later that week.

"There was a headset there and the director said, 'Why don't you just put the headset on, sit in with me, we'll see how you do and we'll figure it out from there.' That led to being in Ogden, Fort Wayne and here in Harrisburg since then. That is really the path."

While Terry was able to shoot up the ranks quickly, he maintains that he isn't sure how he was able to reach Double-A after just a few short years. It wasn't until he made it to the Eastern League that he was able to see how much time and preparation some of the veterans put into the broadcast, and that taught him how to get to the next level as a broadcaster.

Terry didn't go to the Winter Meetings as other broadcasters do to break into the industry, but after a few years of calling high school games, he decided it was time to go for it. He wanted to try calling professional baseball. He used tape from the previous year's state championship baseball game and scoured Joe Block's now-defunct Call of the Game website. He was late in the application process. Most broadcasting gigs in professional baseball are interviewed and filled between November and January, but Terry didn't start sending his reel out until March. He sent out the tape to four or five teams, two of which were Pioneer League clubs and the rest of which were independent organizations.

He initially got an offer from Berkshire, a team that went underwater the next season, but about a week later, Ogden showed interest in hiring him, and the Goldklang Group, which owns the Charleston River-Dogs and also owned the Evansville Otters at the time, were interested in hiring for the Otters' broadcast position. He was reprimanded by the hiring person from the Otters because of his age, 39.

"He kind of ranted at me. He said, 'I don't know how old you are, but looking at your resume, you're probably my age. It looks like you have a really good job with this medical organization and you probably make good money. Is this sort of a you want to get your willies off for a season, take this job from somebody, get a radio job for a year and go back to your regular life?'" Byrom recalls.

He says that he confirmed that he was going to try to do this for the remainder of his career, and the employer then told him everything that was wrong with the position: Byrom would have to move, he would take a severe pay cut and he would be working incredibly long hours. But Byrom stood firm, saying that that was what he wanted to do.

After that, the interviewer said, "Okay, because you're really good. The tape is really bad, but it is easy to tell that you are very good. So, if you want to do this, you're going to get a job and you're probably going to move up pretty quickly because you're really good."

He had been advised to take the first job he was offered, regardless of what league it was in, whether it was affiliated or not, so he could gather good tape.

Then, Ogden came back into the picture. The Californian was in the final two for the Raptors' broadcast position, and one office executive wanted to pick Byrom, while the other preferred the other candidate. How were they going to decide who to pick when both executives were determined to go with their own pick? They asked the owner's girlfriend which candidate she liked more. She didn't know much about baseball, but she preferred Terry's voice, so she picked Byrom and he got the job in Ogden.

"That's the randomness of how it all started. That's what I tell people,

5. Terry Byrom

that we sit and analyze all these things and we think that it's because all these big-name teams know better than us and sometimes that's not the case at all. Who knows how we get chosen over people who don't get the job sometimes," Byrom adds.

It wasn't until after his first year in Fort Wayne, with the Wizards, that Terry decided to go to the Winter Meetings for the first time. He had gotten the Fort Wayne job after hearing about their opening through Pioneer League connections, and he made a couple of calls to get in contact with team president Mike Nutter to secure the position.

In his first offseason, Fort Wayne sent three employees to Winter Meetings, and Terry went along with them. There, he met Mike Capps, who had just begun his journey with the Round Rock Express. Like Terry, Mike was older and had a varied background, and the two had drinks together and discussed baseball.

"The following February or March, Mike called me and said, 'The job in Harrisburg is open. I've already called them, you need to call them right now,'" Terry recalls.

He talked back-and-forth and made a connection with Harrisburg in 2004, but the general manager decided he didn't want to make a long-term decision just a month before the season, so they hired someone temporarily for the season and told Byrom to contact them in the off-season. He waited, interviewed for the job a second time in December following his second season with the Wizards and secured the position he has had for 15 years now.

Now that Terry is nearing 20 years in the industry, he's had the opportunity to learn a lot about himself and the industry as a whole. The way he sees it, yes, a broadcaster's voice and description of the game are important, but he views preparation as the most important thing for a broadcaster to focus on.

"It's [about] not overwhelming me with statistics, and not really overwhelming me at all. To treat it as a one-off game ... helps me to enjoy it more," Terry says. "I listen to a lot of MLB games throughout the season as one-offs and I'll listen to a couple minor league guys in the same way. It's really just knowing enough to keep me interested in listening to you."

Part of it is that the way baseball is consumed today is very different from what it used to be. Thirty to forty years ago, fans knew everything about their team and they knew who all the players were from listening to the radio every night. Byrom maintains that that has changed, and people consume the game much more casually in 2020.

Play-by-Play from the Minors

Many things have changed in the last 30–40 years, but one constant that has remained is a stronghold that Byrom had a chance to visit early in his career. When the Californian thinks of his favorite road city, he goes almost immediately to one of the first towns he visited in Minor League Baseball. In the Pioneer League, he loved to travel to Great Falls, Montana, and the reason for that was receiving a chance to go to the Sip 'n Dip Lounge, which isn't far from the team hotel. The Sip 'n Dip Lounge has adopted a tiki-bar theme since its opening in 1962, but a few constants remain. The table and bar tops are decorated with oceanic themes, and the main attraction is a pool behind the bar, encapsulated in glass so that the customers can see the mermaids who swim in the pool on weekends. Local celebrity Patricia Sponheim, known as Piano Pat, played the three-keyboard organ from the time the Sip 'n Dip opened until her death in her mid–'80s in 2021, playing year-round to entertain the barflies who flock to the town.

The tiki bar is wildly popular for an attraction in a town of 60,000 people. In fact, in 2003, *GQ Magazine* ranked it as the #1 bar in its list of "Top 10 Bars Worth Flying For." Then, in 2013, the bar was recognized again, this time in a story on CBS's *Sunday Morning* where they hailed the spot as one of the top historic bars in America.

Terry recalls his time at Sip 'n Dip and remembers Piano Pat: "Age becomes a relative thing as you get older, but there was this woman who was at least 70 years old playing this three- or four-level organ that you can make different sounds on, and it was just fantastic."

While that bar makes Great Falls Byrom's favorite road city, in the Eastern League he really enjoys visiting Portland, Maine, and Annapolis, Maryland. The Bowie Baysox have visiting teams stay in a hotel in Annapolis, which is only about 15 minutes away.

Byrom's favorite restaurant along the circuit was the Gordon Biersch Brewery Restaurant in Annapolis, now closed. "I started going to Gordon Biersch when I was still going to Candlestick Park. There was a Gordon Biersch under the Bay Bridge in San Francisco. They did those garlic fries at Candlestick that started the whole garlic fry revolution," Byrom details. The company operates 18 restaurants in America, now called Rock Bottom Restaurant Breweries.

Although Byrom enjoys many of the travel aspects of broadcasting, he stays very glued to what is happening on the field during the game. In other words, he doesn't take in a ton of what is happening with the promotional aspect of the industry. With that being said, he still has a few favorite promotions he remembers being a part of and seeing while on

5. Terry Byrom

the road. One that was particularly special to him came about almost by happenstance. In September 2015, the Senators had Red Land, the local Little League team, out to the park on the day of its clash with the Akron RubberDucks. Red Land showed up early and took batting practice on the field, where fans were able to spectate. Following batting practice, two sponsors, PennLive and the *Patriot-News*, distributed pictures of the Little League team that fans got autographed by the players prior to the Senators game.

"At the end of a pretty bad season where we were out of it, ordinarily we would have had 3,000 people, but instead had around 7,000 people," Byrom comments. The Little League team brought in people and there was plenty of interest following the team's loss to Japan in the Little League World Series the month before.

When thinking of promotions he has seen on the road, Byrom claims, "A lot of the promotions are different, but the same. They help bring people in, and it's cool to see some of these things and talk to some of the local celebrities and have them on-air."

Asked to pick a favorite that he remembers, he leans toward the first time he saw the Cowboy Monkey Rodeo—a mainstay of Minor League Baseball promotions. The event stars a white-headed capuchin monkey, Whiplash, who rides a dog as though he is a cowboy and the dog a horse.

The event has been touring America, and even Europe, since 1990, and has been on ESPN, *Good Morning America* and *The Today Show*. Whiplash's popularity really took off when he starred in an ad campaign for the national restaurant chain Taco John's. To give you an idea of how much of a cult following the monkey has, in late January 2009, Whiplash attended the annual St. Paul Winter Carnival in Minnesota and was "knighted" in front of the giant crowd.

Yes, the Cowboy Monkey Rodeo is a special event that has held America's attention for a long time and has been steadfast in Minor League Baseball throughout the twenty-first century, but a more historic promotion from Bowie jumps out for Terry. Each year since 2008, the Baysox have hosted a tribute night to the All-American Girls Professional Baseball League (AAGPBL). They have women who played in the league come out and sign autographs, a pre-game ceremony honors the women and their contribution to baseball as we know it and then everyone enjoys an Eastern League showcase at Prince George's Stadium.

Of course, the night hinges on the popularity of the '90s classic *A League of Their Own*, inspired by the AAGPBL and starring Tom Hanks,

Play-by-Play from the Minors

Madonna, Geena Davis and Lori Petty, and the Baysox have hosted legends from the league, including Jean Faut, who had a 1.23 ERA to pair with her 140–64 record in the regular season from 1946 to 1953 while playing with the South Bend Blue Sox. They've even had Sarah "Salty" Ferguson, who played for the Rockford Peaches in their final two seasons in the league in 1953–54.

While the 17-year industry vet has seen many different promotions that are great for local areas but forgettable experiences for him, there is a bus ride from back in his lone season in the Pioneer League that Byrom will never forget. The Raptors had a trip going from Medicine Hat, Alberta, back home to Ogden, Utah. The Raptor's manager, Tim Blackwell, had never been to Yellowstone National Park and saw that it wasn't too far out of the way to get to the northwest corner of Wyoming. The trip from Medicine Hat to Ogden is normally 775 miles, primarily along I-15 southbound. To trek through Yellowstone adds about 100 miles to the journey, placing it at just about 900 miles, but the staff and players on the bus believed it was a worthwhile adventure.

While in Montana, the bus needed to switch drivers due to regulations limiting how long a single bus driver could drive in one shot, but beyond that, the team sailed smoothly into Wyoming. The team made it through Yellowstone and past the Grand Teton, pushing on to Jackson Hole, Wyoming, when it got dark.

"We were on this two-lane highway in Wyoming and I had finally given way to falling asleep, and the bus started skidding on the shoulder. Then we hit something," Byrom remembers. "This driver wasn't the usual bus driver because they had switched in Montana, but we asked, 'What the hell happened?' and he said, 'This steer came out of nowhere!' I thought, this 1,000-pound steer came out of nowhere? Well, it's not a frickin' cat!" The team figured the driver had dozed off, was surprised by what he saw on the side of the road and turned hard, skidding into the animal.

Now it was around 1 or 2 a.m. and the team checked out the bus, which had minor damage—not enough that they couldn't drive, but a light was broken and other parts of the bus were also damaged. Meanwhile, the steer was still standing on the side of the road and seemed completely fine. One of the players called 911 and found out that there was only one sheriff on duty for the county because not many people lived there. Typically, there weren't many sheriff calls in the county, which census data shows had only 18,300 people living in it despite a massive 4,000-square-mile footprint.

5. Terry Byrom

The sheriff was already on a call about 50 miles away, so the team had to figure out what they wanted to do.

"We finally convinced the bus driver that we needed to go. It probably took about an hour to convince him that we would take pictures and sign affidavits, and lo and behold, then the sheriff showed up. We were there for two or three more hours. When we got back to Ogden, it was still dark, but it was pretty late in the morning."

The team had traveled from Medicine Hat on an off day, but they didn't find their homes until the morning of their next game day and then before they knew it, it was time to go back to the stadium for practice. On the opposite end of the spectrum, Byrom said he had a wonderful time flying with the Nationals from Washington, D.C., to Atlanta and back for a four-game series while he was filling in for the big league broadcast. "After that, I understood why everyone wants to be in the majors."

While the travel is different from what you see at the major league level, the players provide a glimpse of the future, and while they are still raw, there are plenty of incredibly talented guys on the teams that Harrisburg's call-man has seen. Although Byrom didn't get a long look at Juan Soto, the outfielder certainly left an impression. On his meteoric rise to The Show, where the 20-year-old climbed from Class-A to Major League Baseball in just 39 games, Soto spent eight of those contests in Pennsylvania's capital. In those eight appearances, the lefty slugged a pair of round-trippers, recorded 10 hits and drove in 10 runs.

Soto's impression on Byrom was cemented in his first at-bat. "He hit a line drive to right field that the right fielder moved in on and it went by him after his second step in," Byrom recalls. "It was like, okay, that was wow. Then in his second game he had two hits, including a home run that went a fairly long way at our ballpark, and on top of those things, the way he physically looked and the way he prepared. He was just different."

Not far beneath Soto, he remembers Anthony Rendon as the best hitter who has come through Harrisburg. In addition to that, Byrom says that he has to mention the talent from a trio of first-round picks for the Nationals: Stephen Strasburg, who drew hype all the way up to his debut for the Nationals against the Pittsburgh Pirates; Bryce Harper, who was revered as the next top power hitter baseball would see as he climbed the ranks; and Ryan Zimmerman, who was the Nationals' first draft pick as a franchise when they selected him fourth overall in 2005.

Play-by-Play from the Minors

Zimmerman's glove at the hot corner stood out to Byrom immediately. "The first guy that batted for the Akron Aeros that night laid down a bunt, and Ryan charged and threw on the run to first base, and when he came up, he was a Gold Glove–caliber third baseman, and I just immediately thought, 'That was a big league play.'"

The player who laid down that bunt was Franklin Gutiérrez, a center fielder who would play just under 1,000 games in the bigs, including seven in 2005, when Zimmerman made his way to Harrisburg.

Individual players are memorable, but the end goal for every group of guys is to try to win a title. That takes talent and teamwork across the board. In nearly 20 years of calling games, Byrom has had the opportunity to see a lot of teams that played well together, but the 2013 Harrisburg Senators take the cake for the most talented team he has seen. During that campaign, 14 members of the Senators got called up to the Nationals, and a few of them have become MLB mainstays. Rendon, Sandy León, Blake Treinen and Steven Souza all started the year in Harrisburg, were called up to Washington and have been traded from Washington or signed with another team since, but all found themselves on a major league roster for the 2020 season seven years later.

The Senators finished 77–65 in 2013 to win the Western Division regular season title, and made it all the way to the league finals before bowing out to Trenton in a three-game sweep. The strength of that team was its starting pitching, and seven starters found their way to the big leagues. A few of them find themselves in the bullpen now, but Nate Karns, Treinen, Taylor Hill, Robbie Ray, Taylor Jordan, A.J. Cole and Brian Broderick all made at least seven starts for Harrisburg in 2013. Broderick is the only one from that group who only played a single season in the majors.

"What made it special was that these weren't just guys who just got to Harrisburg. They all made a mark to put together a pretty good pitching staff. We didn't have much offense that year outside of Stephen Souza," Byrom says.

The pitching staff compiled the lowest team ERA in the Eastern League that season, a 3.43 mark, with an astounding nine complete games—which was also a league-best mark. They paced the circuit in shutouts (15) and finished second with 1,168 strikeouts to a loaded Binghamton Mets staff that had 1,185 strikeouts that year. The absolute top-to-bottom skill on the hill for the 2013 Senators made them an all-time Eastern League team to watch.

Although the players are more developed in the Eastern League,

5. Terry Byrom

the most dominant team Terry saw was in the Pioneer League. When Byrom thinks back to his days in Ogden, he remembers the five future major leaguers who were on the roster. Headlining the list is Prince Fielder, a player who would start gracing *Baseball America*'s Top 100 Prospects list in 2003, but the team also boasted Craig Breslow, Manny Parra, Dennis Sarfate and Callix Crabbe.

One guy that the casual fan wouldn't have heard of but that Byrom thought was the best unsung talent on the roster was Khalid Ballouli. Selected by the Brewers in the sixth round out of Texas A&M, the 6'2" righty could hurl a ball in the mid–'90s, and locate it well, too. An added level of interest about Ballouli is that he is a legacy professional baseball player. His grandfather, Dick Fowler, played for a decade for the Philadelphia Athletics, and was the first Canadian-born player to throw a perfect game.

"There was a scout who said he could make it if he could keep his arm healthy," Byrom recalls. Unfortunately, the Texas native couldn't stay off the injured list. After five seasons in Minor League Baseball, he hung up the cleats and earned a PhD, and he is currently an associate professor and PhD program director in the Department of Sport and Entertainment Management in the College of Hospitality, Retail and Sport Management at the University of South Carolina.

Another standout role player that Terry saw was on a Harrisburg team. When Byrom reached Double-A, he believed that Dan DeMent, a former Rule 5 draft pick by the Nationals, deserved more of a look. The University of Alabama product spent parts of three seasons in Harrisburg, and played the role of the super utility player.

"He was a good clubhouse guy. Put up really good numbers and was more than good enough to have a shot at the Big Leagues, but never got that opportunity," Byrom says.

The righty's best season in Harrisburg was his first year, 2005. He averaged .328 and clubbed 14 homers while driving in 44 runs in only 71 games. DeMent won an Eastern League Player of the Week Award in June of 2007 and was an Appalachian League All-Star in 2000, but outside of that was never able to distance himself enough from his peers to find a shot at the majors or receive another award.

DeMent never got the call-up to The Show, but Byrom did, and the moment from his career that Byrom will hang on to forever comes from his four-game stint with the Nationals in 2018. During the Saturday contest against Atlanta, the game went deep into extra innings. When it reached the 14th inning, the Nationals offense rallied behind

Play-by-Play from the Minors

Max Scherzer, who pinch-hit and singled to spark the team. Following that, Wilmer Difo tripled him in to put the Nats up 4–3. Spencer Kieboom was able to follow that up with a base knock past the third baseman to give the game its final score, 5–3.

"All of that is on must-see with my calls and it's still on the MLB website, so that's pretty cool for me," Byrom says. It was particularly special for Byrom because it showcased one of his favorite things to call. "I like triples. I think we all have those things that we think we do well, and I think of all the things I call well, I call triples really well. I think I could have had a little more emotion, but I think that the call really matches the video, so I'm really happy about that."

It helps that Scherzer was the guy who scored the go-ahead run in a situation where you certainly wouldn't have expected a pitcher to go to the plate, much less a Cy Young winner and the Nationals' ace.

It takes a lot to go from sitting on your couch, or even working in the corporate world, to calling those big league games. And Terry would have been the first person to tell you back when he was first breaking into baseball that he had a lot of experience with baseball heading into his first year in Ogden. He played growing up, watched and listened to plenty of games throughout his life and coached high school and American Legion baseball for years before he sat behind the mic in the Pioneer League. But it couldn't prepare him for everything he would see calling baseball on the day-to-day beat.

"After being in Ogden for a week, I realized I really didn't know anything. I don't know that it was really one big moment [of realization], but it was pretty clear that professional baseball was on a completely different level than anything that I had ever experienced with just how everyday life goes," Byrom says.

Just looking at how good the batting practice was for the professionals, compared with the kids who weren't much younger than the 18- to 20-year-olds he saw in Ogden, was an incredible wake-up call. To put the level of talent in professional baseball in perspective, Terry draws back to his time in Fort Wayne.

"Even if the guys don't look that good on the field, when you look down at those players, a lot of them are the best players that came from their hometown, maybe ever, and certainly while they were there. So, even to be a guy who never would get to play above A-ball is still really, really good," Byrom states.

To Terry, the biggest learning moment that he's had behind the mic in baseball wasn't necessarily something about the rule book. In this case, it was seeing just how elite those guys on the field are compared to the other baseball players you witness on sandlots across America.

It's more than just talent on the field that makes these players special. A lot of them retire after just a season or two in the game and become salesmen, mechanics or marketing gurus. More become fathers and coaches to future generations in the game. Over the years, Byrom has met a lot of guys with incredible personalities and has made some great friends. One of the first names that comes to mind for him happens to be a guy who got a lot of national attention for his role in the Nationals' World Series run in 2019. It's the same Aaron Barrett who had a sensational rookie season in 2014 for the Nationals prior to needing Tommy John surgery in 2016, and then, while rehabbing, broke his humerus and had to start his MiLB career over, not making it back on the field again until 2018, and not pitching in the bigs again until rosters expanded in 2019. Barrett lives in Atlanta, and when he heard that Terry had been in Atlanta in 2018, he told him that if he ever makes it back there, he has to stop by and he and his wife would have him over for dinner.

"You hear that over the years from different guys, and you know when it is genuine and when it is not, and he is just a good guy and we enjoyed our time together," Byrom says.

Terry was there the day manager Matt LeCroy told Barrett that he was going back to the majors. The moment later went viral, as LeCroy and Barrett both wept tears of joy and the entire team mobbed the unsuspecting pitcher. Meanwhile, the Harrisburg Senators staff was able to catch it on camera and share the moment with baseball fans worldwide. Terry also remembers Media Day in 2019 with Barrett. At this daylong event, the players eat lunch with the front office, and then record the clips and headshots fans see and sign everything that the team will distribute throughout the season. Following that, the media comes to do interviews with all the players. Before Barrett's second Media Day, Byrom approached the veteran and asked if he wanted to take part. Because he had been with the team before, they already had a lot of stuff from Barrett and didn't necessarily need to use him for everything. Barrett's response was, "Terry, I'm a member of this team. I'm going to do whatever everyone needs to do. If you have any trouble with any of the guys, let me know and I'll be able to help you with them." Not only is he a great guy, but he is a solid leader whom his teammates respect, Terry says.

Now that you know Byrom a bit better, you can understand what he appreciates and looks for in a baseball game. When Terry looks back at the history of the game, the one moment he would wish to call would be the Bill Mazeroski homer in Game 7 of the 1960 World Series. While Byrom contests that he could never do a re-creation because he needs the event to transpire in front of him to capture the raw emotion, he picks this specific moment in baseball history because of how much of an underdog the 1960 Pirates were compared to the Yankees.

Truthfully, no one thought they were going to win the Series. Even the scores of the games were super-lopsided. Pittsburgh came out with a Game 1 victory, 6–4, before losing the next two contests 16–3 and 10–0. They eked by the Yankees, 3–2, in Game 4 to even the Series and claimed Game 5, 5–2, to take the lead prior to the Yankees blowing the doors off the hinges and winning Game 6, 12–0.

Game 7 was truly a classic. The 10–9 contest was back-and-forth, but Byrom would love to have called Bill Mazeroski's homer to finish it off.

"I think what I would have focused on would have been him running around Forbes Field with all the people of Pittsburgh. Just like when Hank Aaron hit the homer to break Babe Ruth's record. I would have called both of those the same way, just focused on them running around the bases with Mazeroski's emotion and [fans] starting to run over... He was the first person to end a World Series with a walk-off home run, so I would have also stated the significance of that."

6

Robert Ford

Currently with the Houston Astros
Previously with the Binghamton Mets,
Kalamazoo Kings and Yakima Bears

If you look through Robert Ford's resume, you'll see that he was in Binghamton at the same time that Terry Byrom was starting his tenure with the Harrisburg Senators, but the two broadcasters go back even further. They initially met broadcasting college football in the Midwest prior to their move to the Eastern League. However, Ford's broadcasting and baseball dreams go back even further than the chance meeting of two broadcasters who shared a market early in their careers.

Robert Ford became a baseball fan as a kid from the Bronx who rooted for the New York Mets. When it was time for him to leave the Big Apple, he didn't go far, traveling to upstate New York to attend the prestigious S. I. Newhouse School of Public Communications at Syracuse University. Ford has been the Houston Astros radio play-by-play commentator since 2013 and, prior to that, he worked for the Kansas City Royals for a handful of years, manning the pre-game and post-game shows for 610 AM KCSP. Before making it to the big leagues, he went through Minor League Baseball to compile his tape and learn how to put out the most successful broadcast he could. Through over 800 games in Binghamton, Kalamazoo and Yakima, Ford developed his style of calling a game that made him a two-time Frontier League Broadcaster of the Year (2003 and 2004) and allowed him to climb the ranks and eventually make it to Houston.

I know some New York baseball fans ignored the remainder of the last paragraph to think more about how the first sentence was possible. So, how did a young kid in the Bronx become a Mets fan? Well, his parents were both from Queens, and his entire family had rooted for National League teams dating as far back as Jackie Robinson breaking

Play-by-Play from the Minors

the color barrier for the Brooklyn Dodgers in the late 1940s. In addition to his family roots in baseball, when Ford was growing into a young baseball fan, the Mets were one of the most exciting teams to watch. The teams of the '80s included stars such as Gary Carter, Keith Hernandez, Dwight Gooden and Lenny Dykstra, but Ford has a special connection with one of the all-time greatest Mets, Darryl Strawberry.

"Strawberry hit a walk-off homer at the first Mets game I ever attended in 1985, and he's always been my favorite player ever since then," Ford recalls.

One big difference between Ford and other New Yorkers is that

despite being a big Mets fan, he isn't a Yankees hater. Whereas most people picked a New York team and then rooted against the other team that shared the city, Robert attended plenty of games at the old Yankee Stadium and utilized the Yankees as a way to keep up with what was going on in the American League, because at that time, the only interleague play fans could see was in spring training, the All-Star Game or the World Series. The diehard Mets fan even goes on to say that he misses old Yankee Stadium more than Shea Stadium, which he really doesn't miss.

One thing that Ford did pick up from the Mets, though, was broadcasting. Gary Cohen and Bob Murphy were the Mets' radio broadcasters while Ford was growing up, and Ford still considers Cohen one of his broadcasting idols.

Robert Ford has been in the bigs for more than a decade, but this Bronx native may surprise you. He's a New York Mets fan through and through and has found one of his favorite delis in Akron, Ohio (photograph courtesy Robert Ford).

84

6. Robert Ford

"Whether it was consciously or not, I really think I modeled my style of play-by-play after Cohen. He's a good storyteller, but you always know what's going on on the field. You always have the nuts and bolts. He's extremely well prepared and he's just really easy to listen to," Ford relays.

He also had the good fortune to watch the Mets' TV broadcasts, which included former player Tim McCarver. The backstop spent 21 seasons on the field, primarily for the St. Louis Cardinals, prior to setting up shop in the booth. Although he is primarily known for his network brilliance, which has pushed him to win three Emmy Awards, the 2012 Ford C. Frick Award winner spent 1983–1998 calling games locally for the Mets. What made McCarver special was a style that has become commonplace since he brought it to the table.

"He really was one of the first guys to do what is known as first guessing—that is, to think along with the manager, with the strategy, as opposed to second guessing, or talking after the fact about what happened and why it worked or didn't. This mindset got me thinking about the game in a different way too, because it had me thinking about strategy and thinking along with what the manager might do in a given situation or about why a certain player was in at a certain time or why certain players weren't," Ford explains. While listening to Ford's radio broadcast in Houston, you're certain to notice hints of that New York influence sprinkled over the airwaves.

How did a big city guy find himself traveling all over small-town America in the Minor League Baseball circuit? After graduating from Syracuse in 2001, he spent close to a year working back home in New York City before traveling to the Winter Meetings in Boston that December. It didn't take long for Ford to find something in affiliated ball. He accepted a position with the Yakima Bears in the short-season Northwest League for the summer of 2002. Ford didn't have a lot of tape from college, so during the summer of 2001, while he was home, he picked a handful of Yankees games to attend and brought a cassette recorder to them to archive himself calling the games from the bleachers. At those Winter Meetings in Boston, most of the young broadcaster's demo came from a Red Sox–Yankees game play-by-play that was pulled off the clunky recording device that made it through the gates of old Yankee Stadium.

Twenty-two-year-old Robert Ford definitely would not have seen himself in the position he is in today with the Astros, In fact, he says, "I wouldn't have envisioned myself in Yakima either. I think I was just open to wherever the opportunity was, and that's how I've been throughout my career. I don't think I would've envisioned myself in Houston either, but it has worked out really well. I love Houston, it's a great city and I like working for the Astros."

Following that experience with Yakima, Ford moved to the Frontier League for 2003–04, moving to independent baseball from short-season ball. The broadcaster was able to secure the Kalamazoo gig through a local radio conglomerate that had him broadcast on four different stations in western Michigan. There he was able to broadcast high school and small collegiate sports, as well as do some radio reporting and anchoring work for the group. He moved to the Eastern League in Binghamton the next year and stayed there for the remainder of his time in Minor League Baseball. In 2009, Ford received an offer to do the pre-game and post-game shows for the Kansas City Royals' flagship radio station, which ended his run in the minors.

The offseason was different for Ford. He was a big grinder, and called 10 years of college basketball. He did a lot of sports for the two years he was in Kalamazoo for Kalamazoo College and the Kalamazoo Christian High School Comets. While for the most part the broadcaster was able to find freelance work for the years where he wasn't affiliated with the radio conglomerate, he remembers not being aggressive enough at applying for positions his first year in Binghamton, and as a result, for the first few months that he lived back in New York, Ford delivered pizzas for Papa John's.

While it started off as a winter without a lot of broadcasting for Ford, he eventually found some high school work around the Binghamton area and lucked into a position that opened up with the College of Saint Rose in Albany—about a two-hour drive away. After grinding out men's and women's team doubleheaders at the college and in the high school season, Ford had called significantly more basketball than he was accustomed to.

"I sat down to figure it out, and that winter I called 75 basketball games and I loved it," Ford remembers.

After that season, Ford switched roles a bit. He was able to get a play-by-play job at Binghamton College, and for the next couple of years, he became a substitute teacher for the local school district.

"When you love broadcasting and play-by-play, you're trying to get as many reps or opportunities as you can and you'll do some pretty crazy things to make it happen, and I definitely did that the season I called the College of Saint Rose games," Ford says.

6. Robert Ford

A 20-year radio vet, Robert Ford has called a lot of games on the radio, and he has consumed a lot of additional games turning the dials. To him, the most important task of a broadcaster isn't in any of the specifics that you do on-air; rather, it's in a simple fact about the position from the start: a broadcaster has to be entertaining.

"Anybody can put on a headset and try to tell you what's happening on the field, but what sets you apart from anybody else is being entertaining. Now, that comes from your preparation and having knowledge—knowing facts about the game and the players. That paints the picture. That also comes with finding what you do well and finding your voice," Ford says.

He continues that it's also about letting your personality show through the broadcast. While John Sterling, the New York Yankees' broadcaster, is known for eccentric home run calls, and it works very well for him, Ford maintains that if he did that, it would sound weird. Why? Because that is Sterling's personality, and it is authentic, where for Robert, it would be more of the Astros' call-man pretending to be someone he is not.

Entertainment is important for Ford, and off-air, he had a tough-to-beat city to travel to in the Northwest League when he first entered Minor League Baseball. Back in 2001, Vancouver was in the travel schedule for the short-season league—a fortunate draw, to say the least. In 1999, the city played host to a Triple-A team, and also had an NHL team that it supported. Because of the aforementioned circumstances, it isn't a surprise that the city is much larger than the average city in the Northwest League. For example, Yakima had a population of about 83,000 people at the turn of the century, according to census data. In comparison, Vancouver had around 550,000 residents at the same time.

Not only was the young broadcaster fortunate to be in the same league as Vancouver, but he also visited Vancouver for his first-ever true road trip. Yakima first went to the Tri-Cities to face off against the newly named Tri-City Dust Devils, who played about an hour and a half away from Yakima in Pasco, Washington. Because the trip was so close, the team treated it as a commuter trip, where they would bus back and forth on the same day to save money on a hotel. The team then traveled to Vancouver to play a five-game series—a once popular format in Minor League Baseball that became a rarity reserved for rescheduling postponed games from prior series.

A few additional things made this trip to Vancouver a big success

Play-by-Play from the Minors

for the Syracuse graduate. First, Vancouver had a long-standing tradition of playing Wednesday day games—they refer to the games affectionately as "nooners." So, the Bears had their only day game of the season in the middle of a series. What this meant was that Ford had the opportunity to spend an entire night to do whatever he wanted in Vancouver. Twenty years later, Ford says that he can't recall what he had to eat while he was in Vancouver, although he is sure that it was good. He does remember stumbling through downtown Vancouver, exploring all the sights and sounds of the area, though. The young man found himself in a Canadian strip club, and noticed that some things were a little off inside.

"They had a big-screen TV behind the stage, and when nobody was dancing, they put the TV on, showing the Blue Jays game. There weren't a lot of women going to the stage, and I thought to myself, 'This is weird.' Eventually a woman who worked there, a Black woman with a British accent, approached me," Ford recalls.

The two chatted a bit about where they were from and how they were doing before she asked him if he wanted to take her back to his hotel for "a bit of fun."

"She obviously saw the look on my face, and she goes, 'Oh, you know prostitution is legal here?' And I said, 'No. I did not.' I didn't take her up on her offer. I thought, oh, that is not what I was bargaining for, so I left shortly after."

While that unique experience kept Ford out of the Canadian clubs, Vancouver left a longer lasting impression on him from a baseball standpoint. The team that the Bears were visiting was affiliated with the Oakland Athletics, and Ford was in that league right after the Athletics were stripped of Johnny Damon, Jason Giambi and Jason Isringhausen in free agency. That resulted in the A's acquiring eight first-round picks in the 2002 draft, all of whom made their way to Vancouver at some point during that season. Because the A's had so much money and draft capital running through the Northwest League, their GM, Billy Beane, made it to quite a few Canadians games.

Not only was Ford able to interview Beane while the two were in Vancouver, but he had an interesting run-in with a third party who was along for that entire ride. He noticed that someone was hanging around Beane in the press box, and he asked one of the press box workers who it was. They quickly told Ford that it was a writer working on a book about Billy Beane.

"I thought to myself, 'Who the hell would want to read a book about Billy Beane?'" Ford recalls. "Well, the guy was Michael Lewis and

88

6. Robert Ford

the book was *Moneyball*, and myself and many others have now read that book."

Of course, the book gained a lot of popularity outside of the tight-knit baseball community when Brad Pitt starred as Billy Beane in the 2011 movie directed by Bennett Miller. "It was cool when I read the book a few years later, and I knew the guys that they talked about. All of those first-round picks came through Vancouver that year and I got to watch them play," Ford says.

While Vancouver was Ford's favorite overall city to visit, in his tenure at Binghamton he really enjoyed going to a restaurant in downtown Akron near the hotel they stayed at when the team was in town to face the Akron RubberDucks. The old arrangement in town had a hotel that was walking distance from the ballpark, and a small, aging brick building with a granite entryway and a red-and-green striped awning welcoming you to the Diamond Deli, a hidden gem only open from 9 a.m. to 3 p.m. Monday–Friday. Despite being so close to the ballpark, the name actually doesn't come because of its proximity to the grass-and-dirt diamond. Rather, it is so named because the building used to host a jewelry store. Growing up in New York City, Ford has high expectations whenever going to a delicatessen. That's because his first taste of delis was in the famous kosher delis of New York. While walking around on his first trip to Akron, the broadcaster was looking for a bite to eat and passed the shop at the corner of East Cedar and Main Street.

"It had a sign in the window that said 'Try our famous corned beef.' I love corned beef and pastrami and all that stuff," Ford explains. "There was also a line of people waiting to get sandwiches, which is perfect. There's a line, so it must be pretty good. Well, I ended up trying it and it was really good. It's one of the best delis I've been to anywhere, and I would visit it anytime I visited Akron."

Through frequenting the deli, Ford ended up getting to know the owner relatively well. A lot of times after the final game of a series when Ford would leave town, he would stop by the deli one last time to grab a sandwich, and the owner would chat with him. Knowing that his deli was so close to the stadium and seeing the minor leaguers frequent his shop, the owner would hand Ford 10 cookies with his order and tell him to give them to the guys on the bus so they could enjoy them.

"He was a really nice guy, and very friendly. Those are the things that you really remember about traveling and doing this. It's the people you meet in different places, especially when you go on the road. You look forward to some of the people that you're going to see and some of

89

the restaurants or bars that you enjoy going to, and you develop a routine," Ford says.

When he went there initially in 2005, the downtown Akron area was not doing well. Many of the places around the ballpark were struggling or boarded up, but every time the team returned to the city, there seemed to be a new store or restaurant open. There were a few great spots to go to when Ford visited northeastern Ohio, but he always made sure to stop by the Diamond Deli when he was in town.

The things you remember are the people, and the good people far outweigh the bad people in baseball, but a few of the really good guys stick out. Two that stick out to Ford are Daniel Murphy and Brian Bannister. While both were guys who made Ford's job easy to do because they were smart and fun to be around, it's how thoughtful they were that really made them special. One example of this was one day, before a game early in the season for Binghamton in 2008, when the team was on the road in Erie, and Murphy approached Ford in the clubhouse.

He said, "Hey, Pop enjoys listening to you." At first, Ford didn't realize exactly what he meant, and he said, "What?" Murphy repeated the sentiment before Ford realized that the Jacksonville, Florida, kid who manned third meant that his dad enjoyed listening to the games on the radio. So, Ford said, "If Pop is happy, then I'm happy." Then Murphy cracked a smile before the two went back about their business for the game.

It's always a joy to hear that people close to the team think you're doing a good job. Parents of players and season ticket holders will let you know how you're performing on the mic and will tell you plenty about what would be good for future broadcasts. But the bulk of the people crowding the stands typically don't know much about the individuals between the two chalk lines separating the fans from the players. For a lot of people, it's about an affordable option for a family of four or five that could be enjoyable, and every once in a while, it's about something really fun going on at the diamond that attracts new people to the park for the first time.

Thinking back to one of the most fun evenings he's had at a ballpark in Minor League Baseball, Ford's mind quickly goes to Altoona, where the Curve play. He recalls that team being more creative than most Double-A teams. The key there was having fun with promotions to help get fans into the stands. One promotion that has since spread around Minor League Baseball far and wide is Awful Night. The Curve came up with the promotion for the 2003 season, and went on to host a

6. Robert Ford

total of six evenings that challenged fans with all types of awful things you don't expect when coming into the ballpark. In 2007, the Curve gave away sporks to fans who entered the gates, and another year they gave out cups with no bottom. One year, the general manager, Todd Parnell, affectionately known as "Parney" throughout Minor League Baseball and famous for a variety of loud pants that he sports to the ballpark and to business meetings, was the main feature of the giveaway. The first 1,000 fans through the gate on Awful Night received a picture of Parney's gallbladder, which had been removed in the offseason.

The fun didn't stop after first pitch, though. "Instead of putting up batting average, they put up failure percentage, so if you were hitting .300, they put up that your failure percentage was .700," Ford reminisces. "I remember in the mascot race, the mascots quit in the middle of the race. Whenever they would do something in between innings like that, they would put on the board 'That's Awful.' It was just really creative and really fun."

Ford has to think back to his time in independent ball to remember a truly "awful" night. During his time in Kalamazoo, the team visited Ohio's first capital, Chillicothe, for the Fourth of July. It was a stormy day, and the two teams sat in a rain delay for a significant period of time before being able to begin the game. The Fourth of July is one of the biggest nights of the year for most teams. They shoot off fireworks, which always helps draw fans, and because the next day a lot of people typically are off from work, they flock to the ballpark to grab a hot dog and celebrate America's birthday. This night was no different, and despite the rain, the Paints had a bustling crowd. Following the hour or two delay, after a few innings, the leadership group for the Paints noticed there was going to be a problem. A lot of smaller markets—like Chillicothe—have curfews on how late loud noises such as fireworks or music from a concert can be made. Here, on the Fourth of July, it appeared the game would not end in time for the fans to see fireworks, so the staff decided to call an audible.

"Chillicothe tells everyone that the curfew was at 11 o'clock, and the game didn't start until 9:30, so we weren't going to finish the game," Ford explains. "So, they said, 'Once an inning ends around 10:30, we're going to pause the game to shoot off fireworks. It'll be 15 minutes and then we'll resume the game.'" Around the fourth inning, they stopped the game and shot off the fireworks, which created a whole new problem for the team.

"They didn't account for all the smoke that the fireworks caused. It

91

hung around the field like a giant fog. So yeah, the fireworks show was 15 minutes, but then it was another 15–20 minutes before the smoke lifted enough for people to be able to see the game. So, it wound up being a 35- to 45-minute delay before the game resumed and mind you, we already had a lengthy delay prior to the game. And of course, once all the fireworks are shot off, everyone leaves. So not only do we have this long delay on what was already a long night, but now we have to play the rest of the game with no one in the stands. That was certainly one of the more unique situations I encountered in the minors."

While Ford is a major league broadcaster and has seen all the best players not only from the Houston Astros organization but the best that Major League Baseball has had to offer, he still can recall being wowed by a couple of players in the minors. One in particular has spent a few recent years of his career with the Houston Astros.

Justin Verlander only spent one season, in 2005, in Minor League Baseball. In 2004, he was selected second overall by the Detroit Tigers out of Old Dominion. The stud flew through the Florida State League as a 22-year-old, fanning 104 batters in just 86 innings and earning a 9–2 record to pair with his 1.67 ERA across 13 games. Then he got called up to Double-A Erie to play in the Eastern League. Verlander would only pitch in seven games, to push his minor league total to 20. One of those seven games just so happened to be a June 26 matchup at Binghamton. The game occurred just 10 days after the righty got the call-up to Double-A, and he had tossed just one game prior to it: on June 21, making his Eastern League debut against the New Hampshire Fisher Cars, he went seven innings, allowing just one hit, while striking out 11 batters.

In his game against Binghamton, Ford recalls, "He was just on a different level. You didn't have to be much of a scout to realize that he was going to be very good. Every pitch was in the upper 90s, he had the great curveball and that was pretty much all he needed. He was just dominant."

The righty spun seven scoreless frames and rung up seven batters while allowing just four hits against the Mets affiliate. Of course, Verlander and Ford would cross paths again, 12 years later, and this time, the star on the mound would be playing for our broadcaster's team.

"One of the first times I ever talked to Justin after the Astros traded for him in 2017, I mentioned to him that I saw him in Binghamton and we talked about it briefly," Ford says. "It was cool to see that. It's always kind of neat to say to guys, 'You know, I saw you wherever.'"

6. Robert Ford

It just so happens that 2005 was also the season that Ford came across the best team he has seen in Minor League Baseball. While the Detroit Tigers sent the best prospect Ford has seen to Erie, the Boston Red Sox set up a loaded Portland Sea Dogs team. The team had quite a few young, talented players, including a few 21-year-olds who went on to have stellar major league careers. Dustin Pedroia, Hanley Ramirez, Brandon Moss, Jon Lester and Aníbal Sánchez were all 21-year-olds who played large roles in the success of the team, which finished 10 games over .500 (76–66). Ford remembers holding some bragging rights after Binghamton handed the team their first loss following a 10–0 start to the season. For the majority of their season, four-fifths of their rotation would go on to play in the majors. Lester, Sánchez and Jonathan Papelbon anchored the front end of the staff, and David Pauley and Kason Gabbard filled in when guys eventually moved up, or prior to Sánchez getting the call-up to Portland.

Lester was the glue of that rotation. He finished the season with an 11–6 record and a 2.61 ERA across 148.1 innings, while striking out 163 batters. Those numbers were good enough to win Eastern League Pitcher of the Year honors. The pitching staff would go on to have 11 MLB All-Star seasons, and the hitters would add an additional eight to the team resume.

While the Red Sox system was certainly good that season, boasting four of the top 77 prospects in baseball according to *Baseball America*'s post-season rankings, Ford also got to see some players who became unsung heroes as they climbed the rungs of the system. The best example he remembers was Marco Estrada.

The righty was selected out of Long Beach State in the sixth round of the 2005 draft by the Washington Nationals. It took him just three years to climb the ladder and make his major league debut as a reliever for the Nationals in 2008, where he recorded an ERA near 8.00 in 11 appearances. After that, he bounced around for a few years with the Nationals and the Brewers before latching onto the Toronto Blue Jays in 2015. That started a three-year run of the best success he had at the big league level. In 507.2 innings of work across those three years, Estrada maintained a 3.62 ERA. The run allowed him to sign a few extensions with the Blue Jays that averaged $13 million annually.

Looking back, it seems easy to say that the nine-year major league veteran was always set up to have some success, but it didn't seem that way early on in his professional career. He started off in the New York–Penn League in 2005, and he had a 5.08 ERA in nine games. The Sonora,

Mexico, native got a rude awakening to professional ball. In his first outing, a start against the Tri-City ValleyCats, he only lasted two innings, but allowed seven runs, all of which were earned. Batters teed off against him, going 6-for-12 with three walks and a hit by pitch, and not one batter struck out. Things didn't get much better initially. After three outings, his ERA hung around 24.75 before he was able to adjust to the league and get it to a respectable number. It helped that he allowed only one run in his last 10 innings, which spanned a pair of outings. In that stretch, his ERA dropped from 6.85 to 5.08.

His second year in MiLB didn't fare much better. He was moved up to Savannah in the South Atlantic League midway through the season and his first start seemed very familiar to the scouts and players around him. Facing the Lexington Legends, he allowed eight runs off 11 hits and a pair of walks in just 3.1 frames. Ford had the opportunity to see Estrada in his breakout season. After an even-keeled 2007, where the starter spanned three levels and kept his ERA at 4.85, he made his way to the Eastern League in 2008. The broadcaster and pitcher were in the same stadium just once while in the minors, and Estrada didn't disappoint. He fanned six batters in a six-inning shutout showcase against the Mets affiliate. When thinking about the players he saw while broadcasting in the minors, Ford reminisces, "There were definitely more guys who I thought were going to be better and have more of a career in the big leagues ... than there were guys that surprised."

Moments are in a way the opposite of players. We see guys performing in the minors and have incredible visions of what they could be in the future. Oftentimes, those dreams are derailed due to injuries or other circumstances completely outside of the player's control. The moments that broadcasters call, though, are engraved in stone. There are so many great moments to look back upon that it's sometimes difficult to narrow it down to the best moment we've had on-air. Although not all broadcasters have had the good fortune of calling a World Series.

When Ford thinks about the greatest moment he has called on-air, it doesn't take long for him to pull the rabbit out of the hat. While he has gotten the opportunity to call a lot of great moments, nothing beats getting to call a pair of World Series runs, including a World Series Championship win, which he got to broadcast in 2017. It's easy to say that a championship is the top moment that you've been a part of. Kids playing in their back yard don't pretend to be playing in a game in April. People dream of being a part of a World Series, but Ford maintains that it's even better than a fan can imagine.

6. Robert Ford

"Whether you work in this business or not, we all know that a World Series is really cool and we can all say that getting to call a World Series seems like it is a really cool thing. Well, it's 10 times, maybe 100 times better than you ever could have thought it was. Getting a chance to call those games, with the atmosphere—you just can't beat it. The entire baseball world is watching, it's the only game in town. This Series is what it's all about and this moment is why we get into the game."

Everyone from a player to a coach, a trainer, a broadcaster—they all enter the game to accomplish the goal of eventually winning a World Series, and for that reason, Ford says, there is nothing that can top a Series.

On the other hand, we are all growing older and more experienced each time we put the headset on. One thing that the New York native credits himself with as his career has progressed is going down and asking umpires questions that he has. He typically won't do it following a game, but prior to the next day's game he will head down and have a conversation with the umpires to clarify any rules questions that he may have.

One person who really helped Ford become more comfortable asking for clarification was Steve Palermo, whom Ford met while he was in Kansas City. At that point, Palermo was an umpire coordinator for Major League Baseball, but in the '80s and early '90s, Palermo was thought to be one of the best callers of balls and strikes in the bigs. One night in 1991, the umpire was in Dallas having dinner at Campisi's Egyptian Restaurant, when some robbers started mugging two waitresses in the parking lot. A bartender came into the crowded dining area and asked for help, and Palermo, along with a few other gentlemen, rushed out to apprehend the robbers. During the scrum that ensued, Palermo was shot in the back and left paralyzed from the waist down, never umpiring a Major League Baseball game again. Despite the horrible injury, Palermo remained a vanguard of the sport, and as an umpire coordinator he spent a lot of time in Kansas City, where he and Ford would talk about the game. "He was a great resource to me because I could ask him anything about umpiring. He loved talking about umpiring," Ford says.

Ford was able to ask Palermo questions about the game, like a wonky walk-off that threw him and a Reading, Pennsylvania, broadcaster off a little when he was with Binghamton. On June 20, 2007, Binghamton finished a doubleheader at FirstEnergy Stadium in Reading. Game 1 was picked up where it was left off the previous day after a storm hit the eastern Pennsylvanian town, and it ended in a Bingham-ton win. In Game 2, heading into the bottom of the seventh inning (the final inning for MiLB doubleheaders), the game was tied. Mike Spidale led off the frame with a base knock, prior to a sacrifice bunt, a pair of intentional walks and a force out. That brought organizational catcher Jason Hill to the dish. Hill hit a weak grounder to third, and the ball was thrown to first for what most in the stands believed to be an out that would lead to extra innings.

"Then I looked down and I see players celebrating at home plate and I think, 'What the heck just happened? Why are they celebrating?,'" Ford paints the picture. Luckily, the broadcaster hadn't gone to a commercial break to set up the top of the eighth just yet. "Then I realized what happened. There was catcher's interference, and the bases were loaded, so it forced in a run. So, the Reading Phillies won, and it's still the only time I've ever seen a walk-off catcher's interference."

Sure, it's a little unorthodox, but many of the moments broadcasters dream of calling are rare feats and incredible things that you don't see every day as a baseball fan. So, in a way, the crazy plays we see, but cannot explain immediately, help prepare us to call the unbelievable, great moments that come along throughout a broadcaster's career.

What would a broadcaster who has called two World Series and a walk-off catcher's interference want to broadcast if he could broadcast any moment that has already occurred in baseball history? Ford looks back to one of his favorite calls of all time, when Tom Cheek narrated Joe Carter's 1993 walk-off home run in Game 7 of the World Series. The famous line "Touch 'em all, Joe, you'll never hit a bigger home run in your life," rings loud and clear eternally for Ford.

"I think it's one of the greatest calls of all time because calling a World Series in and of itself is great, but getting a moment like that? And he absolutely nailed the call. It's just perfection and I don't know that anybody else could have done a better call than Tom Cheek had in that moment."

Then, Ford looks back at his own career and prides himself on being a guy who just reacts to whatever is going on directly in front of him. The closest moment to that Carter homer for Ford was when José Altuve hit a walk-off homer in Game 6 of the American League Championship Series in 2019 to send the Astros to the World Series.

His call for the famed blast went, "That's driven, deep to left-center field, Gardner is going baaack. LOOKING UP, SEE YOU LATER, SEE YOU LATER, SEE YOU LATER! THE ASTROS ARE HEADED BACK

6. Robert Ford

TO THE WORLD SERIES!" He then recapped the ninth inning and noted the Series record while the crowd cheered on the home team in the background.

"That's one of the reasons that I prepare the way that I do. It's because when you have any moment, you want to be prepared for whatever it is: if it's a great moment or a not-so great moment, whether it's something mundane in a random game in July, you want to be as prepared as you can for it to call it accurately and to paint the picture."

7

Josh Whetzel

Currently with the Rochester Red Wings
Previously with the Albany (GA) Polecats,
Kinston Indians and Binghamton Mets

Like Ford, after being introduced to Minor League Baseball in the lower levels, Josh Whetzel found himself in Binghamton, calling games for the Mets in upstate New York before he made it to his latest stop in Rochester. Despite both broadcasters working for their entire adult lives in baseball and even calling games for the same team, Whetzel couldn't have grown up in a place more different than the Bronx.

Josh Whetzel grew up in Parsons, Kansas, a small town about a two-hour drive east of Wichita. Whetzel grew up in Jayhawk territory, and pushed his way through the South Atlantic League and Carolina League to make it to Binghamton for a brief stint before earning the gig in Rochester, where he has spent the last 18 years. Prior to his MiLB career, he attended the University of Kansas to earn his degree in Overland Park, around 140 miles north of his childhood home.

Although Josh grew up among St. Louis Cardinals fans in southwest Kansas, his father's family had rebelled against Josh's grandfather and started to root for the Los Angeles Dodgers. At first, they did it just to get a rise out of the elder Whetzel, but eventually it stuck. Down the road, Whetzel's uncle played minor league ball for the Dodgers, and that cemented most of the family into Dodgers fandom.

When Whetzel was growing up, it was difficult to find Dodgers games on television. Out in the country, most families were only able to get three channels on television and this was prior to games being readily available on the internet for fans to consume. If the Kansas native was listening to radio, he would primarily pull in Royals games, but on occasion, while scanning the dial, he would be able to find some other games out there as well. Where his family differed from other families

7. Josh Whetzel

that lived in his neighborhood is that they had a satellite dish.

"My Dad bought one of those big satellite dishes. It was primarily to watch Dodgers games. Now they have those DirecTV little dishes, but this was about an eight-foot dish like the ones you would see outside a TV station," Whetzel remembers. "You could move it around and pull in all sorts of different games. At the time, the Dodgers were televising about 60–70 games a year that we could get."

While he could watch Vin Scully's *Game of the Week* on NBC and some of Scully's Dodgers games, Whetzel didn't get to listen to him very often on the radio. So it makes sense that, particularly when he first started broadcasting, friends and listeners would say that he sounded a lot like Denny Matthews, who has been the voice of the Kansas City Royals since the team's inception in 1969. Matthews holds his own among the elite broadcasters of the last quarter-century. He is a 2007 Ford C. Frick Award winner and he was inducted to the Royals Hall of Fame in 2004 and the Missouri Sports Hall of Fame the following year.

Josh Whetzel has journeyed from a small town in Kansas to Rochester, New York. During his time in baseball, he's been fortunate to broadcast for both Vladimir Guerrero, Sr., and Vladimir Guerrero, Jr., as they made their way up to the bigs (photograph courtesy Josh Whetzel).

Matthews certainly isn't a bad guy to be compared to, but Whetzel says that he didn't intentionally mold himself after the Royals call-man. "I think some of it I just absorbed through osmosis by listening. I wasn't doing it consciously, but there were certain things I said that sounded like the way that he broadcasted things," he says.

99

Play-by-Play from the Minors

The younger Whetzel also was molded a lot by a co-worker when he got his first radio gig while in junior college. "The guy I would do games with was the local sports announcer. He would use some phrases and, particularly when I worked basketball and football, I would use some similar words and phrases... Some of the stuff he said probably bled into what I did."

That's where the journey started. He worked at a small station near his hometown in Parsons while he attended junior college, and it began a career that has spanned a few decades and resulted in Whetzel moving from the Midwest to the East Coast and, slowly, further and further north. The 2015 *Ballpark Digest* Broadcaster of the Year Award winner started his career in Albany, Georgia, moved further north to Kinston, North Carolina, and crept up the coast for a stop in Binghamton, New York, before making it to his longest-tenured stop, in Rochester. His baseball journey began a bit earlier, though, and its roots, like his own, are in Kansas.

After college, Josh packed up his bags and moved to Liberal, Kansas, a town of about 20,000 people in the southwest corner of the state. Liberal may be best known for Dorothy's House and the Land of Oz—a replica of scenes featured in the 1939 film *The Wizard of Oz* that plays host to an annual festival, OzFest. During his tenure in Liberal, Josh worked in a collegiate wood bat league, the Jayhawk League, which is a member of the National Baseball Congress (NBC), as the play-by-play voice for the Liberal Bee Jays. The Bee Jays are five-time NBC champions and have had many MLB players pass through town, including Satchel Paige and their 2007 and 2008 manager, Mike Hargrove. While Whetzel worked for the team, which played a short-season schedule from June through August, he was also the sports and news director for the radio station in Liberal.

Because his goal all along was to work in professional baseball, Whetzel used his time with the Liberal Bee Jays to gather tape for a demo reel that he could send to affiliated ball clubs. He attended Winter Meetings in Dallas in 1994 and interviewed with a handful of teams, most memorably the Southern Oregon Timberjacks, an A's affiliate in the Northwest League located in Medford, Oregon. He wasn't able to secure any of the jobs he interviewed for in Dallas, so he called around to see if any teams had an opening, applied to a handful of jobs and eventually was accepted for a position with the Albany (Georgia) Polecats, who played in the South Atlantic League for a handful of years in the '90s.

100

7. Josh Whetzel

That may seem like a piece of cake, but Josh's journey didn't come without a speed bump. With about a month left in his first season in affiliated ball in 1990, Whetzel and the rest of the Polecats' front office found out that their team was being sold and moved to Salisbury, Maryland, where they would become the Delmarva Shorebirds. The new ownership group wasn't going to take anyone from the old front office with them, so the entire organization found out that they would be looking for new jobs come the offseason. Josh decided to reach out to his college advisor, Tom Hedrick, who wrote *The Art of Sportscasting: How to Build a Successful Career* and broadcast for the University of Kansas's football, baseball and basketball teams; the Kansas City Chiefs; Cincinnati Reds; and Dallas Cowboys over the course of his career. Tom found a job at a Nebraska radio station for Josh and the young broadcaster stayed diligent, sending out tapes and applications while he passed the time doing more work for a station.

The next year, Jim Rosenhaus, the current Cleveland Guardians broadcaster, got a job with the Buffalo Bisons, who were the Pirates' Triple-A affiliate at the time, and the domino effect of broadcasters taking new jobs and others climbing up the ladder behind them left the Kinston Indians job open in the Carolina League. Whetzel sent his tape in and was able to earn that job to return to Minor League Baseball. He spent four years with the Kinston Indians before making the move to Binghamton, where he would wait three years before accepting a position in Triple-A with Rochester.

He knew that Dan Mason, the GM of Rochester, had family who lived in Binghamton and would come to a few Binghamton Mets games each year. So he had that connection from meeting Mason at games, and the GM in Binghamton at that time had worked in Rochester years prior. When the Rochester job was open, Whetzel networked a bit to get his tape listened to. After those in the hiring process listened to his tape, it was easy to select the current voice of the Red Wings as their new broadcaster.

The journey to Rochester taught Josh more than just how to network. Through his nearly 30-year journey in baseball, Josh has learned quite a bit about the sport and how to tell the story of a game to the audience. He believes that broadcasters starting out in radio need to first find out how to accurately describe what is happening on the field, but what sets great broadcasters apart from good broadcasters is: "Having that personal connection with the listener. It's hard to define, but it's what separates a lot of good broadcasters from great broadcasters."

Whetzel continues, "It's the ability to make some sort of a connection and feel like you're actually talking to the listener as opposed to broadcasting, so it's more of a conversation." If you can combine that connection to the listener with the added flavor of strong, connecting anecdotes and stories, that's how you can climb to the next level.

Like broadcasters, only the greatest players can climb to the next level and continue their playing careers. One conversation that many broadcasters and fans of the game have is: Who is going to be the next great player? Spending 18 years in Triple-A, Josh has had the amazing opportunity to introduce the final level of prospects to MLB fans. After a stud has spent a few years polishing the gleam of his game, Whetzel has seen him taking his final steps to becoming the next big star. If he thinks back to all the guys he has seen, the guy who had the best career and who played on a team Whetzel broadcasted for was Vladimir Guerrero, Sr. Funnily enough, the veteran broadcaster saw Guerrero Sr. come through Albany in his first year in affiliated ball, and he got to see Vladimir Guerrero, Jr., in the last week of the season in 2018.

The two came up in different eras of baseball. Vlad Jr. was maybe the most hyped prospect of all time. He was a legacy and had his father's name, so people knew who he was, and his immense talent and personality helped to market that. He was also one of the first top prospects to come up when social media coincided with good, clean video of games he played at nearly every level. His father, however, played in an era when *Baseball America* was a small magazine that operated out of Durham, North Carolina, and was one of the only ways, other than traveling to a minor league ballpark or looking at box scores in a local paper, that you could keep track of prospects as they climbed the ladder to success.

Vlad Guerrero, Sr., played in the South Atlantic League as a 20-year-old, just one year after making his professional debut in the Gulf Coast League and just one year before he would go on to play nine games for the Montreal Expos in his debut season in The Show. We all know how the 2018 Hall of Fame inductee's major league career progressed. He finished with an incredible .318 batting average while pummeling 449 home runs and earning nine All-Star awards. How was his year in the South Atlantic League? In 110 games, he hit .333, launched 16 homers and drove in 63 RBI—all of which were career highs at that point.

"That was my first year, so obviously I thought he looked like he was pretty good, but I couldn't have predicted that he was going to be a Hall

7. Josh Whetzel

of Famer," Whetzel remembers. No doubt about it, Whetzel saw one of baseball's greats in his first season, but he remembers a few more players who certainly wowed him when he saw them. CC Sabathia, the lefty drafted out of high school by Cleveland in the first round of the 1998 draft, didn't have great numbers in his seven starts in Kinston in 1999. In fact, he had an ERA hovering at 5.34 and walked 19 batters in just 32 innings. But Whetzel will tell you that the stuff was always good for the Cy Young Award winner and six-time All-Star.

Sabathia was always viewed as a top player. One guy who slid under the radar, and is largely thought of among baseball's inner circle as "the best player that no one has seen," faced off against Sabathia in his first professional appearance. In a 2013 *Sports Illustrated* article by Michael McKnight titled "The Best Player You Never Saw," Sabathia is quoted as saying, "Brian Cole was the player who showed me I needed to develop an off-speed pitch."

Whetzel can confirm that Cole is perhaps the best prospect he has ever seen. Although I think that Cole more likely fits in the unsung hero role here. Drafted by the Mets in the 18th round of the 1998 draft, he was handed a $100,000 signing bonus and surprised everyone he saw. Cole wasn't ranked by *Baseball America* as a Top-100 prospect at any point during his career until about two weeks prior to his death in 2001. With that being said, the 170-pound outfielder from Meridian, Mississippi, was special, and he proved it to everyone who played with him or against him. In 1999 with the Capital City Bombers, Cole hit .316, as a player who was nearly two years younger than the average player in the league. As if that weren't enough, he smashed 18 homers, scored 97 runs and drove in an additional 71 RBI in just 125 games. Oh, by the way, he stole 50 bases as well. To put that into perspective, until 2022, the last person to steal 50 or more bags in the South Atlantic League was Eric Jenkins, who was selected in the second round of the 2015 draft, and he stole 51 in 2016 for the Hickory Crawdads.

"The Mets' big prospect at the time was Alex Escobar, and he was clearly better than him," Whetzel remembers from Cole's first campaign in Binghamton in 1999. "The next year he was supposed to be our lead-off guy and center fielder, and the Mets were letting him leave spring training to drive home to drop his car off and then fly up to Binghamton." Of course, fans already know what happened to Cole: He was driving back home and, according to a state trooper who was on the scene, pulled off the road onto the median in Jackson County to avoid a collision with another driver. When he drove the car back onto the road, it flipped into the air and rolled. Cole died later that day. "He was going to be really, really good," Whetzel explains. You can travel far and wide and wait years and years before you find another player whose lore and statistics will line up again with the late Cole, who grew up in poverty in football country, Mississippi, but beat the odds and made it to the pros. Unfortunately, the accident robbed his family of an incredible human being, and him from having what was sure to be an incredible career.

Far from Mississippi, Whetzel has enjoyed his time on the baseball circuit and some trips he made while broadcasting Buffalo basketball for the Mid-American Conference. There, he was fortunate to travel to a number of great towns and cities. One advantage of calling collegiate ball is going on the tournament trips that a lot of teams take to places such as Hawaii, the Cayman Islands, Alaska, and Northern Ireland. While these are all great vacation destinations, the International League has some great cities to visit for three to four days at a time that can rival any other work trip the average person would have to make. If Josh were to have to pick just one town out of the many Western Division cities he enjoys to visit, it would probably be Louisville, Kentucky.

"If you can't have fun in Louisville, you can't have fun anywhere. Louisville should never lose home games because it's the International League version of Las Vegas," Whetzel says. There's so much that Whetzel enjoys about Louisville that he finds it difficult to narrow it down to just one place or one district that makes it special. "It's the bourbon capital of the world, basically, because you're in Kentucky. Which is good. They have a lot of good restaurants too. There's a place called Doc Crow's and I get a shrimp po' boy for lunch there all the time."

Doc Crow's is a Southern smokehouse and bar located on Main Street in Louisville, just a few blocks over from Louisville Slugger Field. The food runs the average customer about $12, plus you'll probably want to have a beer or two while you're there. They sell just about everything, from tacos and wings to salads and burgers, but you'll certainly want to try their smoked meats. They offer ribs, brisket and pulled pork that receive nothing but positive reviews from the customers who come through the establishment.

After he finishes lunch or before he heads out for a night on the town, Josh works the ballgame. Especially in the last couple of years, broadcasters get tasked with more and more things to do during a game, such as live Tweeting, cutting highlight reels to send out to the media or preparing for a post-game interview. With all of that on his plate, Whetzel admits that he doesn't pay too much attention to a lot of the promotions that take place on the field between innings, because he is typically focused on another aspect of his job. He does remember one promotion from the start of his career in Minor League Baseball that the former Jayhawk wishes he could see more of today: the diamond dig promotion.

The promotion is relatively simple. The event would be sponsored by a jeweler and the team would bury, say, a diamond ring. Following the game, they would allow fans who had registered or purchased tickets to the event to try to dig up the diamond. The event would go until someone found the ring or necklace or whatever was buried, and the person who found it could take it home. This was a promotion that fans could enjoy with little risk, but they could also leave with one of the highest monetarily valued rewards available at a minor league ballpark.

"I've seen it happen a bunch over the years and it really fires fans up. People have stopped doing it—probably because it tears up the infield. The grounds crew probably hates it. It's probably just not the best way to do it," Whetzel says. Although it is rare, some teams still participate in a diamond dig. In 2019, the Amarillo Sod Poodles teamed up with local store Barnes Jewelry for a diamond dig, but that's just one team out of 160 that decided to go with the once popular promotion.

While the different promotional nights and between-inning promotions don't typically blow Josh away, he has noticed a lot of success in Rochester with Throwback Nights. The most popular type of Throwback Night is when the Red Wings change their logos and jerseys to those of a former Rochester baseball club identity. One that they use semi-frequently is the Rochester Hustlers, who played in upstate New York from 1908 to 1920 and joined the International League in 1912.

"The new trend are these alternate team names and jerseys, which a lot of teams have done. We've had a lot of success with the Rochester Plates. The name is because the local food delicacy around here is called the Garbage Plate," Whetzel explains. "Every Thursday home game, we are the Rochester Plates and we wear different uniforms and that's been a pretty big success."

The standard Garbage Plate is a couple of hamburger patties with home fries and mac salad and meat sauce on top. It was first sold in Rochester around 100 years ago and was initially named Hots and Po-tots after the restaurant that started the tradition, Nick Tahou Hots. Years later, a lot of people who came to Rochester for college would want to order the menu item and would say, "Can I get that plate with all the garbage on it?" The name stuck, and now people all over upstate New

Play-by-Play from the Minors

York crave this piece of Rochester history. The first time the Red Wings suited up as the Plates, they had about 12,500 fans at the game. Needless to say, the promotion is a hit among the local fans.

Whetzel, along with other fans, hopes that the local food delicacy/ alternate identity nights continue to be a big trend in Minor League Baseball, but he certainly wishes he could put some bad flights and bus rides behind him.

Besides something that happens at least once each year—when players' equipment doesn't make it to a ballpark in time for a game because it got shipped separately—normally travel inconveniences only wear on you for a couple of days. Whetzel remembers a trip back from Gwinnett, Georgia, that did not go as planned. The Red Wings were going to play the Columbus Clippers in Rochester that night and José Contreras was making a rehab start for the Clippers, who were Yankees affiliates at the time. Rochester tends to sway to Yankees fandom, so its team receives an attendance boost whenever a Yankees player is in town. That day, because of a flight delay, the team didn't make it to the stadium until the gates were already open and there were around 10,000 fans circulating the ballpark.

"We didn't land until about six o'clock for a seven o'clock game and we had to rush from the airport to the ballpark. We went in right through everyone outside the ballpark. They had to pave a way for us to get into the ballpark and then they had to delay the game for about an hour for us to get ready before we could play," Rochester's call-man remembers. He has a handful of stories about games that have been canceled because of delays, or planes haven't been able to take off and flights have been outright canceled, but only one time has Rochester lost an off day due to travel.

The team rode to the Durham, North Carolina, airport after a day game, ready to fly back to Rochester to enjoy their off day the following day, and the flight was canceled. The airline was able to reroute a handful of tickets to make it to their destination, but not enough for the full team to get back in time for the next game, nearly 48 hours later. The Red Wings decided to allocate the tickets by major league service time, so the handful of players who had spent the most time playing big league ball got to fly home while the rest of the team had to take a 10-hour, 650-mile bus ride home on their off day. The ride was long enough that they had to switch bus drivers halfway through the trek. Normally if the team had planned to make a trip that far, they would have taken multiple buses, but that wasn't the case for this emergency trip. The trainer worked out a deal with a busing company, but it resulted in the majority of the team not making it home until 9 or 10 in the morning the next day—and that was after the team had played in a day game the day before, not a game with a 7 p.m. start time.

Sure, Whetzel would like to forget a lot of the bad travel moments he has encountered over the years, but there are a couple incredible moments on the diamond that he has witnessed that are unforgettable. One that instantly enters his mind doesn't come from Minor League Baseball. Whetzel had the opportunity to get called up to the bigs for a handful of games in his career, and one of them just so happened to be a big night for MLB's all-time saves leader, Mariano Rivera. On September 19, 2011, the Yankees entered the final frame of a ballgame with a 6–4 lead and put in their trusty closer, Rivera. He needed just 13 pitches to complete a perfect inning for his 602nd save, putting him in sole possession of the most saves in MLB history, climbing over MLB great Trevor Hoffman.

"When I knew I was going to get a chance to call that game, I looked at where Rivera was and I thought, 'Wow! He's going to be close to the saves record by the time that game comes around.' Then sure enough, he was one away from it and he set the saves record that game, which is pretty cool. I actually have an autographed baseball from that game. The trainer, who I knew, thought it was cool that I got to call that game, so he got an authenticated signed ball for me," Whetzel says.

While he didn't call that moment, he was the play-by-play guy for the middle innings, and Whetzel remembers that he was still rooting that Rivera would get the record that game, and in the middle innings he was hoping that the game wouldn't progress to a blowout, so Rivera would get the chance to do it while he was there. It all worked out for the star in the end.

That performance by Rivera was memorable, and despite the fact that Whetzel hasn't been able to call a championship-winning team in his 25-year career, he had the opportunity to call a couple of really talented teams while he was in Kinston in the late '90s. In 1996, 1997 and 1999, the Kinston Indians put together some incredibly strong teams, finishing more than 20 games above .500 in both 1997 and 1999. Unfortunately, both of those teams lost a lot of talent late in the season, as the major league Indians were vying for deep postseason runs and players were called up to reinforce higher levels as rosters expanded.

The 1996 season was particularly strange, though. The team finished the abridged regular season 76–62 despite having only four future

Play-by-Play from the Minors

big leaguers on the roster. The name of the game for that year's team was offense. The player who would go on to have the best MLB career was Sean Casey, who would play in the bigs in 11 seasons and hit over .300 as a major leaguer. Casey had played minor league baseball for Cleveland, and even six games as a September call-up with the parent team, but after he was dealt to Cincinnati in a trade for pitcher David Burba, he never played for Cleveland again.

With Jack Mull at the helm, Tim Jorgensen led the squad with 17 homers and Chip Glass was able to walk 40 times to set up innings for the big power hitters behind him. Jaret Wright and Noe Najera were a tandem to be reckoned with on the bump, combining for a 2.61 ERA to lead the rotation through the regular season. The season didn't get strange until the playoffs.

That year the Carolinas were devastated by hurricanes and tropical storms. In the first round of the playoffs, Kinston faced off against the Durham Bulls. They played the first game at home and won before heading to Durham for the second and third games of the series. While they were there, Hurricane Fran bulldozed through Kinston and did a great deal of damage to the Indians' ballpark. The city of Durham lost power and the team was trapped there for a few days without being able to play any additional games because of the damage from the hurricane.

"We eventually played a doubleheader in Winston-Salem to determine who would move on. They won the first game and we won the second game to advance," Whetzel remembers. "But after that we couldn't use our ballpark. The right-field fence had been knocked over, so we drove from Winston-Salem to Wilmington, Delaware, and played the entire championship series there. We would have had homefield advantage had games been played in Kinston." Wilmington would end up winning the championship that year and Kinston finished the season on the road for close to 10 days. To top it off, because it wasn't planned, most guys had only packed about three days of clothes for the trip. So, the team kept having to do laundry on the road. Imagine having to wait in the hotel for all your laundry to get cleaned every couple of days during a work trip. It's just something that makes life a little more hectic and takes a little more wind out of your sail.

Our broadcaster hasn't been able to call a championship-winning team despite being around a boatload of talent, but one thing he has been able to do quite a bit of is call no-hitters. He's had the opportunity to be on-call for 10 no-no's throughout his career. In Minor League Baseball, a lot of no-hitters are either combined no-hitters, where three

7. Josh Whetzel

or four guys have thrown for the team that hasn't allowed a hit, or they are only seven innings in length because they're part of doubleheaders. That doesn't bug Whetzel, though. He confirms that he gets a buzz from being a part of those games and going along with the rare moment.

The best prospect to throw a no-hitter that Whetzel called was in Binghamton on August 13, 2001. The Portland Sea Dogs started the Florida Marlins' 1999 second overall pick, Josh Beckett, on the bump. After cruising through the Florida State League to the tune of a 1.23 ERA in 12 games, he was called up to AA and was still holding a sub-2.00 ERA. Less than two months after making his Eastern League debut, the dominant righty went seven frames before handing the ball to Brandon Bowe and Aaron Scheffer. The Marlins would call him up to The Show on September 4 to finish the season, and, outside of a few rehab stints, he wouldn't look back for his whole 14-year career.

On the other end of the spectrum, no one could have expected that Jeremy Cummings, who played for the Scranton/Wilkes-Barre RailRiders in 2006, would be the first player to throw a no-hitter at Frontier Field. The 21st-round pick out of Charleston, West Virginia, was a solid organizational pitcher who tossed over 1,000 innings in minor league ball but never threw a pitch in the majors. He would even pitch for the Red Wings the next season, as he played for four different farm systems in his final four seasons in baseball. But on September 3, 2006, Jeremy Cummings had it going. He hurled 137 bullets to earn his eighth win of the season, and he walked four batters and hit another, but he did not allow a single hit in Scranton's 5–0 victory over Rochester.

Looking back, only three of the 10 no-hitters Whetzel has seen were thrown by one pitcher, and that was one of them. He remembers a few wonky games that turned out way different than the first inning would have suggested, too. "The first one I called, Luther Hackman pitched against Kinston for Salem in '96. He was so bad in the first inning that Kinston scored a run against him and he got a mound visit … from his pitching coach. After that, he settled down and was able to throw a nine-inning no-hitter. That was before they started posting pitch counts and that sort of thing, but I'd love to know how many pitches he threw in that no-hitter because it had to be a ton." Most baseball fans haven't watched a baseball game that has ended with no hits, and some broadcasters go a full career having never called a no-hitter, but Whetzel can boast 10 of them. He's had 10 once-in-a-lifetime experiences to learn from on the field, but one guy taught him a lot about the game while he was getting grounded in Rochester.

Play-by-Play from the Minors

Whetzel has learned a lot from his Red Wings on-air partner Joe Altobelli, who won a World Series as a manager of the Baltimore Orioles in 1983. Altobelli played sporadically in the majors from 1955 to 1961 before working on coaching staffs in the minors in the mid–60s. He would work his way up to the majors and keep coaching until 1991, when he went back to Rochester, the place where he spent 1971–1977 managing the team. He was the team's general manager in this stint in the early '90s, focusing more on ticket sales and promotions than worrying about wins and losses. He fell into the booth in 1998, right before Whetzel joined the team, and remained there until 2009, when he announced his retirement after spending 69 consecutive seasons working in organized baseball.

Whetzel views Altobelli as a mentor in many ways. "I learned a lot of baseball stuff from him, just in general from being around him and being so close to him for all those years. Nothing that necessarily sticks out as a specific thing, but so many different baseball stories and strategy things that maybe I wouldn't have thought of that I would get from him."

He started to learn a lesson in Kinston that he continued to learn further from Altobelli and his experiences in Rochester about being critical of a manager's decision on-air. "Normally when those guys make a decision and it doesn't seem right, there's actually a pretty damn good reason why they made that specific decision. Just because the fans or the broadcaster isn't privy to the reason why they decided to do it, doesn't mean it was wrong." Of course, what Whetzel is talking about is when guys are playing banged up but it isn't information that was shared outside of a coach's office. Another example could be up the ladder, when someone has told the manager that they can't use multiple lefties in the pen in one day, because one might be called up the next day and needs to be available to pitch. Information like that often travels behind closed doors and factors deeply into coaches' decision-making process as they manage a game.

Altobelli taught Whetzel a lot, and he is a beloved member of the Rochester community, a guy who has spent time in a variety of roles and capacities on the team, engaging with fans and making each night at the ballpark memorable for those who flock to see the Red Wings. While Whetzel only knew Altobelli as an established member of the baseball community with decades of experience in the industry, he met Brian Dinkelman when he was just starting his journey in baseball.

Dinkelman was an eighth-round pick of the Minnesota Twins in the 2006 draft. He'd spend seven years in affiliated baseball, and even got to play 23 games in the majors. The outfielder hit .301 in his cup of coffee with Minnesota in 2011, but retired after the 2013 season, when he hit .215 in 89 games with Rochester—his fourth consecutive season with the Triple-A club. Although the outfielder was never the best player on the team, he played a vital role in the Twins organization, a role that continues to this day as the manager of the Cedar Rapids Kernels, the Midwest League affiliate of the Minnesota Twins. His role is to be himself, a great locker room presence and a veteran to help the team stay loose—of course, in addition to being a super utility player at both the minor and major league levels.

"He was a hilarious dude, everyone loved being around him and he created a great atmosphere in the locker room," Whetzel remembers. Another guy Josh remembers spending a lot of time in Rochester, and who he enjoyed interacting with, is Trevor Plouffe.

Whetzel remembers a tradition the Red Wings had while Plouffe was playing there in 2008–2012. When a player was being interviewed on the field after a game for the television broadcast, some of the other players would sneak behind him on-air and pie him in the face with a shaving-cream pie. One player, Brock Peterson, did not want to get pied in the face while he was on-air, so Whetzel assured him that if he saw one of the players coming, he would say a code word to alert Peterson so he could avoid it. A few moments into the interview, Whetzel saw someone sneaking out of the dugout and said the code word, which allowed Peterson to look over his shoulder and avoid the pie.

"So Plouffe and a few other guys said they were going to get me the next time something like that happened," Whetzel explains. "So, another game, later, we get to the post-game and we're interviewing someone on the field and the door to my booth opens up. Sure enough, Plouffe, Luke Hughes and Steve Tolleson run in with shaving cream and a towel and just smash it all over me. They snuck up the back stairs of the ballpark and got into the press box that way to do it. I have a tape of that somewhere—I should try to find it." Whetzel laughed it off and admits, although sometimes that stuff can get annoying, that was a pretty funny moment. As a broadcaster, you need those moments and those laughs during the grind of the everyday season. Not every night has an extraordinary walk-off ending or a pitcher who is just shoving and wiping away the opposing lineup, and if you can smile with the team because of one person's actions, it gives you an extra reward and some fun memories to look back upon.

Play-by-Play from the Minors

Josh has plenty of memories to look back on, but he's a huge base-ball history buff and if he were given the opportunity to call any moment in baseball history, he looks to the major leagues and back to his Dodger fandom. The first moment that comes to his mind is Kirk Gibson's home run in Game 1 of the 1988 World Series. He admits that it would be tough to compete with Vin Scully's call, "In a year that has been so improbable, the impossible has happened." If he were to call it, though, he would draw attention to "just the surprise in general of see-ing him come to the plate in that situation [with an injured leg]. He was visibly in such bad shape after hitting a couple of foul balls up the first-base line and barely being able to make it out of the batter's box. Just the fact that he was able to hit a ball halfway up the pavilion in right is just amazing. You just hope you don't screw up those moments, you know?" Whetzel reflects.

So, a small-town kid from Kansas would imagine calling the most-replayed moment caught on television for the second-largest market in the United States. A day when an iconic player left his mark on baseball in his final at-bat of that Series, which the Dodgers would go on to win in five games over the Oakland Athletics.

8

Scott Kornberg

Currently with the Jacksonville Jumbo Shrimp
Previously with the Quad Cities River Bandits,
Winston-Salem Dash and Myrtle Beach Pelicans

When Josh Whetzel was spending his summers in Binghamton, New York, broadcasting games for future Mets players in the late 1990s and early 2000s, Scott Kornberg was growing up just a little ways south, getting ready to cheer for those same players. During the Subway World Series in 2000 and through the career of the Big Apple's prized backstop Mike Piazza, Kornberg grew his fandom as he prepared to become the broadcaster he is today.

Scott Kornberg is an East Coast product who has climbed the ranks, beginning as a television broadcaster for Colgate University Athletics. The University of Maryland graduate spent two years as a broadcast assistant, first in the Midwest League with the Quad Cities River Bandits and then in the Carolina League with the Winston-Salem Dash. After one season in the Carolina League, he drew enough attention to earn his first lead broadcasting gig with the league and began a three-year stint with the Myrtle Beach Pelicans in the 2016 season. It didn't take long for the talented broadcaster to earn Co-Broadcaster of the Year honors for the Carolina League in 2017, and in the winter of 2018 he made his latest move, accepting a job with the Jacksonville Jumbo Shrimp in the Southern League.

In the offseason, Kornberg has occupied a variety of media relations and play-by-play roles, most recently with the Jacksonville Jaguars. He spent four years as the broadcaster and sports information director of the Western Illinois Leathernecks before starting a similar position with Jacksonville University and the University of North Florida in 2018.

Kornberg was born on Long Island and lived there until he was four years old, when his family moved to New Jersey, first to Somerset and then to Montgomery Township. That spot was within easy reach of a lot of bigger scenes nearby, only a couple of hours from Manhattan, about an hour from Philadelphia and an hour from the beach—the famous Jersey Shore. His parents emphasized education from a young age, so the young baseball and basketball player needed to have his grades in order to participate in sports. He remembers reading a lot growing up and enjoying trips to the local library.

Although baseball is currently Scott's favorite sport, it wasn't always that way. Most of his early memories come from watching basketball rather than baseball. "Growing up in the

'90s, Michael Jordan was the guy, so everyone was a big Michael Jordan fan. I always tell people this, especially younger kids, it is impossible to relate [anything else in any sport] to that era in the NBA.... I was a Nets fan, but I was also a Bulls fan. No matter what city you grew up in, you were a Bulls fan because of Michael Jordan. I had a full [set of] Michael Jordan jersey[s], the black Bulls jersey and a red one. My earliest memories are playing in the backyard, wearing those jerseys and pretending to be Michael Jordan," Kornberg reminisces.

Scott Kornberg got his big break after he emailed every team in Minor League Baseball looking for an internship. A few years later, he found himself in one of the most enviable locations in Minor League Baseball, working for the Jacksonville Jumbo Shrimp (photograph courtesy Scott Kornberg).

Growing up near Manhattan, Kornberg became a huge Mets fan, following his dad's fandom. He also tuned in to the Nets and the Jets, and, prior to the NHL lockout in the 2004–05 season, he really liked watching Devils games before falling off the wagon as many Americans did after that lost season. While Vin Scully is Kornberg's idol, he grew up in an era where a kid on the East Coast couldn't listen to Dodgers games. He was a big fan of Gary Cohen, who is currently the Mets' TV guy, but when Scott was young, he called games on the radio. "His prep is great, but he's also really good because he was a Mets fan. He understands what it's like to be a Mets fan because he was going to Shea Stadium and sitting in the upper deck. I think that's why anytime there's a big moment—like Johan Santana's no-hitter or, when I was a kid, it was Robin Ventura's 'grand slam single'—he relates so well to the fan base, and I think that is a great quality to have as a broadcaster," the longtime listener reflects. He also points to Ian Eagle, who used to call Jets games when he was a kid. Scott appreciates the enthusiasm that Eagle adds to the broadcast and the way he uses his inflection in big moments.

It wasn't until he came home from his freshman year at college that Scott heard Vin Scully for the first time, but the famous broadcaster taught Kornberg one of the biggest lessons that he has learned so far. Late at night, the teenager was scrolling through channels on TV and saw a Dodgers/Padres bill on the MLB Network, where they were broadcasting a simulcast. Kornberg had heard of Scully through his grandparents, who were avid Brooklyn Dodgers fans, and decided to give him a listen. "I tuned in, and it was a commercial. I remember thinking, 'This guy probably stinks anyways.' Then when they came back from commercial break, there was a close-up shot of a full moon, and Scully was silent for a second before saying, 'Isn't it amazing we put a man up there.' With those nine words, I was hooked. From that point on I couldn't get enough of Vin Scully, and I think the thing that I really took from him was detail. He knows everything, and I know that it is my responsibility as the broadcaster to know everything about people's background and the other things historically or culturally that can apply and relate to what you're broadcasting. That's because people relate to people." And that is how a broadcaster on the opposite coast from Scully and nearly 60 years younger than him has learned and grown from listening to him.

Scott's path to Minor League Baseball is pretty traditional, but he did have a special moment when he was younger that helped inspire him to continue to pursue the field. Kornberg has a few younger brothers, including one who was in the Cal Ripken World Series. It just so

Play-by-Play from the Minors

happened that the coach for his brother's team was Tom Verducci, a broadcaster for the MLB Network, writer for *Sports Illustrated* and analyst for Fox Sports. Scott's dad told him to ask Verducci questions about his job with *Sports Illustrated*, so the high schooler did it. When Kornberg's brother made it to the series in Louisiana, he took a recorder to the games and "broadcast" them all. "I still have them on my computer somewhere, and I think it will be really cool for my brother and I to look back at those a few years from now."

Kornberg has come a long way from bringing a recorder to his brother's baseball games. He chose to become a Terrapin after looking at a couple of schools because Maryland would let him broadcast and gain experience right away, whereas other schools made freshmen wait a year or two before letting them in front of a camera.

Scott believes that the University of Maryland was the best possible fit for him, not only because it is a good academic school, but also because so many alumni come back to talk to current students. He recalls alumnus Scott Van Pelt, who anchors *SportsCenter* for ESPN, visiting for the annual Sports Symposium on campus. A gesture Van Pelt made did not escape Kornberg's attention: "This guy could be doing whatever he wants when he comes to visit, but instead he stays three or four hours after the symposium ends just to talk to kids who want to work in sports. He stayed until the janitors kicked us out at midnight or one a.m."

Kornberg was able to intern for stations in Washington, D.C., and Baltimore, and the local student radio operation had both a mix-talk station and a station solely for sports. The dynamic was very hands-on because of all the access students had to local media, and Kornberg credits his success as a broadcaster to what he learned in the scrum with local professional media and other student interns.

The New York native knew he wanted to do play-by-play when he entered Maryland, and it had a broadcast station dedicated to having students do live play-by-play of the university's sports. Kornberg began broadcasting softball as a freshman, but not many people wanted to call the baseball games, because the team was miserable at that point. So Kornberg, who was always extremely ambitious, received the opportunity to broadcast a couple of baseball games very early on. He worked his way up the ladder not just on-camera but also behind the scenes, becoming the station director in his senior year and also calling football and men's basketball games for the station. Off campus, Kornberg was able to find plenty of play-by-play opportunities as well. His first one came with the High Point-Thomasville HiToms, of the Coastal Plain League. He was able to parlay that experience in summer league base-ball into a role with the Colgate Raiders of the Patriot League directly out of college.

He got a break and was able to work under Marco LaNave in the Quad Cities for his first minor league job, prior to moving to the Carolina League for the next four seasons. Despite a quick rise among the ranks of baseball broadcasters, Kornberg remains humble: "It wasn't because I was good. It was because I was really aggressive. I literally sent an email to every Minor League Baseball team and college wood bat league team when I was a senior in college. Most of them you don't hear back from, but some of them you do. One was the HiToms. I got a call from a North Carolina area code while I was cooking dinner one night, and it was the owner. He called and interviewed me on the spot, and I got that job later."

He had a similar plan of attack for Quad Cities. He sent an email to the office and was later interviewed for a job that was never posted. He ended up interviewing twice to be an assistant with Quad Cities before landing the gig. His experience with Quad Cities would prove crucial later, when LaNave left Jacksonville to broadcast games for the Akron RubberDucks in 2018. When broadcasters leave a team, if they are in good standing with the front office they typically leave a short list of broadcasters who would be a good fit to replace them. In Jacksonville, LaNave left only one name, Scott Kornberg, who says, "To some extent, you make your own luck, and I worked really hard. I think because of that hard work, a lot of people were willing to vouch for me."

The Terrapin will tell you that announcing is never about the broadcaster. Scott isn't looking to draw attention to himself, but rather tries to give attention in the best manner possible to the players between the chalk. The players on the field are important when you're starting out, but to take it to the next level, Scott believes, a broadcaster needs to know how to utilize the crowd. "The best broadcasters know when to shut up, they know how to use few words in a way that is the most impactful, and that allows them to be quiet so that the crowd can tell the story." At the end of the day, isn't that why most of the people who attend sporting events are there, to cheer along with the roar of the crowd and to experience group entertainment?

Kornberg elaborates, "We all want to be connected to other people … and the crowd is the best way to do that. As a fan, the crowd is what I remember. As a kid, I remember booing Chipper Jones at Shea Stadium and the 'Let's go Mets' chants. Those are the things that you remember."

Play-by-Play from the Minors

The beauty of Minor League Baseball is that different towns have different makeups, identities and traditions that form their personalities. For example, Kornberg's favorite road town that he has traveled to for college athletics is Fargo, North Dakota, which plays host to North Dakota State University. Scott maintains that the atmosphere at the games and around the town is absolutely incredible. The best MiLB road city, though?

Kornberg points to Raleigh, North Carolina, the home of the Carolina Mudcats. There are lots of beer gardens and parks near the ballpark and hotel to walk around and explore, particularly when the weather is nice. Prior to a game, one can visit Pullen Park, one of the world's oldest amusement parks and the first registered park in the state of North Carolina. Avid hikers can hike along the Mountains-to-Sea Trail, which cuts through the northern part of the city and is part of a 1,000-mile hiking trail that spans almost the entire width of the state. Another off-the-beaten-track place to visit is the Juniper Level Botanic Garden, just 12 miles away from the city, which draws visitors from all over the world for its Open Garden Days.

While Raleigh is a wonderful city, it was not home to the greatest restaurant Kornberg has visited while on the road. That was in Salem, Virginia, although it has closed down since Scott was in the Carolina League. During Kornberg's tenure in Myrtle Beach, there was a family-owned restaurant in Salem called El Cubanito. A Cuban immigrant founded the restaurant, and in 2015, Nick Basto, a player for the Winston-Salem Dash, was eating its food in the dugout before a game. "It smelled so good and I asked him what it was, and I ended up going with him, Eddy Alvarez and Keon Barnum. It was amazing, so the next year, I got the job in Myrtle Beach, and I told one of our Cuban players that there was a great Cuban place there and he ended up ordering six dishes. He said that the lady who did the cooking cooked just like his mother, and that's how I knew it was authentic Cuban," Kornberg remembers.

The popularity of the restaurant ended up spreading throughout the Pelicans' roster. It was so popular that the team would put a trip to El Cubanito on the schedule and send a bus to it each day. The Pelicans' call man would try to order something new each time he went, but his favorite dish that he remembers was chicken marinated in pineapple juice and served with plantains and rice. Since El Cubanito is closed, Kornberg also highly recommends The Grumpy Monk in Myrtle Beach. He found it while living in Myrtle Beach, so it isn't necessarily his favorite road restaurant. He adds, "If you talk to people in the Carolina League, I would venture to say that they will tell you the Grumpy Monk is their favorite place. That place is my favorite restaurant outside of Savannah, Georgia. They have 60 beers on tap, the best buffalo wings I have ever had outside of Buffalo, New York, great sushi, chicken and it has a great atmosphere."

Sure, a good sports bar is a great spot to spend a few hours with friends, but a professional ballpark's atmosphere is a little more compelling than that of a local bar. When trying to get fans to visit the ballpark, the Jumbo Shrimp radio guy prefers a classic promotional evening over the many wacky ones he has seen. Two for Tuesday is a simple idea that a lot of teams employ to get a few more fans in the seats and to sell more beer and hot dogs. The draw is that fans can get two tickets, hot dogs or beers for the price of one. When Kornberg joined Jacksonville, he was able to see the promotion's effect on a lower-drawing night to encourage fans to attend the game. In 2019, Jacksonville took it to another level, though. For a July 30 contest against the Pensacola Blue Wahoos, they had a Two for Tuesday where they only allowed a pair of fans into the ballpark. The two fans were Josh Ribeiro, Jr., and his father. Both received Jumbo Shrimp jerseys, as the evening was also dubbed "Authentic Jumbo Shrimp Jersey Giveaway Night," and Junior got to throw out the first pitch.

The Jumbo Shrimp teamed up with the Dreams Come True organization and Community First Credit Union to make the evening a special one for Junior, a young child who was fighting cancer. The entire stadium, though empty, was still decked out for the game. Concession stands were open and hawkers were perusing the empty stands yelling out the products they would usually sell to a crowd full of people.

"It was really cool. You could see the kid smiling from ear to ear. You would talk to him and he was the sweetest boy. You saw him fighting this serious disease, but he had such a positive outlook on life, and he was such a happy kid. If that doesn't melt your heart and show you how much good there is in this world, then you have a heart of stone," Kornberg says. Junior picked the songs that came on between innings, and everything inside the gates was tailored to him for the evening. Outside of the Baseball Grounds of Jacksonville, the Jumbo Shrimp hosted a block party where they sold concessions, played music and broadcast the game on monitors for the fans to enjoy. Once the game became official after five innings, the attendance was posted as two and the Jumbo Shrimp opened the gates for other fans to join in the fun with Junior

119

and his father, who sang "Take Me Out to the Ballgame." "It was a ... heartwarming event that I was ... grateful to be a part of, because he is a really special kid," Kornberg recalls. While this promotion was indeed heartwarming, most promotions are done to try to pack the seats with a crazy idea that interests fans. As a broadcaster, you see many of these promotions multiple times a year, catching them at different stops along your road schedule.

There's one zany promotion that Kornberg still can't believe, Cowboy Monkey Rodeo night. Like Terry Byrom, Kornberg was wowed by the fans' enthusiasm for the event. "People love it, they go crazy for it. I personally don't understand the appeal, but to each their own." Those road trips to a new city for a weekend to play a game and see a fireworks night or a creative promotional evening like Cowboy Monkey Rodeo before skipping town can put some strain on the players, coaches and staff members. It always helps when a promotional evening results in a big amped-up crowd to cheer the players (and provide energy for the broadcasters) on one of those trips.

While Cowboy Monkey Rodeo generally goes pretty smoothly, Scott recalls a trip from Kinston, North Carolina, home of the Down East Wood Ducks, that did not go well. The trip from Kinston to Myrtle Beach really isn't much of a trek. The journey stretches just over 150 miles down the shores of North and South Carolina. Normally, it would take around three hours depending on traffic conditions along Route 17. This time, at around two or three in the morning, the bus had to stop on the side of the highway. "Everyone got off the bus, and actually it was really fun, because everyone was hanging out together. We got a few big circles of people and everyone was just hanging out."

Kornberg relays that people were walking around, listening to music and just taking advantage of the chance to get to know one another better. Even though the remaining distance was short, getting a new bus typically takes a while. Not only does the company need to get the driver who is on-call to drive to the bus company, but they also need to get a bus ready to go out and find the broken-down bus on the side of the highway. Needless to say, the process tends to take a minimum of a few hours.

When the new bus comes, the players need to move all of their stuff from the broken bus to the new bus before they can resume the drive. "All of the stuff is in the bottom of the bus, but our bus [driver] for whatever reason locked the bottom compartment, and we couldn't unlock it, because it needed the bus to be running for it to unlock, and our bus

8. Scott Kornberg

wouldn't start. I'll never forget, we had two players, Connor Myers and Eloy Jiménez, [who] rigged up all these hangers and they were trying to pick the locks of the compartment part of the bus. I was sitting there thinking, here we have this prized prospect, who's the future of baseball, a top-10 prospect or whatever he was at the time, and he is picking a lock to this bus. He did it, and it was remarkable. He got so excited when he did it, he picked the lock and just started jumping up and down and celebrated. That's one of my favorite moments with Eloy, him and Connor Myers picking that lock at four in the morning and how happy they were."

After they picked the lock, the team crawled into the bottom of the bus and pulled all the bags out and placed them on the side of the road, where they sat until the next bus picked them up and brought them back to Myrtle Beach.

Eloy Jiménez wasn't only a guy who is able to pick a lock with a coat hanger, but he was largely considered one of the top prospects in baseball and surprised many in his first two seasons in Major League Baseball. When Kornberg thinks back to Jiménez's time with the Myrtle Beach Pelicans, he remembers, "He was just so good, and to me it was unfathomable that he could be traded, because he is everything that you could possibly want in a superstar. He's not just an amazing player, he's a remarkable, intelligent and well-spoken person, who everyone gravitates towards in the clubhouse."

Jiménez joined the Pelicans at the end of the 2016 season, getting the call-up from South Bend for the playoffs. Kornberg is aware of the 2017 video where Jiménez hit a ball into stadium lights in the Carolina League Home Run Derby in Salem, Virginia, but that isn't the most impressive moment he saw with his own eyes from the budding star. In fact, the broadcaster even points out that it is less impressive than other times he has seen the outfielder accomplish the same feat. During a home run derby, someone is lobbing meatballs toward home in the hope that you crush the ball, but Kornberg recalls a batting practice in Kinston where the Dominican Republic native was aiming to hit the lights, and was able to accomplish the feat multiple times.

In batting practice, the coach isn't just lobbing a ball hoping you crush it, but Eloy's talent is so immense that he tried to go above just hitting the ball out of the park; he wanted the ball to hit the stadium lights beyond the outfield fence. Hitting the lights isn't the most memorable moment Kornberg can think of, though. He goes back to thinking about Jiménez's first batting practice, coming to the team for the

121

playoffs in 2016. The Pelicans were playing the Lynchburg Hillcats, and Jimenez stepped up to the plate. This 6'4", 235-pound player is huge, and his hair was styled with a big blond mohawk as he joined his new team. He hit the first ball, and "the crack of the bat sounded like a cannon. It was huge. I've never heard the ball sound like that off the bat," Kornberg remembers.

The first two pitches that Jiménez hit were at least 50 feet over the left centerfield wall, but the third pitch the prospect hit was a laser that glanced off the top of a huge, 20-foot wall that occupies the outfield in Lynchburg. The broadcaster contends that the ball had not yet reached its apex, and at that point, everyone else began to take notice. Nobody was running the bases or fielding ground balls, as is routine during batting practice, and the entire Lynchburg roster was peering from the clubhouse, trying to decide if they could believe their eyes. It's the only time that Kornberg can remember every player from both teams stopping and watching someone else hit, and he also remembers the reaction of the Pelicans' hitting coach, Mariano Duncan, a 12-year major league veteran, who just sat laughing and shaking his head. What else can you do when you see such a naturally gifted player?

Kornberg remembers the day that Jiménez was traded. Funnily enough, he was traded across town from the Chicago Cubs to the Chicago White Sox. He was also traded across the field, as the Winston-Salem Dash happened to be in town playing the Pelicans the day that the Cubs executed the trade, so the star outfielder just had to switch dugouts to join his new team. The trade went down early, around lunchtime, and Kornberg was at a table with Brian Boesch, the Dash broadcaster at the time, and his assistant, Joe Weil. The two Dash broadcasters figured Kornberg was going to be excited, but he was extremely upset. Scott recalls being incredulous at lunch, believing that the Cubs had made a huge mistake, even though they had reeled in an MLB All-Star pitcher in the deal. A month later, Boesch pulled Kornberg aside prior to another game between the two teams and said, "I just want to tell you something. When I saw your reaction at lunch after the trade, I thought you were crazy, but now that I have seen Eloy play, oh my god, you were right."

Although many people knew about Eloy Jiménez long before he ever made it to Chicago, David Bote didn't have that type of fortune. The corner infielder was picked up in the 18th round of the 2012 draft by the Cubs and was dancing along a string when he finally made it to Myrtle Beach four years later. (At that point, Bote had been in Minor

8. Scott Kornberg

League Baseball for four seasons. He wasn't an everyday player, even in A-ball, and people didn't know his name because he wasn't a coveted high-draftee or a guy who had eye-popping numbers. A normal Minor League contract is only six years long after being drafted and if Bote wanted to make a Big League debut, he had to go all the way from Myrtle Beach to Chicago in just two seasons.) Kornberg watched him in the Midwest League when he worked for Quad Cities when the team visited Kane County. At that point, Kornberg says, Bote was essentially a nobody. He never played, so Kornberg didn't need to pay much attention to him. Once Scott became familiar with working in the Cubs system, he noticed that Bote seemed to be a roster filler. He went to Daytona for four games in 2013 and Iowa for a series in 2015 because he was always the last guy on the roster and nobody else would go somewhere where they wouldn't play to just be there for a couple of days. Bote had been "phantom DL'ed" a number of times, but that was just the way his career was going when the third baseman and Scott's careers matched up in Myrtle Beach. A player is phantom DL'ed, or placed on the disabled list despite not actually being hurt, to allow another player to take their spot on the roster temporarily, or sometimes permanently until the player is cut or their contract is up.

During this time, whenever Bote would get moved, he would be flown from point A to point B, and his wife, Rachel, would pick up anything he needed from the clubhouse and fill up her car with everything before she and their baby would drive to Iowa, Tennessee, or wherever she needed to go to support Bote. At one point, a sequence of events moved Bote from the last man on the team to an infielder who needed playing time. Gleyber Torres got traded to New York and Ian Happ, who played solely second base in 2016, was called up to Tennessee during the deadline. All of a sudden, Myrtle Beach had to find playing time for David Bote. Bote received a trial opportunity.

He got to play the final 60 games of the season as a regular in the lineup, and it paid major dividends. "He hit .367 in the last 60 games and he had all the highest exit velocities, everything like that. It was ridiculous. He put himself on the map." Kornberg maintains that this is a heartwarming story for a few reasons. Obviously, it's incredible to see a guy go from the bottom of a High-A roster to the bigs over the course of a few seasons, but it also could not have happened to a nicer guy. Bote was really into the community wherever he went and chose to help others. Kornberg adds, "This isn't just a story of him. This is a story about his entire family. When he made it to the Cubs, he said, 'I couldn't

123

have got here without my wife.' I got to see that personally because literally every single day she was at the ballpark." Since getting the call to The Show, Bote has had a positive impact in the Windy City, hitting .240 with 24 homers in just under 250 games. Prior to the start of the 2019 season, he was able to ink a five-year contract extension worth $15 million, so all those trips for Rachel and all those years waiting for an opportunity certainly paid off for the kid from Longmont, Colorado.

While Connor Myers helped Eloy Jiménez pick the lock after the bus broke down on the side of the highway that evening while Kornberg was watching, the player supplied more than just one comical memory for the tenured broadcaster. Myers fit the bill for a great organizational player. He always volunteered to do service work or to hang out with kids before the game or in the community. He was the first in line to hop on-air for an interview with the broadcaster. He even went the extra mile and texted Kornberg on his birthday each year and let the team know when Kornberg won Broadcaster of the Year in the Carolina League, so that the rest of the team would know to congratulate him.

Myers's popularity dates back way further than just baseball, though. Scott recalls visiting the Frederick Keys, who are close to Myers's hometown in Maryland, and fans would give the outfielder a standing ovation whenever he stepped up to the plate or made a big play—a feat that is extraordinarily rare in Minor League Baseball. "Connor Myers is one of those guys where he is going to be a winner no matter what he does in life, because he is a great player, but he's an even better person. That is why he is my favorite player in Minor League Baseball, and I think it is going to be impossible to dethrone him." Myers had arguably the best season of his career in 2019, when he hit .263 and had career-best marks in doubles, triples and homers while playing his first full season in Double-A with the Tennessee Smokies. The 27th-round pick out of Old Dominion defied the odds, carving out a role in Double-A ball before his retirement in 2021. That's what makes the gig so enjoyable to Scott, and that's why when he thinks back to his favorite moments working in baseball, he doesn't necessarily think about accolades or achievements; he thinks of the people that made up those great teams and why they are special to him.

Sure, calling a championship season for the Myrtle Beach Pelicans was an amazing experience, but it wasn't the East Coaster's favorite moment he has been fortunate enough to broadcast. Kornberg had the opportunity to broadcast an even rarer moment with the club for an iconic Minor League Baseball manager. In 2016, Buddy Bailey reached a

8. Scott Kornberg

career mark with the Pelicans when he won his 2,000th game as a manager of a minor league club. The milestone 5–4 victory came after the Pelicans' late rally from being down 4–1 against the Down East Wood Ducks on August 24, 2017. Only 11 managers can claim that milestone, and the former player is one of them.

His journey is really impressive, too. Bailey spent four years playing in Minor League Baseball, never making it up to the bigs before he began to manage in the late '80s for the Atlanta Braves—the team that drafted him as a player in the 16th round of the 1979 draft. For those who know the heralded manager, it is no surprise that Bailey was a pioneer coach, who spent a few years in the Southern League before the Braves started having major league success for the first time in decades. Fast forward a few years and Bailey was awarded the International League Manager of the Year trophy in 1996 and 2003. He is one of the few people who has a ring from when the Boston Red Sox broke the Curse of the Bambino in 2004 while sweeping the Cardinals in the World Series. If that wasn't rare enough, he is one of just seven people who have a ring from that World Series and the Cubs' 2016 World Series that ended the 108-year drought for the Windy City. The most well-known name in that list of seven people is Theo Epstein, but Bailey's accomplishment is exactly the same.

"When I look at that guy, he is a baseball lifer and an absolute legend, but he looked at me as a friend. On the road, we would go out to dinner after the games and we would just talk about life," Kornberg reminisces. Bailey chatted with Scott about his girlfriend and their engagement and even suggested songs for their wedding. Thinking about Bailey's 2,000th win, Kornberg reveres the milestone because of its significance in history, but also because Bailey is a special person to Kornberg. The two still keep in touch, even though Kornberg isn't working with the Cubs organization anymore, and both celebrate their accomplishments when they come around. As it stands, Bailey has the fourth highest number of all-time wins for a Minor League Baseball manager, with 2,282. The record belongs to Stan Wasiak, who is the lone manager to reach more than 2,500 wins before he retired in 1986 with 2,530 career victories.

Kornberg, who called games for the 2016 Carolina League champion Myrtle Beach Pelicans, will tell you that the most talented team he has ever seen in Minor League Baseball did not win a championship. It was the 2016 Salem Red Sox, who were loaded with future All-Stars. Headlined with Andrew Benintendi, the fifth highest-ranked prospect in baseball in 2016, according to MLB.com, and Yoán Moncada, who was the top-ranked prospect in all of baseball, the team also carried Michael Kopech, who was put 30th overall on that same list and fanned 82 batters in 52 innings that year, Rafael Devers, a 19-year-old catcher who hit .282 with 11 bombs and 32 doubles, and 10 other future major leaguers, including Michael Chavis, Ben Taylor and Trevor Kelley.

The team had the star power on paper. They were also the final team to see all of these players on the same field together, as the Red Sox traded Moncada and Kopech to the White Sox to acquire Chris Sale that winter. The Salem squad put together an 87–52 record to combine with a +69 run differential over the course of the regular season, but by the time the playoffs rolled around, Moncada and Benintendi were playing in Double-A Portland and the team fell out of the playoffs in the semifinals before Myrtle Beach would scoop up their second consecutive championship on their third straight trip to the Carolina League Championship. That season, Myrtle Beach was the top team that Kornberg has had the pleasure of calling. What made that team so good, though? "We just gelled," Kornberg says. "Part of that was David Bote. We lost our starting center fielder, who was really good, we lost Gleyber Torres and Ian Happ, who were amazing. So from a talent perspective, we weren't the best. We were about .500, 49–48 when we lost all those guys, and the rest of the season we played .700 baseball. We came to the ballpark and we just knew we were going to win."

Scott has called plenty of great moments during his time in baseball, but he had the opportunity to call one moment that most people wouldn't believe possible unless they've been following Minor League Baseball for quite some time. He was put in a situation where there was a doubleheader where Winston-Salem was considered the road team for the first game, but then was the home team for the second game. In Minor League Baseball, this typically happens when a game is postponed near the end of a series in one town and the two teams don't play at the same venue again for the remainder of the season. In this case, a pair of games was played in Winston-Salem on July 19, 2015, and the first game was being completed after being suspended on June 27. So, Game 1 of the doubleheader, even though it was played at BB&T Stadium, the home of the Dash, featured the Lynchburg Hillcats as the "home team." For Game 2, the teams swapped who got to bat first and who went out to the field first, and the Dash were the home team. It was a learning moment for Kornberg, who didn't know that that could happen until talking over the rules following the game. "It just taught me to be careful, because you don't know everything

126

and you should get all the facts before you say something over the air," Kornberg remembers.

So, there's a look into what Scott Kornberg has accomplished and seen during his six-year Minor League Baseball career. If the broadcaster were able to have the opportunity to call any moment in baseball history, he would be tempted to call one of the great New York Mets' moments, but after meditating and reflecting, the former Terrapin thinks he would want to call something that was bigger on the all-encompassing scale of Major League Baseball in America. The moment that he ultimately reflects upon is Jackie Robinson's first game for the Brooklyn Dodgers in 1947. "Not just for the cool factor of getting to call Robinson's debut or because Ebbets Field is a legendary place. I hope that during that time I would have had a way of calling it like Red Barber did. He was so good; he said, 'Here comes Jackie Robinson coming up to the plate. He's most definitely a brunette'—or something [of] that nature," Kornberg says. "I don't think I would have been that poetic, but ... I would [want] to have called it knowing the cultural moment and being on the right side of that history."

While Scott believes he would have been on the right side of history and even says that his grandparents, who grew up in Brooklyn, enjoyed watching Robinson play, he also understands how important the event was beyond baseball. "It is a landmark moment, not just in baseball history, but in American history, and I think it would have been really cool to call that game, to understand that it isn't just impacting the players, but it's impacting our country at the time, and all the people who are depending on Jackie Robinson for civil rights. It shows how sports are transcendent."

9

Jay Burnham

Currently with the University of Massachusetts
Minutemen and Worcester Red Sox
Previously with the Hagerstown Suns, Pensacola Pelicans,
Asheville Tourists, Trenton Thunder and
Richmond Flying Squirrels

Right before Scott Kornberg moved to Jacksonville, the Jumbo Shrimp operated under the name the Jacksonville Suns. The Suns played in an older ballpark, the Samuel W. Wolfson Baseball Park, from 1962 until the 2002 season, when they moved to the new Baseball Grounds of Jacksonville, and were eventually rebranded in 2016. Funnily enough, right around the time that Jacksonville built a new stadium, Jay Burnham found himself in the dilapidated Municipal Stadium for two years with the Hagerstown Suns, in Maryland. He spent some time in Florida, too, in Independent ball, to figure out how to get to where he is today.

Burnham once believed a career in broadcasting was unattainable. Luckily for us, in college the Massachusetts native went from listening to Red Sox games on the radio to taking his first steps toward broadcasting games professionally. To move from listening to different broadcasters across the country to actually broadcasting games himself took some time, but Jay eventually elevated himself from avid listener to elite broadcaster. The rest is history: Burnham did a couple of internships before he received his first job as an unpaid intern for the Suns. That started a 16-year journey in Minor League Baseball that ended when Burnham accepted a job as the voice of the University of Massachusetts Minutemen, effectively bringing him back home and moving him from Minor League Baseball to NCAA athletics full-time.

During his 16 years in baseball, Burnham became a decorated member of the club of broadcasters. In 2011, while with the Trenton Thunder, he won *Ballpark Digest*'s Broadcaster of the Year Award, and in 2016 he won *Baseball America*'s Best Broadcaster Award, taking home, within a five-year period, two of the top honors a Minor League Baseball broadcaster can obtain. What else can you expect from a guy who transitioned from a temporary role in Hagerstown to a spot in an American Association of Professional Baseball booth, then back to the South Atlantic League, where he built a broadcast for one of MiLB's most iconic teams? Burnham worked out a deal with a local station to end a nearly 40-year hiatus of Asheville Tourist games being broadcast on the radio, a deal that has lasted for over 10 years now. Burnham's journey wasn't always sure, though, and at times, it definitely didn't appear linear.

When Burnham was 17, he graduated high school, and, like a lot of teenagers, he wanted to get as far away from home as he possibly could. So he rebelled and decided to attend Hawaii Pacific University for a year. His big goal while he was in Honolulu was to figure out what to do with his life. "Part of that was listening to games on the radio via internet broadcasts, utilizing Hawaii's six-hour time difference to listen to more games. You could listen to every radio station in the country streaming online back in 1999. Then I started to figure out that maybe I could be something in radio play-by-play for baseball." Once he figured that out, he had to transfer to a school that was more communications-based and eventually earned a degree from Elon University after attending Kansai Gaidai University in Japan and Greenfield Community College in Massachusetts.

Despite being a guy who grew up in Massachusetts, Jay certainly isn't a homer when it comes to influences. He spent that first year of college trying to figure out who he was and was influenced by radio in its earliest stages on the internet, so it only stands to reason that when he got his first job that he would continue to look to the dial for influence. When Burnham started his first job, he bought an XM radio transmitter.

"It was the newest technology that they had and I got it at Circuit City for about 600 bucks, and it took me like 10 years to pay it off my credit card, but I would just listen to everybody. I wanted to learn what to say in different situations and how I should sound in big moments," Burnham explains his purchase. While scanning the dial, he appreciated a lot of different broadcast teams. He used to rank the broadcasts; the Orioles, with Joe Angel and Fred Manfra, were high on the list. He admits that as he listens now, he favors broadcasters who have spent time in the minors. One of his favorite teams to listen to these days is the Tampa Bay Rays, who have Trenton Thunder alumnus Andy Freed as their lead broadcaster.

Play-by-Play from the Minors

Jay Burnham has done it all, from working in Indy Ball and Hagerstown with the now-defunct Suns to calling games for the Woo-Sox. Burnham primarily works as the voice of the University of Massachusetts Minutemen today (photograph courtesy Jay Burnham).

If Jay had to pick a favorite, though, there was one broadcaster who stood out more than the rest for him. It was the San Francisco Giants' Jon Miller. "His ability to deliver a big moment and his ability to make you interested by the tonality of his voice and how it would change up or down in pitch is astonishing. When I listened to him, I thought: I need to figure out how I could utilize the things he did with his voice and how I could do it myself in baseball," Burnham remembers.

Burnham's love for baseball started before his year in Hawaii. Prior to scanning the dial for broadcasters everywhere and prior to his XM radio transmitter, Burnham wanted to be Jerry Trupiano. Growing up in Massachusetts, Jay was a big fan of the Red Sox and so he listened to Trupiano and fell in love with his enthusiasm for the game. Trupiano had a lot of fun while he was on-air with Boston from 1993 to 2006, and Burnham wanted to be like him. Despite being influenced by listening to many other broadcasters, you won't hear Burnham utter one of their catch phrases on the radio. That influence comes from elsewhere.

"I always thought that [the] things that people associate you or your broadcast with had to be unique to your experiences in life, and that's how I have pulled things together," Burnham explains. So, the ardent classical literature reader has been influenced a lot by his reading over the years. "John Kennedy Toole wrote a book called *A Confederacy of Dunces* that he won a Pulitzer for posthumously, and there was the word 'perfidious' in it. It means an attempt to trick, so a curveball could be perfidious."

It took a lot to move Burnham from the pages of his favorite books to the airwaves in Minor League Baseball. When he was at Elon University, he asked the student radio station if he could start a broadcast for the baseball games, and they told him that they didn't have the capabilities for it.

"Later I found out that you really just needed a phone line to do it, so it turned out that they really didn't want to bother with it or I didn't push hard enough, one of the two. So, I started trying to contact people via email in the early days of it. Eventually, Will Smith was generous enough to respond to me. He later brought me on and helped me through every step in my career." For Burnham's first year with Hagerstown, they didn't have any broadcast openings, so he volunteered to work as a general intern to help out with other things and worked some broadcasting into it. He would come back to Hagerstown the next summer, but this time he was hired as the unpaid number two broadcaster.

Yes, it was a struggle initially for Burnham. Most broadcasters starting their journey in baseball need to be resilient enough to work long hours for little to sometimes no pay, they need to have unwavering support from their family and friends and they have to be able to find the joy in what they're giving to the community and to the game. Burnham's love for Minor League Baseball developed long before he ever worked in baseball, though. When he was eight years old, his parents had a birthday party for him at a Pittsfield Mets game. The young Jay felt so excited to be a part of the game. He got to throw the first pitch and Bob Feller was there and signed an autograph for Jay, who, admittedly, didn't know who he was at the time. That formed his initial emotional tie to the game as a kid, and it only grew stronger as he aged.

Jay believes Minor League Baseball is incredible because you can be a sports person who watches, say, Mid–American Conference football and Mountain East Conference basketball and still be drawn to the sport, but there's a whole different segment of Minor League Baseball fandom that comprises people who are interested in the business side of the sport and the quirkiness of the industry as a whole. "One of the first books I read about the business was [the autobiography] *Veeck as in*

131

Play-by-Play from the Minors

Wreck, and it explained what Mike Veeck was doing with the Browns, the White Sox and Disco Demolition [Night]. When I finished reading it in college, I wanted to be Mike Veeck—not Mike Tirico, I wanted to be Mike Veeck," Burnham says. It's the quirkiness of Veeck and his style that continues to push people like Burnham into the loving arms of the industry.

Despite leaving the industry a handful of years ago, Burnham says that he still is attracted to the passion of those who work there. There isn't an industry that works harder for the show to continue. "People outside of the industry still work hard, but they'll never believe that when it rained July 3, 2011, and my parents are in town. ... I get a call at 4 a.m. that says: 'Hey, we have to put the tarp on the field because Derek Jeter is playing shortstop for the Trenton Thunder the next day.' As I headed out the door, my family goes, 'What are you doing?' but you just do it out of duty for the 9,000 people that are going to be in the ballpark the next day," Burnham explains. "It's hard to explain to people the dedication it takes."

The same attributes that make the industry so intoxicating for Burnham are the same traits he believes make up an elite broadcaster. When he's listening and he can tell that someone is good, the first thing he thinks is, "Are you passionate and are you able to tell the story of the game?" Especially in today's day and age, where people are drawn to short highlights and video as opposed to the old, rhythmic melody of the game on-air, more and more sports, like hockey and basketball, are moving to simulcasted games—a game where one announcer broadcasts to both a television and a radio audience. It is important that the game is delivered well, and because of that, Burnham prefers to listen to tone and tenor to judge how well a broadcaster is doing rather than their knowledge of some obscure detail about something.

Burnham knows that the stories of yesteryear like Vin Scully going ice skating with Jackie Robinson aren't told anymore in our increasingly digital era where anything someone says may get blown up into a potentially negative story. It's fine if young broadcasters don't have those kinds of experiences, but they should certainly tell the stories that are available to them. For example, the best prospect that Burnham has ever seen in Minor League Baseball was Daniel Bard, who he got to see in 2008—Burnham's first year in Asheville. Bard would eventually go on to play for the Rockies organization, which Asheville was affiliated with for 25 years, but at the time, he played for the Boston Red Sox, who selected him in the first round of the 2006 draft.

132

9. Jay Burnham

In 2008, the flamethrower was coming out of the bullpen, and the Asheville Tourists got to see him in Greenville for his eighth appearance of the season. Coming into the game, Bard had punched out 19 batters in 11.1 innings and had not allowed a run to cross the plate. To top it off, he had only walked three batters and allowed five hits in that stretch.

"I saw an immaculate inning thrown by Bard in Greenville and I thought he was unstoppable. I'm glad he got a shot at redemption [after losing control of his pitching earlier]," Burnham says. "I was just in awe of his entire performance. He was throwing like 100, just blowing guys away." A lot of times, guys who dominate at those lower levels have one or two of the five tools people are looking for, and they get by with that, but then they turn out not to be the greatest prospects in baseball. A few years after Burnham saw Bard, he had the opportunity to see Manny Machado on his way through Bowie. The third baseman and shortstop was a more prolific prospect than the pitcher, and Machado eventually blossomed into a player the Padres handed $300 million to.

Machado was just growing into his bat, and started showing off power for the first time in his career. He went on to hit 11 home runs, a career high for him in 2012. Machado was one of the top prospects in baseball at the time, and he was ready to make a jump to the big leagues when Burnham and the Trenton Thunder got the opportunity to see him on August 4. He was the hottest player in the Eastern League. The first week of August, he hit .462, with two homers, two triples and two doubles in just 26 at-bats—all while striking out just once and drawing four walks. Burnham won't forget Machado's August 4 performance anytime soon.

"He hit a home run to give Bowie the lead in the eighth and it also gave him the cycle. He got promoted to the majors the next week," Burnham remembers. Machado ended the game going 4 for 4, scoring three runs and driving in three more in what became an 8–7 win for the Baysox.

Of course, everyone saw Manny Machado coming. Machado was the third overall pick in the 2010 draft, continuously ranked as one of the top prospects in baseball, and he made his major league debut as a 20-year-old. But there was a player in Asheville who had one of the top individual seasons in Tourists history in 2008 that absolutely no one could have seen coming. Darin Holcomb was picked up by the Rockies in the 12th round of the 2007 draft out of Gonzaga, and never appeared on a top prospect report. In fact, Holcomb would only go on to play four seasons of organized ball, finishing his career in 2011 at Double-A Tulsa after an injury cost him his 2010 campaign.

Hailing from Spokane, Washington, Holcomb was playing baseball across the country from his home in Asheville, but he sent out a spark that those from the Lilac City were sure to notice. "He was unstoppable until he had a back injury that eventually knocked him out of the game," Burnham remembers. That season, the third baseman played in 137 of the Tourists' 140 games and hit .318, while walking an incredible 65 times to push his on-base percentage to .400. His 46 doubles and 14 homers were enough to help him drive in over 100 RBI while scoring an extra 89 runs himself. The rest of his career, Holcomb never hit over .271 again, but Burnham will remember that magical season when the Washington native was able to take the league by storm.

Holcomb was only able to sustain that success for one season, but Burnham had the chance to connect with another minor league legend who many people haven't heard of. This first baseman sustained his level of success for a little longer than Holcomb, but Burnham wouldn't catch up to him until he was an assistant in the American Association. He was a guy who had so much success that never got recognized on a big scale, but continued to do his job and light up minor league scoreboards for years while playing in Harrisburg. Talmadge Nunnari met Burnham in his hometown, Pensacola, Florida, after quite an impressive minor league career. Nunnari was picked up by the Expos in the ninth round of the 1997 draft out of Lurleen B. Wallace Community College in Andalusia, Alabama. The first baseman became something of a legend after hitting .325 between the South Atlantic League and New York–Penn League in his first season and ending his career with a .291 average in 600 games in the minors.

"There was this guy named Talmadge Nunnari, otherwise known as 'T,' and he hit like .330 for multiple seasons in Minor League Baseball as a first baseman, but back then, if you didn't hit 30 homeruns as a first baseman, you didn't get any recognition," Burnham explains. "So, T ended up getting a cup of coffee in the majors—five at-bats, then tried to hit for more power and ended up not being able to make it and eventually started to sell advertisement[s] for an independent team."

His top season came in 1999 when he hit .344 in 134 games, 63 of which were in the Eastern League. If the .344 average wasn't enough, his on-base percentage was .423, something that would have analytics departments frothing at the mouth today. To put that into perspective, according to Baseball-Reference.com, the MLB average on-base percentage in 1999 was .345, which is the highest mark since .346 in 1950.

"His numbers in MiLB alone are insane. I'm sure he doesn't think about this, but I do. Had he been coming up now, as opposed to then, what type of analytics would they have used to track his exit velocity, his ability to get on base and all those things that weren't a factor in the mid–90s that probably would give him a 10-year Major League Baseball career?" Burnham asks. "Maybe I think about it because he was a friend of mine, but I think about him and what would have happened had the numbers been there like they are now." People have written books about the run that the Senators had in those days, and MayfliesandBigflies.com talks extensively about the top moments of those late '90s Harrisburg teams and the things that they were able to accomplish.

T got his cup of coffee with the Nationals, but not everyone does. Burnham was never able to call a championship-winning game for a team he worked for, and the great walk-off home runs and no-hitter moments become rarer and rarer as the "three true outcomes" tactics of baseball become more prevalent. Those outcomes are walking, striking out or hitting a home run, and the rise in the rate of all three has decreased the amount of time that the baseball actually gets put into play. Jay did have the opportunity to call one nine-inning no-hitter, though.

In July 2008, the Tourists were wrapping up an eight-game homestand against the Lakewood BlueClaws. The starting pitching matchup was nothing to marvel at. Two pitchers, both with ERAs hovering around 4.00 and picked in the later rounds of the 2007 draft, were going to battle it out: the Tourists' Bruce Billings and the BlueClaws' Julian Sampson. It seemed to be a pretty typical Wednesday evening game for fans in the South Atlantic League.

Burnham had a feeling early on that Billings had the stuff and could make something happen. "Optimistic Jay, I think I was starting to think about it in the fifth inning. My boy that I called 'Dolla Dolla' Billings had a no-no going and it was almost more [like] counting down outs to get to Wedge Brewing after the game, but the game was just flying by. It was about a two-hour game. You know those getaway games where you start to get the vibe early."

Everything was going seamlessly for Billings, who ended the game with a walk, which he issued to the third batter he faced, leaving him a ninth-inning error away from a perfect game. The Tourists ended up winning handily, 10–0, and the last out still sticks out to Burnham. "The last out was crushed to deep left field. The left fielder stumbled in and made the catch. I was locked in. It was great, and I was so excited."

In the last couple of years, complete-game, nine-inning no-hitters have become rarer and rarer. This stems from organizations paying more attention over the last 10 years to pitch counts and utilizing strategies involving openers or bullpen days. With these strategies, even if a player is dealing through a significant portion of a game, he could get pulled due to the analytics a situation presents. In theory, that's to help the individual development and health of a player more than just worrying about creating championship teams. Despite that, everyone still hopes to win a ring at the end of the season, and the best team that Burnham saw played in Asheville in 2008 when his career was just beginning.

After having the opportunity to see that nine-inning no-hitter, Holcomb represented the Tourists as the South Atlantic League MVP that season. Those Tourists won 83 games and outscored opponents by 111 runs. The one problem that the team ran into was the Augusta GreenJackets, and, more specifically, a young Madison Bumgarner. In two meetings against Asheville in the regular season, the lefty offered 14 scoreless frames while fanning 20 hitters. When they met in the first round of the playoffs, they saw Bumgarner for Game 1.

"We didn't get a single run off of Bumgarner in a few opportunities. We played him in the first game of the playoffs, so it's like, yeah, you lose there, but it's best of three, right? Then they beat us at home. I think on their championship rings they had their record inscribed on it because it was such a good squad," Burnham says. The GreenJackets finished with an 88–50 record. Jay still is looking to be on call for a championship-winning team. That journey can take a long time for a broadcaster. Much like sitting on a bus on the next road trip, there are plenty of surprises that impact how you get to your destination.

Although Jay has spent time in the Atlantic League, Eastern League and South Atlantic League, when he thinks of the best road cities he has had the opportunity to travel to while in baseball, they are definitely in the South Atlantic League. He has worked in Hagerstown and Asheville, but considers Asheville the top destination in the league. "In my opinion, Asheville is one of the top five towns in America," Burnham explains. "You have Savannah; Charleston, South Carolina; and Asheville in the same league. It's hard for another league to have those types of awesome cities."

When you think of Asheville, North Carolina, it's hard not to think

9. Jay Burnham

about the plethora of breweries situated about the "Tourist"-y town. Burnham mentions Green Man Brewery as one of his favorites to visit. It is one of the town's original breweries and has been in the same location along Buxton Avenue, just a hop and a jump away from McCormick Field, since 1997. Along the way, it has birthed some award-winning microbrews like ESB Special Amber Ale and the Green Man Trickster IPA. There is one place in Asheville that is a bit more special for Burnham, though.

In West Asheville, across the French Broad River, on the corner of Haywood Road and Michigan Avenue, sits "a chill venue for eclectic American fare," according to a Google Maps review. The Admiral is the spot where Jay met his wife, Cheyenne.

"It used to be a weird hipster, fine dining $2 PBR place. Now it's hard to get into, but back then it was one of those places where at nine o'clock they would move the tables from out of the dining room and it would be like a dance floor," Burnham thinks back. He met Cheyenne in The Admiral and they've been together ever since, through moves to Richmond, Virginia; Trenton, New Jersey; and now to Massachusetts— although the family still owns a house in Asheville.

Sure, after traveling around the country calling baseball in a handful of towns for 16 years, there are many places that feel like home—but when Burnham has been on the road, he has had some wild experiences. One of his favorite parts of working in Minor League Baseball is going to All-Star Games. It's normally a three-day period when executives from teams across the league sit back and have a party to celebrate all of the hard work they've done throughout the year. For broadcasters, they get to see a lot of the people that they've met while traveling on the road and typically have more time to hang out, grab drinks and share stories.

In 2009, Jay had a bit of a wild experience getting to the South Atlantic League All-Star Game in Charleston, West Virginia. Asheville ended the first half of the season in Bowling Green, Kentucky, a league outlier a hundred miles west of any of its other teams. The trick was that most of the Hot Rods players were staying in Bowling Green, and most of the Tourists players were going to go on the bus back to Asheville—out of the nearly 60 guys on the two teams, six had to make the five-hour trek to Appalachian Power Park. The leadership groups of both teams didn't want to pay for a bus for so few players. Burnham was planning on going to the All-Star festivities anyway, so they rented a van for the 24-year-old, who was too young to rent it by himself. Following the final game of the first half, Burnham hiked east to Lexington,

137

Play-by-Play from the Minors

Kentucky, hopped on Route 64 and after 340 miles found himself in Charleston, West Virginia.

There were two big names in that van: 19-year-old Tim Beckham, who was selected first overall in the draft the year prior and signed a $6.15 million bonus with Tampa Bay, and Chris Andujar, whose dad, Joaquín Andujar, was a four-time MLB All-Star with the Houston Astros and the St. Louis Cardinals in the late 1970s and early '80s.

"I'm driving the whole crew and I'm sitting here and going to West Virginia. Some of the guys back there signed for a lot, and so there was a lot of value to their organizations back there. We stopped at Zaxby's so we could get some lunch for the guys and eventually I pull up to the Ramada in West Virginia and we unload around six All-Stars from the back of the van. I just thought, all right! My job is done. I've delivered the package here safely," Burnham laughs as he recalls the task. Of course, after the task was over, he was able to get to the usual All-Star festivities, heading to the hospitality room to drink and network with the league executives.

Having to drive a van wasn't the worst thing that Burnham has had to do to get from point A to point B in his career. While he was in the American Association, there were teams the Pelicans traveled to play that were literally all across the United States. The closest opponent to Pensacola was in Shreveport, Louisiana. When the Pelicans played in the Captains' stadium, they were only 460 miles from home—about a seven-hour trip.

After a poor situation in the Pelicans' first year in the league that resulted in players being left behind at their home airport trying to fly to El Paso, the team decided to just bus to El Paso for their annual trip out west. Typically, the team would have a 12-day road trip where they would drive all the way out to El Paso to play a series and hit two other opponents for series on the way back to Pensacola, where they would finally get the chance to play a home game. El Paso, Texas, and St. Paul, Minnesota, were the two farthest trips they had to take, and both journeys took nearly a day.

The El Paso trip was a nearly 1,300-mile odyssey that with today's regulations in Minor League Baseball and the busing industry would take three drivers to drive straight through. But the Pensacola Pelicans had just one bus and one bus driver, James Bonds. Maybe Bonds wasn't a secret agent, but he certainly performed some incredible feats of will.

"We would do a 24-hour bus trip across the state of Texas, across Louisiana to get to El Paso, where we would play a six-game series. This is

9. Jay Burnham

1000 percent illegal," Burnham chuckles. "We had one bus driver, James, and the way the rig was set up was similar to a truck pulling a tractor trailer, with a separate cab. That was our set-up, where you could walk between the two."

Most of the players would sit in the back and try to sleep or play Pluck or other games to pass the time. This was back before buses had reliable wi-fi and cell phones that let you hold the world in your palm, so the biggest entertainment on the bus was the people it contained. The back typically didn't have enough room for the broadcaster, so Jay would sit up front, in the compartment with the driver.

"James would ... smoke cigarettes and drink Mountain Dew and just drive all night long," Jay remembers. "I would sit with him trying to keep him entertained and awake. Then, around two or three in the morning, I would fall asleep, but sure enough, he would get us to where we were going. Those off days that we spent on a bus, those are the things that in hindsight I wish Facebook or Twitter was a thing or I had a camera on my phone back then. I wish I could have captured those types of journeys."

The team would finally arrive at where they needed to go, Mr. Bonds having smoked many packs of cigarettes and drained a handful of bottles of Mountain Dew, and it would be time to play baseball. Unlike the players, the fans who attended the game the next day wouldn't need caffeine or nicotine to stay awake. The crack of the bat and the promotions would be enough to charge up the roaring crowd, who never had to endure a 1,300-mile bus ride to attend a game.

Maybe fans aren't completing marathons to get to the park, but a lot of fans will race to the gates to ensure that they can get the latest bobblehead or T-shirt giveaway prior to a game. One promotion that Burnham loves isn't one that fans have to race to the park to see, but they will be cheering on one racer to finish strong. Promotions are dime a dozen, and Minor League Baseball has so many different, strong promotions, but Jay says he gravitated toward the mascot races that are now so common during games. He's thinking specifically of the Milwaukee Brewers' Sausage Race and the Washington Nationals' Presidents Race that the teams hold at each home game. When Burnham got to Asheville, part of his job was obtaining a set amount of sponsorship dollars each year, and one of his ideas in his first year was to have a themed race for the breweries in the downtown area.

"I got yelled at for doing this—for a variety of reasons, but I wanted a brewery race and I wanted five breweries to race in the seventh inning.

Play-by-Play from the Minors

Through hook and crook, we [were] able to get it to go," Burnham explains. "I gave each brewery an opportunity to design their own costume. One brewery was the French Broad River Brewery, which was named after the river in North Carolina. They came up with a raft, so the contestant had to wear a raft. That ended up putting them at a disadvantage, though, because Green Man Brewery was a woodland creature, so they just had to put a mask on. It ended up that French Broad River lost almost every time because the poor contestant had to run with a whole boat raft around their torso."

Those breweries don't only represent the racers for each game in Asheville; they are a huge part of that North Carolina community. Today, almost every park in America has an ode to Thirsty Thursday, but those local beers and breweries are why the Tourists brand a lot of their events around alcohol. People who have gone to games, particularly on Thirsty Thursday, know that in Asheville, it's an incredible event—it is even trademarked there. Burnham loved seeing the race late in those games because fans would really get into it and it was great exposure for the breweries that decided to hop on board for the promotion. While it isn't the craziest promotion he's been a part of, it's certainly the one that he's most proud of because it was his vision start to finish. It was an adaptation of the broadcaster's favorite promotions he's seen with a local tie and it was great for sponsorship revenue and exposure for the team. As shown by the mascot races and local tie-ins that inspired Burnham's favorite promotion at one of his parks, quirkiness plays a big role in what he enjoyed seeing on the road.

When traveling in independent ball, Burnham always admired the St. Paul Saints' operation. The team is another leg of the Goldklang Group, and is perhaps the most electric of all the teams because of the added freedoms they can perform, not being in affiliated baseball. When the Massachusetts native worked in Pensacola, he had to take a 20-hour, 1,200-mile bus ride to St. Paul each year—and when you factored in breaks for the driver and the traffic that the bus hit along the highway, it typically ended up being around a 24-hour trek. That drive was entirely worth it for Burnham, though, who was completely in awe of all the different promotions that St. Paul had.

He specifically remembers a promotion where a fan would get strapped to a billboard beyond the outfield wall. There were two ways for fans to win prizes. First, if the fan on the billboard caught a home run ball, everyone would get to take a prize home, and second, if the fan stayed up longer than a specified time—for example, if they stayed strapped to the billboard for say, three innings—then beer was fifty cents cheaper for the rest of the night.

"So, there's this person that's strapped up on the billboard, which, legally, I don't even know how they were able to do it, but that was the coolest [promotion] I've seen there," Burnham remembers. "I've always admired St. Paul, and when the All-Star Game was in El Paso that year, I asked Mike Veeck for his autograph. He's the only person I've really approached as an adult and asked for an autograph. He was part of the ownership group there, and everything they did there was so cool."

Jay would try to take some of those ideas and bring them back home to wherever he was working at the time. Bringing ideas back from the road is easy. The hard part is finding creative people who are okay with fostering those types of ideas and implementing them in a fun, unique way. Burnham says that his time in Richmond was the closest he ever got to the promotional atmosphere in St. Paul. A big part of that had to do with Todd Parnell—the Flying Squirrels' general manager while Burnham was there. This is the same "Parney" who was the inventor of Awful Night, which Robert Ford talked about.

Yes, Burnham would learn a lot from his travels, but he also tried to learn a lot from the players that he came in contact with throughout his career. There were plenty of guys he learned life lessons from, but one veteran who just understood his role well and was fun to be around was Flying Squirrels catcher Steven Lerud.

"After the games, we'd be in Parney's office and he would come up with some of the funniest things. He bought into the way Minor League Baseball worked, but he would always put a barb into it," Burnham remembers. "If we gave him stuff for having a bad game, he would come back with the fact that he had to wear a waffle jersey for brunch day. He was the mouthpiece of the team, so he was one of my all-time favorite guys. Sometimes it's about who you can count on to do an interview or a media appearance, and it may not mean anything to getting to the major leagues, but those are the guys who I like. We have the most interaction with them, but they have helped me and it makes my job that much easier."

At the end of the day, baseball is always about the people for Burnham. So when he thinks about calling one moment in baseball history with no repercussions and with the knowledge that he has today, the decision is easy. The voice of the Minutemen would pick Jackie Robinson's debut.

"And I might go on a rant about ..., not only the game, but the

141

foundations and systemic racism that [have] been put in place to keep people of color down for hundreds of years," Burnham explains. "Today we romanticize the Negro Leagues, but when we talk about them we need to talk about why they existed. They existed because they didn't allow people of color to play Major League Baseball."

Burnham is a huge advocate of today's civil rights movements and an ardent supporter of the Black Play-By-Play Broadcaster Grant and Scholarship Fund that was founded by Adam Giardino, a University of Connecticut sports broadcaster, following the 2020 Black Lives Matter protests. Burnham's goal is to afford people opportunities that they may not have received due to their race when he was breaking into the industry. He points out that segregation really isn't that far away from our current day.

"The SEC in football, there were schools that didn't have a Black player until the '70s. That is [on] the cusp of my lifetime," Burnham says. "There's a difference between what people say and where people put their resources. Are people and owners living their values or are they just saying one thing and doing another?"

When you look at Jay and how he lives his life and directs his career, it follows exactly how he talks, and that is why calling Jackie Robinson's debut makes so much sense for the veteran broadcaster. The moment is about more than just the game that we use to distract ourselves from our daily lives; that particular moment is about a step forward our nation took. A step forward that started with the game of baseball and that still impacts our culture today.

10

Joshua Suchon

Currently with the Albuquerque Isotopes
Previously with the Modesto Nuts and Watertown Indians

Jay Burnham and Joshua Suchon found two different ways into broadcasting. After an initial start in broadcasting, Suchon used the written press, which was booming in the late '90s, to create his platform. On the other hand, Jay Burnham stuck it out in independent ball and the low level of the minors to get to where he is today. Both broadcasters have ended up extremely successful despite opting to take different routes early in their careers.

After getting his start in Minor League Baseball in the New York–Penn League in 1996 with the Watertown Indians, it took Suchon a while to find a long-term home in the minors. He ended up earning that and more in Albuquerque, where he has spent the last seven years. Josh has also branched out more recently and is the host of the "Life Around the Seams" podcast, which has put out over 50 episodes since 2018. The podcast follows Josh through his life on and off the diamond while he interviews fellow workers in the industry who have unique backgrounds. The West Coast product has also found himself on call for the University of New Mexico's women's basketball team and worked with AT&T SportsNet to bring fans coverage of the Colorado Rockies' spring training in 2019.

In addition to his work in baseball and behind a microphone, Suchon is an accomplished writer. One can find freelance credits to national publications such as the *Washington Post*, ESPN.com, *Baseball America* and *Sports Illustrated* dating back to 1994, but he also spent 10 years with the Bay Area News Group—many of those years as a traveling beat writer for both the San Francisco Giants and the Oakland Athletics. While there is a plethora of shorter written content from Suchon that fans can digest, he has also published a trio of books, the first of which

143

Joshua Suchon has worked for the Albuquerque Isotopes for a decade now, but the play-by-play broadcaster got his start with newspapers in the '90s. Suchon has also penned a trio of books of his own (photograph courtesy Joshua Suchon).

he published in 2002. The subjects of his three books range from Barry Bonds's fabled 2001 season, where he drew a .515 on-base percentage along with 177 walks (plus 35 intentional bases on balls) and 73 homers while driving in 137 RBI, to a cold-case murder in Suchon's hometown, Pleasanton, California.

Joshua grew up in Pleasanton, which is a suburb of Oakland, part of the larger Bay Area and not far from San Francisco. His mother's side of the family rooted for the San Francisco teams, the Giants and the 49ers, while his father's side of the family was pro–Oakland—pulling for the A's and the Raiders. His father is the rare Bay Area person who has immense pride in all the teams. If they are from either San Francisco or Oakland, he'll root for them.

"We ended up liking the Oakland teams more, just because it was easier to get there, and because we were physically closer, it made me want to like the A's more than the Giants," Suchon says. While he was more a fan of the A's, he certainly wanted the Giants to win. The Californian says he was happy as could be when the Giants and the A's met in the World Series in 1989. He recalls a moment from his childhood: "I remember one time about a month into the season in the early '80s or the mid–80s, both the A's and Giants were in first place. My Dad got out the standings from the newspaper and put it on the refrigerator and said, 'You know, we may not see this [again] in a long time.' Which is an indication of how much he cared about both teams."

One doesn't need too many guesses as to who the budding broad-caster's greatest influence would have been growing up. If you glance at the play-by-play guys for Oakland's teams in the '80s, you'll see that Bill King at one point called the A's, the Warriors and the Raiders. At that point, most games weren't broadcast on television yet. King, the 2017 Ford C. Frick Awardee, may be best-known for his signature phrase "Holy Toledo!," but he also called A's games for 25 seasons, beginning in 1981. His tenure at the Oakland Coliseum came at the tail end of his career working with the Golden State Warriors from 1962 to 1983 and the Raiders (both Oakland and Los Angeles) from 1962 to 1992.

The "King" of broadcasting in the Bay Area was Suchon's favorite for a variety of reasons. "Everything about Bill was the best. His vocab-ulary, his enthusiasm, the way he ripped the officials and just the way that he rose to the occasion at the biggest moments made Bill the best," Suchon recalls. Josh maintains that he has probably "stolen liberally" from King without even realizing it. "To me it's a lot about tempo and intensity at certain moments in the game," he says. "I haven't done a lot of football, but I feel like my football is really based on Bill in terms of setting the field—being able to say where the wide receivers are and the tight end. Giving you the snap formations. I can't really say there is a certain phrase I use, but that's because there are probably a bunch that I use."

Like King, Suchon started his career a little differently than most minor league broadcasters. King, an Indiana native, was stationed in Guam during the end of World War II and began broadcasting with the Armed Forces Radio Service. There, he was wired play-by-play of a sporting event and he rebroadcast it as though he was at the game. After spending the summer of 1996 in the New York–Penn League, Suchon struggled to find a second gig in Minor League Baseball, so he returned home and worked at a restaurant for a bit.

"If you were to compare, this is a tape of me broadcasting baseball and this is a story of me writing, my writing was probably further along at that point in my life and there were more opportunities," Suchon says.

145

Play-by-Play from the Minors

He started working with a Pleasanton affiliate of the *Oakland Tribune/Bay Area News Group* that he had stringed for in high school. He asked if they had an opening, was initially told no and a few weeks later began writing about a story a week. It grew to two stories a week, then he was answering phones as well. Shortly after, he gained part-time status and eventually moved into a full-time role with the news group.

After a few years with the Alameda News Group (ANG), another part-time position was offered to Suchon, but broadcasting was also dangling a carrot in front of him. The Modesto A's had an opening for their radio broadcaster and he was interviewing for that position. He first received an offer from ANG, but held out for a while, hoping to hear from the Modesto A's, who had just renovated John Thurman Field. He eventually accepted the writing position, just to get an offer from Modesto three days after starting the new job. Naturally, he accepted his dream position broadcasting with a team and quit the news group— arriving about 60 miles east from his hometown the first week in February, or about two months prior to the start of baseball season.

The first month of the season, the team was playing games at a makeshift field in Lodi—about 40 miles north of Modesto—and the small staff seemed overwhelmed with everything that had to be done. The day prior to the season, the general manager approached Josh and told him that they would not have a broadcast that year, and that they would try again the following season.

"I remember I was pissed because I came there to broadcast. I was willing to do media relations and everything else, but I thought, if I'm not doing the broadcast, then what am I doing here?" Suchon relays. "So I quit, [and] I gave a six-week notice rather than a two-week notice to get them to the opening of the new renovated ballpark." Having no idea what he was going to do, he returned to Pleasanton. ANG found a way to reach him right before he left Modesto—before the era of cell phones, the company called his dad, who relayed them to his aunt and uncle's number. His contact said a staffer had left and they had a full-time opening, and Suchon was first on the list. Naturally, he took the job, and assumed that maybe he was destined to write rather than broadcast.

He would work for the news group for a decade, gaining the opportunity to cover the Giants from 2000 to 2003 before covering the A's in 2004–06. In 2006, ANG merged with two other news groups to become the Bay Area News Group. Feeling burnt out from the grind of producing two stories every day and the other rigors of the newspaper industry, Suchon thought one more time about pursuing his passion in broadcasting. To gather new tape, since he hadn't been on a broadcast since his time back with the Watertown Indians, he was granted a suite way down the third-base line at the McAfee Coliseum (now the Oakland–Alameda County Coliseum) by the A's PR staff. When Suchon was off (he typically covered around 140 games per year), he sat in one of the suites or empty press box booths that are typically reserved for Spanish-language or national broadcasts and just broadcast the entire game into a recorder, eventually using the tape to get a full-time play-by-play gig. The newspaper writer called two games to try to get the quality half-innings required to send to potential employers.

"The first one was horrendous. The second one was a little bit better—it had a few half-innings that I could use, which is all you need," Suchon says. While scouring for news of broadcast openings around Minor League Baseball during the 2006 off-season, Suchon stumbled across a familiar name—Modesto. Things were different this time around, though, Suchon contends. The GM who was there in the '90s was gone. They were affiliated with the Rockies and had been rebranded as the Modesto Nuts by this point, but most importantly, the candidate was actually hired on by the radio station rather than the baseball team.

He eventually accepted the position, where he would spend 2007 as an employee of ESPN Modesto to call Nuts games and prep football. Following the opportunity with Modesto, Suchon called Dodgers spring training games from 2009 to 2011 for Prime Ticket and the MLB Network, as well as working UC Santa Barbara basketball games in 2010–11. His opportunity with the Isotopes began in 2012, when he began calling Los Angeles D–Fenders games, prep sports games and Isotopes games for Spectrum SportsNet, a gig that began in 2012 and carried him through his Isotopes start in 2013.

Throughout his journey, Suchon has also coached young broadcasters, acting as a mentor for those who wanted assistance entering the industry. Josh stresses to those mentees that the most important thing to elevate their broadcasting from good to great is rhythm. "I feel like you're doing a waltz with the starting pitcher and it is just knowing when the starting pitcher is going to throw again." He also iterates that it is important to sound like you're smiling, and to provide context and good detail, but rhythm is equivalent to you being in control of the game.

Just as a broadcast has a rhythm, the ebb and flow of baseball's schedule finds a rhythm. Unlike most other major North American sports, baseball games are played nearly every day, and players and broadcasters often travel on the same days that they are playing games. While the Californian isn't in control of the daunting schedule in baseball, the Pacific Coast League is a perfect fit for him—allowing him to visit a number of great cities that he is familiar with. He likes going to Reno to visit his parents and Sacramento because it's close to his sister, high school friends and Johnny Doskow (the River Cats broadcaster and a good friend of Suchon's). On a different note, while away from his desert home, Tacoma is a nice change of pace because of all the moisture in the air of the Washington city. Suchon considers himself an explorer and adds that he has taken quite a few ambitious trips to take advantage of the travel aspect of Minor League Baseball.

One time, while on a road series against the Iowa Cubs, Suchon left Des Moines to hit a small farming town called Dyersville. About 175 miles from Principal Park, there's a famous baseball diamond—and the movie site for *Field of Dreams*. So, he awoke at 7 a.m. to make the pilgrimage to one of the bucket-list locations for most baseball fans. After spending a few hours on-site, he returned to Des Moines just in time to get to the stadium and start the day of work.

He has also journeyed to the Jack Daniel's Distillery while visiting Nashville, and he has visited plenty of parks and historic areas around Austin, Texas. The broadcaster has gone to the Ninth Ward while in New Orleans, Graceland and the recording studio where Elvis received his start during a trip to play the Memphis Redbirds and he has spent time hiking the Rocky Mountains while in Colorado Springs. He doesn't create a set list of things he wants to do, but the Isotopes call-guy always tries to do something while he visits these cities. Sometimes it's a restaurant, sometimes it's hiking and sometimes it's visiting a historic site or a museum filled with something interesting or cultural.

All in all, most of the experiences he's lived, whether it's going to Seattle from Tacoma, dipping his feet in the water of the Pacific Ocean or hiking around Yosemite, are the centerpieces of someone else's summer vacation. Josh just happens to either precede or follow up those experiences by broadcasting a baseball game and taking care of the media who want access to the team he is working for.

During all these travels, Suchon has sampled many restaurants across the country, but he is never satisfied with what he has already tried. He continues to try to branch out. "I have a rule where every time I go to a city, I have to have at least one meal at a place that I have not eaten at previously," Suchon explains. He convinced a few other broadcasters in the Pacific Coast League to try to do the same thing and share their top finds with the rest of the group. It's been a fun way for the broadcasters to share more than just the game that unites them.

Traveling on the road, Suchon has had the opportunity to see more than just great restaurants. He has also been able to witness plenty of goofy and successful promotions, and he says a lot of them are in one location—Fresno. The Grizzlies' team president, Derrick Franks, is a close colleague of Suchon's and he often gives the broadcaster a hard-time for "picking on" the Grizzlies. Suchon mentions some of their zany promotions on-air, but they have topped the charts with quite a few wild events.

Suchon says that he has also seen his fair share of wonky promotions at the Grizzlies' Chukchansi Park, including a night dedicated to '90s rapper Biz Markie and his song "Just a Friend." The club called the 2015 promotion "Old School Hip-Hop Night."

Suchon remembers the night vividly: "They brought him out to the ballpark and they had him sing the song between innings. You have 90 seconds or two minutes between innings and it takes time to introduce him and he had to say something before he started singing, so by the time he was ready to start singing, the starting pitcher was ready to go and it was a mess." He laughs as he finishes the tale. "It was just awkward.

"On the other side, they do a Fresno Famous tournament at the same time as March Madness, where the [winner's face graced] a bobblehead giveaway in 2015 and a jersey giveaway in 2016. Robin Lopez, who graduated from San Joaquin Memorial [High School] and has played in the NBA since 2008, was the winner in 2015 for the inaugural season. Since then, the tournament has [evolved] and included Fresno foods in 2017, but continues to be a top hit in the market."

Just like the broadcaster group text about food uniting the members of the PCL, promotions are a great way to welcome people of different backgrounds into the gates of a team's ballpark. Suchon has played a part in one promotion championing diversity that towers above the rest in his eyes. The massive promotion, which Minor League Baseball rolled out several years ago, is called Copa de la Diversión, or Fun Cup. It's a season-long event that resonates with the local Hispanic and Latino communities in Minor League Baseball. Each team that participates assumes a different cultural identity with a bright color scheme and embraces the cultures of those who make up over 30 percent of the players and countless fans across the globe.

Albuquerque's identity each year has been the Mariachis de Neuvo

México. The tradition began in 2018, when the Isotopes were one of just 33 teams across the 160-team circuit to be invited to join. After an overwhelming success, including the Isotopes setting a new individual game attendance record, there are currently 92 teams who participate in Copa. The Mariachis go all out for the event. Isotopes Park is commonly referred to as "The Lab," but for Copa games, the brand changes to El Plaza and the concourse is filled with live mariachi bands, flags, streamers and piñatas. The Isotopes' director of public Relations, Kevin Collins, in an interview with *New Mexico Living* in 2019, referred to the nights as having a "Dominican League flair, where you can hear the music all throughout the ballpark and it's fantastic and really unique." This event isn't just about selling tickets and merchandise, though. The Isotopes were lauded as the top Copa identity for both the 2018 and 2019 seasons, and a big reason is because they donated over $200,000 to local Hispanic organizations and invested the most marketing dollars into Copa–specific marketing campaigns among the participating teams. From the booth, what was important to making the night a success was, according to Suchon, "[r]eally the whole ensemble. Setting it up as a success with it being a fireworks night, having the live bands and dancers inside and outside of the ballpark, decorating the ballpark and even having it on Cinco de Mayo for the first one. Doing all of that to create buzz for the future, and doing more than just putting on a hat and playing music to create an authentic atmosphere, made it special."

Although Suchon has spent most of his career in the PCL, a league that does not partake in many bus trips, he can still recall plenty of stories of airport travel that did not work out well for the players and him. A trip from 2016 haunts the voice of the Isotopes more than any other trek. Following a poor start of the season where the Isotopes had fallen behind by nearly 20 games in the standings, a flurry of roster moves set the team up with a few future major leaguers who began to help the team surge back toward a potential playoff position. They finished an eight-game road trip with six wins in Colorado Springs and Oklahoma City in pursuit of El Paso, which led the division.

Coming back from Oklahoma City, the team made the decision to fly rather than take a 550-mile bus trip. There isn't a direct flight, though, so they had to catch a connection in Denver. They had an early morning departure and about 30 minutes into the flight, the captain came on the intercom and told the travelers that they would have to turn back around because there was an issue with the landing gear. "We made it back to Oklahoma City, sat on the plane for a while and then they realized that everyone had to get off the plane because they didn't realize how long the delay was going to be," Suchon recollects. The plane was eventually fixed and they made it to Denver, but they had already missed the connecting flight back to Albuquerque. To put the situation in perspective, when a team that purchases more than 30 tickets on a flight is late for a connection, the airline will usually hold the plane, because that's a significant portion of a flight that is held up by a different flight's late arrival. In this case, though, they did not hold the plane. What Southwest instead decided to do was to create a new flight and essentially arrange a charter flight home for the team.

Despite this effort from the airline, the Isotopes didn't land in Albuquerque until around 5:30 p.m. for a game that was supposed to start at 6:30. The team only delayed the game for a half-hour, so when the bus pulled up to the stadium, they stretched, took some hacks in the cages, got in their uniforms and headed out on the field to play. Suchon recalls the leadership of a veteran member of the team, Chris Nelson, ringing around the bus: "I'll never forget Nelly just kept saying, 'Get your minds right, get your minds right,' as the bus pulled up. He was saying it to everyone and adding, 'No excuses. Get your minds right.' I was super tired and I was thinking, 'Oh no, this is going to be the end of this super good run we have had.' Then when Nelson said that, I just thought, 'All right, here we go. We've got this.'"

They won that night and swept the four-game series to stay in contention that season. Suchon says that was probably the most exciting homestand he has witnessed while in Minor League Baseball—and it all started with a wild plane trek. Great runs like that typically come from a melding of exciting prospects and wily veterans working together under a strong coaching staff.

In AAA, Suchon has had a great opportunity to see a lot of prospects right before they make it to The Show and when they are fine-tuning their skills to compete on the world's biggest stage. One of those players that awed the Isotopes broadcaster was Noah Syndergaard, who played for the Las Vegas 51s in 2014–15. During that time, the future Met played the Isotopes five times, three games in 2014 and two in 2015. The Texas native spun 14 innings against the Isotopes in 2014, allowing three earned runs and fanning 13 batters. In 2015, he worked a seven-inning, two-hit scoreless outing with nine punchouts on April 27 and came back to spin an eight-frame, two-run outing less than two weeks later for his final game before getting the call to New York.

What struck Suchon about Syndergaard's final game in Triple-A wasn't so much his dominant pitching, it was how the 6'6", 250-pound righty mashed the ball. "What made it memorable was that he hit a homer to dead center that went about 460 feet. Then he hit a double to left center off the top of the wall. He also hit a single that nearly decapitated the starting pitcher, and so he came up in the seventh inning with a chance at the cycle. How many starting pitchers come up at the plate with a chance to hit the cycle? And he was unbelievable on the mound."

He also recalls a George Springer visit in 2013. It wasn't so much a performance in a specific game or any on-field act that makes Suchon remember him as a top prospect. It was the reaction he had from the clubhouse that swung Suchon. "He was so good that almost our entire team came out of the clubhouse just to watch him take batting practice. When stuff like that happens, that's when I'm like, okay, that's not normal." That's not to say that Springer didn't play well against Albuquerque; he played eight games against the Isotopes in 2013, and in those eight games, he was held hitless just once. Overall, he finished 9 for 29 (.310 average) while clubbing eight homers, driving in eight RBI and drawing four walks while Suchon called the action. Suchon has seen a lot of great players, but those are the players that stand out above the rest. He says, "I try really hard not to be a scout—to not sit down and break a guy down. I go off the reaction of guys who do that for a living. So, when players go out of their way to do something they don't normally do to show respect for a different player, that's what makes the difference for me."

Sure, Springer and Syndergaard have gone on to become top-tier MLB players who have brought home hardware at the highest level of the game, but, without hesitating, Suchon says Stephen Cardullo immediately comes to his mind as the top unsung hero he's watched come through Albuquerque. Hailing from Hollywood ... Florida, the 24th-round pick of the Arizona Diamondbacks in 2010 was released by the team prior to the 2012 season following two years in the Pioneer League.

From there, he spent four seasons in independent baseball, playing for the London Rippers and Florence Freedom of the Frontier League in 2012 prior to spending the next three years with the Rockland Boulders of the Can-Am League. He got markedly better in each of his three seasons in the Can-Am League, finishing his final season, 2015, hitting .331 with nine homers and 76 RBI in 93 games for the Boulders.

Cardullo was used to being an underdog. As soon as he began looking at colleges, his journey to prove the doubters wrong began. After having no scholarship offers to play in college, Cardullo was able to become a walk-on and play at Florida State. He didn't play much as a freshman or sophomore, but his junior year he started at first base, eventually moved to shortstop and, to top it off, was named a First-Team All-American after hitting .376 and rocking 10 homers for the Seminoles. None of it surprises Suchon, though, and the reason a college walk-on and four-year Indy ball journeyman was able to make his MLB debut with the Rockies the same year he made it back to Minor League Baseball all comes down to his work ethic.

There were a pair of moments where his work ethic stood out to the veteran broadcaster. First, prior to a day game, when there isn't batting practice on the field, Cardullo brought a piece of lumber into the batter's box, just stood there and visualized the game.

"He wasn't in the lineup that day. Here comes Cardullo, what's he going to do today?" Suchon spins the yarn. "I realized he was just there visualizing what was going on in the game. It's not like he never played at the ballpark before—he played in lots of games, but he was just getting himself mentally ready to pinch-hit later that day. Sure enough, he pinch-hit later in the game and got a hit."

The second tale came directly following the All-Star break in 2016. Suchon had taken an alternate route into the stadium that day, through the clubhouse so he could grab his radio equipment, rather than straight up to his office. That trek brought him back past the batting cages to get to an elevator that brought him back to the press box. "It's pretty early, sometime between 11 a.m. and 1 p.m., and walking through the clubhouse, I hear banging going on in the batting cage. I thought, 'Who in the world is taking batting practice right now? Some guys are probably still headed back into town.' No one was in the clubhouse. As I got closer, I started to play the game of who do you think it is. My initial thought was that it was just some clubhouse kids having fun, and then I go, no, I bet it is Cardullo. Sure enough, it's Cardullo, and he is in the cage by himself, and he is just putting the ball on the tee, taking a swing and repeating it." In Suchon's view, this man willed his way to Major League Baseball.

Cardullo is just part of why that 2016 team was special for Suchon. Their run from completely out of contention to nearly making the play-offs was fun to watch. It wasn't just fun for those in the stands, but truthfully incredible to be a part of in the booth. From August 8 to the 23rd, the Isotopes won 15 of 17 games to catch up to the fading El Paso Chihuahuas in the final two weeks of the season. On July 7, the Isotopes trailed El Paso by 17 games, but after 20 wins in August—their most in a single month in franchise history—Albuquerque finished just two games back of the division champions.

Of the 64 players who were on the active roster for at least one game that year, 51 of them played in the majors. The team boasted nine first-round picks, including reliever Adam Ottavino, starting pitcher Tyler Anderson, outfielder David Dahl and pitchers Kyle Freeland and Jordan Lyles.

"If you look at the 2016 team and you see all the future major leaguers, and the major leaguers who have had major impacts at the big league level, the 2016 team, especially in the second half, was loaded," Suchon remembers. "It felt like we were never going to lose. We were just stunned when we lost." A marquee moment for this team, which the broadcaster lauds as the most talented team he has broadcast games for, came directly after the All-Star break. The Isotopes' catcher, Tom Murphy, capped off a 12–8 victory with an eighth-inning triple to give him a cycle. This started a streak where the backstop went 18 for 24 and raised his batting average from a lowly .206 to .283, one of the top averages on the team. In that game, the left fielder, David Dahl, also hit two homers, a sign of the explosive offense that bolstered the second half of the season for the Rockies affiliate.

Brandon Barnes was a huge part of that 2016 team. Barnes was a guy who had spent four years in the majors and was optioned to Triple-A after playing 48 games with the Rockies and hitting .220 with sub-par power numbers. Suchon says, "At Triple-A, there are a lot of guys who are salty. They think they're getting screwed and they take out their frustrations on people around them. Brandon Barnes was the exact opposite. He was there because David Dahl took his job in the major leagues, and it would be easy for him to be upset for that reason." He explains, "When he was an up-and-coming player, he remembered what it was like when a guy came back from the major leagues and was miserable and kind of took it out on everybody else. Barnes didn't want to be that guy. He was upset, but he didn't want anyone to know that. He just wanted to go back to having fun."

And oh boy, did Brandon Barnes have fun in Triple-A. It all started with the locker room setup. He turned the clubhouse into a nightclub, where if they won, they turned off the overhead lights and added strobe lights, flashing LED lights, a smoke machine and, of course, some loud music. The only rule with the Isotopes Clubhouse Club? Everyone has to stay for at least three songs following a win. He bought Spikeball and played with a bunch of his teammates prior to games on the field. "That really translated onto the field. All of that really corny stuff worked. Actually, it wasn't corny because it worked," Suchon says. Aside from having a grade-A personality, Barnes was also able to play in big moments.

In a 10-inning thriller against the Fresno Grizzlies on August 24, 2016, Barnes played hero in more ways than one to seal the Isotopes' fifth victory in a row—their 15th in the last 17 games. Barnes's heroics began with a diving grab in the third frame, when Max Stassi led off the inning of the scoreless contest. It would rob Stassi of extra bases and allowed Albuquerque to take the lead in the bottom of the third. What Suchon recalls, though, began in extra innings.

Tyler White stepped in the box to lead things off and got ahold of a ball on an 0–2 count, sending it looping into the right-center alley. Barnes gathered a full head of steam, leapt horizontally and, with his glove arm fully extended, made the catch before sliding into center field. That ensured that no one scored in the top of the 10th, and fate would have it that Barnes would bat in the bottom half of the inning. With a runner on first and one out, Barnes took the first pitch for a ball upstairs, and here's Suchon's call on the 1–0: "Hit high, deep left-center field, that one is GOOONE! Brandon Barnes, two-run, walk-off bomb, 'Topes win! 'Topes win! 6–4 is the final. The celebration is on! There goes the water cooler, crank up the fog machine. Club Isotopes is about to get rocking tonight, folks!" Albuquerque fans know the game as the Brandon Barnes game, and it is one of the top performances Suchon recalls from his broadcasting career.

Looking back on his career so far, Suchon would tell young broadcasters to make sure they enjoy the job. He believes sometimes you can get caught up in trying too hard to be a professional broadcaster. He says that when he first started, he tried so hard to do the fundamental things, which are important, but didn't spend enough time trying to enjoy what was occurring every day. He sees himself as a salesman of the team and of the sport, and says that in order to be the best you can be, you have to enjoy it.

"I put a sticker next to my TV that says, 'Let them hear you smiling.' It's impossible. They can't hear you smiling—they can hear you laughing, but not smiling. The idea is that when you smile, you come across with more warmth and energy and hopefully that makes people enjoy the broadcast more."

Now that you know the fundamentals of Joshua Suchon's career,

Play-by-Play from the Minors

from Watertown to Albuquerque, as a broadcaster, a coach to younger broadcasters and much more, you can fully appreciate him wanting to tell the tale of a historic moment for America. The one moment in baseball history that Josh would like to call is simple: "I would call the first game Jackie Robinson played in the major leagues. I would try to call it in a way that would set the stage for what this historical moment means, but also just describe what it is that I'm seeing. How the crowd is reacting, how teammates are reacting and how the other team is reacting. I'd tell his story. He was an All-American football player at UCLA, he served his country and played semi-professional football, but most importantly, I'd describe what this moment means to baseball, what this moment means for America and how the fans are reacting to it."

11

Zack Bayrouty

Currently with the Sacramento River Cats
Previously with the Stockton Ports and Reno Aces

Like Suchon, Zack Bayrouty has a different career trajectory than most of the broadcasters in this book. Although the difference between Suchon writing and Bayrouty doing media relations at the start of their careers is more want-based than anything, the two both spent time out of broadcasting before breaking into the industry on the mic. Bayrouty grew up in Worcester, Massachusetts, not far from other broadcasters in Minor League Baseball, but he didn't feel pulled toward broadcasting until he found himself in a booth in Jupiter, Florida.

Coming from the second most populous city in Massachusetts and living just 40 miles away from Boston, Bayrouty grew up used to the bustle of city life and with four significant sporting teams that he learned to live and die by. He was a diehard fan of the Bruins, Celtics, Red Sox and Patriots, and swears that the Red Sox World Series in 2004 was especially special for him. He started working in baseball in January of 2005. "2004 was like my last clean series of just being a fan without working in baseball."

It was a euphoric moment for Zack, who recalls the pain of the American League Championship Series loss a year earlier to the Yankees. "When Aaron Boone hit that home run off of Tim Wakefield in the ALCS, I sat down on the curb of where I was living at the time and cried. That was as a college kid. At that point I figured that I'd never see the Red Sox win the World Series in my life," Bayrouty says. Then, of course, when the team actually won, it was the biggest thrill for not just him, but the entire city of Boston, which reveled after the Curse of the Bambino was finally broken.

Like most broadcasters, Bayrouty's fandom has transformed since his employment in baseball. That soft spot for a favorite team growing

157

up remains, but you appreciate other organizations a lot more as you work with them. One thing that will forever be a part of the Sacramento broadcaster's style is the influence of listening to and watching Boston sports. He only listened to those Boston guys while growing up. "I like that it happened that way, because I think my taste for broadcasters evolved as I moved along," Bayrouty explains. Despite not planning on getting into broadcasting while he was in college, he took a class at Northeastern University with Joe Castiglione in the fall of 2004. He just needed to fill a credit and he wanted to fill it taking a class with someone he grew up listening to on the radio.

Bayrouty wasn't starstruck by the broadcaster, but he learned a lot about why Castiglione did what he did. The Red Sox broadcaster Bayrouty is most influenced by is Sean McDonough, though. "Sean has an easy way about him and there's a quality about him that I just can't put my finger on, but you just felt like he was your guy or Boston's guy," Zack says. "There is just an ease about him that I appreciated."

The Massachusetts native also learned from Gil Santos, who broadcast Patriots games for 36 seasons. Zack thinks about him a lot because of how sound his fundamentals were and how comfortable he was when speaking on-air. Santos was one of the more layered broadcasters of major sports, and a lot of that comes from his start doing news for radio—which is what Bayrouty wanted to do, write for the news. When Bayrouty was younger and listening to the radio hoping for a snow day, if he was lucky, Gil Santos would read his school's name over the air.

Santos's biggest influence on Zack's career came through broadcasting football, though. When the East Coaster moved out west initially, he broadcast a lot of local football games, something he had never done before. When he went on air, he noticed that he was using a lot of the wording that Gil had used in Patriots games. Instead of "direct snap to Brady," it was direct snap to some other quarterback. For Patriots fans, he also set up field goals the same way that Santos would: "Snap. Ball down, kick on the way. It's up and it's good."

Zack's baseball influence didn't really come to the fore until he got to Stockton. Yes, he listened to and watched Red Sox games, but he did that because he was a fan, not because he was analyzing how to broadcast a game from the professionals who were on-air. At Northeastern, students had to complete a co-op program in their industry to graduate. The school year was divided into trimesters rather than semesters to help students achieve that. The idea was that for two trimesters students would take traditional classes, but for the third trimester of

11. Zack Bayrouty

Zack Bayrouty wasn't originally trying to become a broadcaster. He just wanted to work in media relations. More than a decade after his internship in Florida ended, he's on the opposite coast, working for his third team, the Sacramento River Cats (photograph courtesy of Zack Bayrouty).

the year, they would find an internship or a real-world work experience where they could get hands-on training for their future career. The first internship for Bayrouty, who was aspiring to be a writer, was in the financial section of the *Boston Globe*—a far cry from the sports world.

Bayrouty's second internship, which began in January 2005, was closer to the mark, though. He stayed in Jupiter, Florida, at Roger Dean Stadium, which served as the spring training facility of the Florida Marlins and the St. Louis Cardinals. From January to August, Bayrouty helped in the press box for spring training and then, during baseball season, he ran the press box for the Jupiter Hammerheads, who were the High-A affiliate of the Marlins at the time. In other words, he made the schedule for the game day workers who were there; wrote the game notes, game recaps and previews; and organized any media requests that came through. He didn't do anything broadcast-related, but this was on par with what the Northeastern product wished to do when he graduated. Through that experience, Bayrouty met Bo Fulginiti, the broadcaster of the Daytona Cubs at the time.

159

Play-by-Play from the Minors

Because the stadium housed two teams, Fulginiti, who is now out of baseball and is a pastor of Cedar Street Baptist Church in Metter, Georgia, would travel to Roger Dean Stadium quite frequently. About halfway through the season, Fulginiti asked Bayrouty if he could come on the radio for a few innings so he would have someone he could banter with during the game. Bayrouty didn't have much to do since the Hammerheads weren't playing, so he figured he'd give it a try.

"We just hit it off. I had never been on a radio broadcast before, but I was comfortable enough with him," Bayrouty recollects. "It was to the point where afterwards he said, 'Man, I really enjoyed having you on with me and I think you'd be pretty good at this.'" Later, Fulginiti relayed that he was pretty confident that he would get a broadcast job with the Stockton Ports, across the country in California. He asked if Zack wanted to join him as his number two in his first year, to which Zack agreed. So, he went back to Northeastern in the fall, graduated in December of 2005 and joined Fulginiti in Stockton one month later to start his Minor League Baseball career. As fortune would have it, Fulginiti left baseball the next offseason and the Ports asked Bayrouty if he wanted to take his mentor's place.

He did, and he spent the next 13 years in Stockton before making the move to Triple-A Reno in the winter of 2020. Because he really didn't plan on getting into baseball radio as a profession until he agreed to move to Stockton, Zack's influence came from his time in Stockton. There was a local radio station that aired a replay of the San Francisco Giants broadcast at midnight every night, so Zack would listen to Jon Miller and Dave Flemming call the game from earlier that evening on his way home from the ballpark.

"I gravitated towards their style," Bayrouty explains. "I think Jon Miller and especially Dave Flemming had a big influence on me because I didn't really know what I was doing at the time. So I thought, here's the best broadcast in baseball and I can basically take this formula and make it work for me, and that's how I developed my baseball style."

It wasn't until the Ports extended the offer to him that he truthfully thought he wanted to broadcast baseball for a living. Even when he was a broadcast intern for Bo the year prior, he still thought that maybe being the PR guy for a major league team would be the best long-term job for him. Because of that, Zack has a different perspective on what makes a broadcaster great, because he was looking at the position as an outside observer as he went through the motions to become the broadcaster he is today.

"The most important thing for a baseball broadcaster, major league

160

11. Zack Bayrouty

or minor league, is to give the details of the game and to do it well," Bayrouty says. "I know it sounds boring and basic, but if you can give the details of what's going on and paint the picture in a way that brings everything to life for the listener and to do it with vivid detail, I believe that's the most important thing to build the trust of the audience." That leads back to Bayrouty's roots of wanting to be a "professional" journalist, or maybe, better phrased, a journalist who writes stories that get heavily edited and put in the Sunday first-edition sports section or on the 6 o'clock news rather than spoken over the airwaves live with no filter.

That trust of the listener is so important because once you build that, you can do what Zack figures to be the second most important job of a play-by-play broadcaster, and that is to tell good stories. Remember, at the root of all journalism, we are just professional storytellers. A good journalist is able to tell stories of players or people close to the game that can draw interest from the listener or the reader or whatever medium they are trying to tell the story through.

Those stories take many different stops, and that is the beauty of radio. To a listener, their eyes see whatever is beyond their dashboard or past the ledge of their front porch or out the window of their living room. It's Zack's job to try to bring the unique features and the quirks of a team's city or promotional night through the listener's speakers and convey those to them. It doesn't get much easier than when Reno's broadcaster used to travel to Lake Elsinore, his favorite ballpark to visit. Pete Lehr Field at Lake Elsinore Diamond was built in 1994 and has a capacity of 8,000 fans for a game. It has 6,000 red permanent seats in a single grandstand that tracks from first base to third base and that contrasts with the cement walls and columns and green roofing of the suite level directly above it.

"They originally designed it for a Triple-A team, so it had a bigger feel to it," Bayrouty explains. "They would always draw so well, especially on weekends. There's nothing like a sold-out game at Lake Elsinore. The press box is so far up that you need an elevator to get there. You have your own booth and you can hang a microphone down. It just sounds amazing." So, when Bayrouty had to travel, the press box at Lake Elsinore certainly felt as close to home as anything could, and it allowed him to gather plenty of strong tape and highlights to use for the future.

What made Lake Elsinore Bayrouty's favorite city had everything to do with the ballpark and not much to do with the surrounding attractions. His favorite restaurant was in a different town. Bakersfield was home to the Bakersfield Blaze in the California League through 2016.

161

Play-by-Play from the Minors

The stadium experience in Bakersfield is nowhere near as enjoyable as the one in Lake Elsinore. The sun sets beyond centerfield, so oftentimes, games have delays for the sun to set so it is safe for the catcher and hitters to look at the pitcher and have the ability to see what he is throwing. What Bakersfield did have, though, is one of the best Chinese restaurants that Bayrouty has come across in his travels. Rice Bowl is located across the street from Dewar's Candy Shop and about a block over from Pork-Chop & Bubba's BBQ. They're a bit of a hike from the stadium if you're walking; you have to cross Route 178 and the Kern River to get there.

The average dish is between $10 and $15, but they come with massive portions, your choice of meat and carb. If it is your first time going to Rice Bowl, then Bayrouty's suggestion is, "I would get the lunch combo that comes with chow mein and fried rice. Then you get any meat you want. It varies for me, sometimes I get the orange chicken or broccoli and beef. It really just depends on the day. The big thing is that you always get a ton of food for like 10 bucks." It helps that the restaurant was walking distance from the hotel and the food was great. Bayrouty always viewed it as a treat when he had the chance to eat at Rice Bowl, and to this day, if he's driving through Bakersfield, he makes sure to allot enough time to make a stop at his favorite Chinese restaurant.

Bayrouty is no stranger to traveling and hitting the highway in the Southwestern portion of the United States. Outside of his time in the California League, he also has called basketball in the region for a decade. Despite all the trips, the East Coaster is incredibly fortunate and has never had a major delay or a bus breakdown. Early on, he remembers, a bus got a flat tire and the team had to wait for around two hours for it to get replaced, but the bus still functioned and had working air conditioning, so the team just picked a movie and watched it on the bus before continuing their journey.

The one time a bus broke down while Zack was with Stockton, he wasn't on the bus. The team was leaving Bakersfield to go back home for the All-Star break, and Zack and his then-girlfriend (now wife) decided that while they were already in Southern California, they would use the All-Star break to visit San Diego. "Their bus broke down on I-5, so I got a bunch of pictures from guys saying that the bus broke down. Meanwhile, I'm sitting in San Diego thinking, 'Oh man, that sucks,'" Zack remembers. So, in this situation, he may have felt more like the general manager or team president who gets the phone call from a broadcaster or trainer explaining that they are on the side of the road and may need help to get out of their current predicament.

11. Zack Bayrouty

Getting those texts and having that interaction with players is one of the underrated perks of being a broadcaster. You get to meet so many people in this industry from countless backgrounds, and they also just so happen to be world-class athletes. One of those guys that Zack has had the opportunity to be around is Sean Doolittle. The South Dakota native was selected 41st overall in the 2007 draft out of Virginia, and in college he was a two-way player. In other words, he both pitched and played first base as a Cavalier. The Athletics wanted him to stay in the batter's box after draft day, though, so for his first few years in Minor League Baseball, he did.

Sean is a special player and was a first-round pick because of his talent, but he made it to Major League Baseball because of his work ethic. Not only is he the most talented player that Bayrouty has seen, but he also is one of the top locker room guys that Zack has watched go through Stockton's clubhouse. Our broadcaster had the opportunity to see him come through Stockton twice, a few years apart from each other.

He first came through Stockton in 2008. He hit third in the lineup and played first base. The slugger held a .305 average and popped 18 homers in 86 games. Doolittle hit right in front of Chris Carter, who never made the majors but in 2008 led Class A-Advanced hitters with 39 home runs. He had 10 more than Ryan Strieby, who had the second most homers in the California, Carolina and Florida State Leagues with 29 that year.

Doolittle was such a feared hitter in the California League that when future Chicago Cub David Patton and the Modesto Nuts played Stockton on May 4, 2008, and the game went to the 11th inning tied 5–5 with a runner on second base and a pair of outs, the Nuts intentionally walked Doolittle to face off against Carter.

"After that, Sean turned to Chris in the on-deck circle and said something to him like, 'Let's f-ing go,' or 'Let's end this right now.' Then Chris came up and hit a walk-off three-run homer," Bayrouty recalls. "They intentionally walked Sean, that's how good he was. I still maintain that Sean was the most complete hitter on that '08 Stockton Ports team that won the Cal League Championship and had an absolutely stacked lineup."

What really got Sean through to the bigs was how hard he works. Bayrouty can remember leaving the ballpark late one evening—at nearly midnight when no one else other than the cleaning crew was at the stadium—and hearing the loud smacks of someone hitting in the cages. He went over to investigate, and sure enough, there was the lefty, hitting

163

in the pen because he had struck out twice in the game earlier that day. Doolittle was always willing to put in the extra work, even when no one was watching. That's why after he injured his knee in 2009 while he was hitting .270 in AAA, he rehabbed and was able to come back as a relief pitcher and find some incredible success. He's now won a World Series and had two MLB All-Star seasons after being told he wouldn't be able to consistently hit again.

That made the second time Doolittle came back to Stockton, in 2011, even more impressive. This time, the lefty reliever didn't stay long. He pitched in just six games before getting the call-up to AA. In those six games, he worked 10.1 frames and whiffed 21 batters while allowing just one earned run to score. He was electric for the Ports, and it didn't stop there. At three levels in minor league ball before he was eventually promoted to the Oakland A's in 2012, Doolittle had a 0.72 ERA and 48 strikeouts in just 25 innings. He threw up video game numbers while pitching for the first time in nearly five years. Not only that, but he was very approachable, which is rare for high-caliber players.

"He wasn't afraid to talk about anything ... with you. He was big into books and I had a lot of conversations with him about his process in getting back on the mound with the A's," Zack remembers. Zack says that at the end of the day, above anything else, Doolittle always felt thankful and lucky. He felt lucky that he could still play the game and was thankful to the A's for leaving him on the 40-man roster while he was rehabbing, which allowed him to climb back up the ladder more quickly.

While most baseball fans know about the *Star Wars*–obsessed lefty who has pitched in Oakland and Washington over the years, most probably haven't heard of Archie Gilbert. After attending Cal State East Bay, a university that is part of California's 23-campus state college system, he was signed as a free agent by the Oakland Athletics in 2007. He ended up playing for the 2008 Stockton Ports team that won the California League title. He was the lead-off hitter for that team, setting the table for Josh Donaldson, Sean Doolittle and Chris Carter.

"Archie set the tone for what was a really, really talented lineup that year. I mean, there was a major prospect at nearly every spot in the order," Bayrouty recalls. The outfielder also played a massive role in what was the best moment, or, better yet, series of moments that Bayrouty has witnessed on the diamond. The 2008 California League divisional playoff series saw the A's affiliate matched up against a stacked San Jose Giants team that included a lot of the young guys who would go on to win three World Series in the next eight seasons.

164

11. Zack Bayrouty

The Ports dropped the first game of the series 5–3 after ceding four runs in the bottom of the eighth to San Jose. The team had their own late-inning magic in Game 2, though. Trailing 6–4 in the ninth, the Ports were able to score three runs off the bats of Josh Donaldson and Chris Carter to win 7–6. That set up an ever-important Game 3 in a best-of-five series.

Once again, the Ports were down late, trailing 6–2 entering the eighth frame. That's where Archie came in. Gilbert drew a two-out walk to load the bases, which caused San Jose to go to the bullpen. Josh Horton, the next batter for the Ports, laced a ball into the left-center gap that scored a pair and sent Gilbert around third. The throw came in from left field to short and then was relayed to Buster Posey at the plate in front of Gilbert, but Gilbert lowered his shoulder and tried to score the run anyway.

"Gilbert bulldozed Posey," Bayrouty recalls. "Archie didn't care. It was a two-run game. That was an important game and that embodied who he was. He was there to win and he was there to compete. He didn't care who you were, and he was a big, big reason why the Ports won the championship that year." Posey was able to hold onto the ball for the third out of the inning, but the effort play from Archie charged up the team and they were able to score three runs again in the ninth to win 7–6 for a second consecutive night, stunning the Giants.

The Ports would drop Game 4 after a late rally from San Jose, but then Stockton cruised to a 9–4 victory in Game 5 after scoring seven runs in the first two frames. "That series featured a bit of everything. The series went five games, had back-to-back walk-off wins, a massive collision at the plate with first-rounder Buster Posey," Bayrouty explains. "There was high drama and great players in that series. No matter where I go in life, even if I'm lucky to call a World Series at some point in, I'm still going to remember the '08 North Division Championship Series."

That 2008 Stockton Ports team is the only championship-winning team that Bayrouty has broadcast for, but if you ask him, the best team he has ever worked for was the 2014 Stockton Ports. "I'll go to my grave wondering how in the hell that team didn't win a Cal League Championship," Bayrouty laments. The infield for that team was absolutely stacked. A Class A-Advanced team, it had a multi-year future major leaguer at each position. Bruce Maxwell, a German backstop, spent three years in Oakland. Matt Olson played first and has since established himself as a Gold Glove–caliber fielder with incredible power at the major league level. Chad Pinder played second and became Oakland's

165

super-utility player for six years, providing a consistent bat off the bench for a low-budget team that continually competes for the AL West crown. Daniel Robertson manned short, and broke into the bigs with Tampa Bay as a 23-year-old. He's in his third season with the Milwaukee Brewers at age 29. Finally, Ryon Healy played at the hot corner, opposite Matt Olson, similar to what he did in his first two seasons prior to getting shipped to Seattle and eventually Milwaukee before retiring.

Outside of the stacked infield, the team also had Michael Ynoa to bolster the rotation and a rehab stint from Eric O'Flaherty to help ground the pitching staff. The team didn't win the first-half title, but finished the year 85–55 and outscored opponents by 131 runs over the course of the season. Because they didn't win the first half of the season, they had to play Visalia in a best-of-three series to advance to the championship series.

They lost the first game of the series and then found themselves down 2–1 in the bottom of the ninth inning of a win-or-go-home game. Daniel Robertson walked to start the inning. After that, Chad Pinder singled and Matt Olson walked to load the bases with no one out. It was an ideal situation to walk-off the game. Fate wasn't with the heart of Stockton's lineup, though. Renato Núñez, who platooned with Healy at third in the second half of the season, grounded into a 4–2 fielder's choice that forced Robertson out at home to keep the score 2–1. Then Beau Taylor popped an infield fly to give the Ports just a single out remaining. Next, Healy came to the plate and was set down with a swinging strikeout to end the Ports' playoff hopes.

"Visalia had to get through Beau Taylor, Renato Núñez and Ryan Healy to get three unproductive outs with the bases loaded to win that series," Bayrouty says. "That, to me, was the best team on paper. It was nuts. Everyone knew how special that team was, and they went on to win the Texas League the next year, but they fell short in Stockton."

That '14 team fell short at the end of the season, but in 2009, Zack had a team fall short in a single game that felt as though it was a full season. Bayrouty called the longest game in California League history, a 21-inning contest between the Ports and the High Desert Mavericks that lasted seven hours and 34 minutes. Our broadcaster learned about curfew rules in the California League, which have since changed. Back in 2009, though, a game wasn't allowed to go into a new inning after the stroke of midnight, and the two teams would have to resume the contest the following day—similar to when a game gets suspended due to inclement weather.

166

11. Zack Bayrouty

The first night, the two teams played 14 innings and after five hours and one minute, the score was tied 5–5, so they went back to the drawing board the following day, Friday, at 6:05. The Mavericks almost won the game in the 17th inning, scoring the go-ahead run off a bases-loaded walk, but in the home half, Stockton was able to load the bases with a single out and Shane Keough tied it up with a sacrifice fly that scored Frank Martinez. The game marched on for four more innings. The second day of play lasted two hours and 33 minutes—almost as long as the average game time in Minor League Baseball. Then it happened. Joseph Dunigan was on second and Alex Liddi was on first for the High Desert Mavericks in the top of the 21st. The team decided to go for a double steal, and the Ports catcher, Raul Padron, overthrew second base, allowing Dunigan to trot home to put the Mavericks in front, 7–6. Stockton had a pair of singles in the bottom of the 21st, but they weren't able to score the run, and the Ports lost the longest game (by time) in California League history.

Bayrouty learned a lot during that game about curfews in the California League and how to keep an audience engaged in a lengthy contest. A trip to Lancaster on a Thursday evening in the late 2000s would teach him something different. He'd learn about wind speed and how it can affect pricing in Minor League Baseball.

The JetHawks tried a promotion to get fans through the gates each Tuesday based on wind speeds. Beginning in 2006, the JetHawks launched their Tumbleweed Tuesday specials. Prior to the first Tuesday home game of the season, the front office staff, with local meteorologists, would measure the wind speed and would discount tickets by 10 cents for each mile per hour of wind. For example, on April 18, 2006, the wind speed recording read 20 MPH, so the JetHawks took $2 off each $6 reserve ticket for fans who would attend their Tuesday games in 2006.

"Yeah, they were out in the Mojave Desert and they would get to that point where they would do that promotional night. They didn't do it in their later years, but early on that was a promotion that the franchise would do," Zack remembers. That's one of the more goofy promotions in Minor League Baseball, but in Stockton, they tended to engage with fans in a more serious way.

Bayrouty will tell you that he is a historian of the game. He loves to read and research baseball events that occurred before he was born. That makes it easy for him to name his favorite promotional night he's helped organize during his career. The California League has a lot of

167

history, and the Stockton Ports can claim their fair share, according to a 2014 *Baseball Reference* article about the league. It makes sense that Zack became a big part of reaching out to former players and managers to attend the Ports' Alumni Night each year.

"People came from all over and had played for Stockton as far back as the '40s and '50s. Being a guy that appreciates baseball history, it was so cool to meet some of these guys," Bayrouty tells. "There was an original Stockton Port named Charlie Strada who played in 1941, and he played with one of the DiMaggio brothers who played in Stockton. He had stories to tell from 1941 and it was amazing." He remembers those as the best promotional nights Stockton would host. Their success was due to how they resonated so much within the community without having to employ a gimmick to bring fans into the gates.

Most of the work for the night is done early in the year. The Ports have a database of all their alumni and how to contact them. Each year after they pick the evening for Alumni Night, they'll send out a mass email invitation to anyone who would like to come back. The Ports offer to put them up in a hotel for a night if they return for the game and whoever comes back typically gets to throw out a first pitch or is announced to the crowd during the game. Overall, the night markets itself because the Ports have branded themselves as a team and Stockton as a city that is proud of its minor league history. The night is normally a resounding success.

Our broadcaster usually invites one or two alumni into the booth during the game, and he has been very fortunate to have guests who have gone on to have success both on and off the baseball field. In fact, one year, Ron Shelton, who was drafted out of high school in the 39th round of the 1966 draft, came on-air to talk with Zack. Shelton spent parts of three seasons in the late '60s with the Ports and never made it to the majors, retiring after five seasons in baseball, but people may better know Ron for what he did in 1988. After baseball, the Californian got involved in screenwriting and directing. His biggest credit came for being the screenwriter and director of the movie *Bull Durham*, which he based on his own experiences in Minor League Baseball, most of which came through Stockton.

As a baseball historian, Bayrouty is particularly fascinated by 1950s New York City baseball. Three teams playing in the city, the cultural relevance of Jackie Robinson's debut and the way those teams operated before leaving the city are all so intriguing, but if he had the chance to call just one baseball moment, the Massachusetts–bred broadcaster would go back to his roots. He would call Carlton Fisk's infamous walk-off home run in Game 6 of the 1975 World Series.

He would start with the basics by thinking of Dick Stockton's original call of the game. It was simple enough, he remembers: "It's a long drive, if it stays fair," then the ball clangs off the foul pole atop the Green Monster in left field at Fenway and Stockton bellows, "Home run!" Bayrouty really liked that call because it added a layer of suspense to what was happening, "I think Stockton gives you that by not saying too much."

After that, when Bayrouty thinks about adding the layers of information he would sprinkle into the at-bat, he would talk about the anticipation to get to this point for not only the players, but also the fans. The two teams had to wait out three rainouts with the Cincinnati Reds leading the series 3–2 before they could play Game 6, and then they sat in the 12th inning, further ratcheting up the anxiety for both fan bases, making them wait to find out what the outcome of the game and potentially the series would be.

"I think everybody forgets about Bernie Carbo's home run in the eighth that tied it," Bayrouty remarks. He's referring to the outfielder who pinch-hit for pitcher Roger Moret with two outs in the bottom of the eighth. The Red Sox were trailing 6–3 and the count was 2–2 when Carbo smacked the ball deep to center field to tie the game and allow Fisk and the Red Sox a chance at some extra-inning heroics.

"I think the game in its fullest context between the Red Sox and the Big Red Machine with the names and drama that was associated between the two teams is important, and when the game goes deep into the 12th, there's an exclamation point with a home run over the Green Monster that's just fair. That whole game is just baseball magic to me. Everything that happened, happened on the grandest stage in baseball," Bayrouty explains.

It makes sense that the guy who loves baseball history would talk about the two storied clubs in a franchise-altering series for both teams and try to bring you the whole context of that World Series and what had happened leading up to that incredible point where Carlton Fisk shocked the world in one of baseball's most famous moments.

12

Alex Cohen

Currently with the Iowa Cubs
Previously with the Bowling Green Hot Rods,
Idaho Falls Chukars, Melbourne Aces and
Huntsville Stars

Zack Bayrouty had a far journey to move from Massachusetts to earn his first job in Florida. He had an even farther move to get his first play-by-play gig in California, but all of that seems relatively small when you look at the path of the voice of the Iowa Cubs, Alex Cohen. A native of the suburbs of Philadelphia, Cohen has seen his career take him as far as Melbourne, Australia, and he's moved to Alabama, out west to Idaho and back closer, where he has resided since 2017 in Iowa.

Cohen grew up in a sports-centric family and friend group, and was a diehard Phillies fan who played high school baseball, making baseball the first (and last) sport he ever broadcast. He started broadcasting younger than most people do, as a founding member of the Sports Broadcasting Club at Upper Dublin High School. In the club, Cohen was part of quite the prestigious group of broadcasters. One of the three main broadcasters, which included Cohen, who has now broadcast professional baseball for the better part of 10 years, is Josh Getzoff, who is the radio play-by-play broadcaster for the Pittsburgh Penguins today. Getzoff has been in that role since he was named the TV Sportscaster of the Year while serving as WICD's sports director in Champaign, Illinois. Another member of that club was Stephen Watson, who is currently a host on the Bally Sports Wisconsin cable channel. Before that, he was a sports reporter, working the Big 12 Sports team at WISN Milwaukee, where he won an Emmy for his work.

"It was really cool getting to work with all these guys that have had a lot of success in the same field I'm in while we were all still in high school," Cohen gushes. "Seeing Josh go to the Penguins and win

12. Alex Cohen

Alex Cohen has journeyed halfway around the world and back to get to Iowa. After working in the Pioneer League and the Australian Baseball League, he's made Principal Park in Des Moines his home (photograph courtesy Alex Cohen).

a ring in his first two years while calling games with a Hall of Fame broadcaster in Mike Lange has been great. And seeing Stephen bounce around like I have, going to Vermont, South Dakota, and Wisconsin, has been great. He just got married and is about to have a kid. Seeing all of us go through this progression and lean back and forth on each other for now 15 years has been pretty amazing."

With such a prestigious group of co-conspirators in high school, it's no wonder that Alex was challenged consistently early on and was able to quickly find success in the world of broadcasting. It was easy for Cohen to decide his next step after high school, which was attending Indiana University. A lot of people he went to school with went there, and it has a beautiful campus with good sports.

Play-by-Play from the Minors

"I went to visit and it was a 72-degree day in March," Cohen remembers. "So, I fell in love with the campus immediately. It also doesn't hurt that Joe Buck went there. I wanted to get into broadcasting and the biggest name in broadcasting at the time attended IU, so that was pretty cool for me too."

Cohen's journey to baseball started pretty close to home. A journey to a Lehigh Valley IronPigs game at Coca-Cola Park took about 45 minutes for the Pennsylvanian, so even though he started as an unpaid gameday intern for his sophomore and junior years of college, it was a pretty easy decision to get his feet wet. Many minor league employees are familiar with the phrase "other duties as assigned," but Alex was introduced to that slogan right out of the gate. His first task working for the IronPigs was to grab Jon Schaeffer, one of the team's broadcasters, a chicken sandwich from the main concourse because Schaeffer wasn't a fan of the press box food that particular day.

"Yeah, that was my first job on my first day," Cohen laughs. "It went from grabbing chicken sandwiches to helping them with social media, then doing pre- and post-game interviews, writing stories for the program and work back in the studio my first year. My second year we transitioned into a lot more of the on-air work." Cohen is still friends with Schaeffer to this day and chuckles as he remembers one of their first interactions. He lights up in a different way when he thinks about his first professional game on-air, though.

"When the lead broadcaster, Matt Provence, and his wife were having their second kid, I had the chance to fill in on a few games when the team was up in Rochester in 2010, and that was my first professional baseball game that I ever did." The next step for Cohen was to set his own path. He graduated from Indiana and went west to the Frontier League, and, more specifically, the Gateway Grizzlies.

The next stop of Cohen's journey was Huntsville, Alabama, to work for the Stars, who have since rebranded to the Biloxi Shuckers. A long way from home in his first gig where he ran the show after college, Cohen noticed that he had begun to develop some bad habits on-air. The Stars' ownership group decided to sell the team following the 2013 season, so Alex determined that was a good time to step back into an internship role to right the ship. He was happy with his overall development, but felt that he needed to take one more step before making another large leap. That step was sitting behind two incredible broadcasters in Oakland as a broadcast and media relations assistant.

"I just sat in the booth every home game and listened to Ken

12. Alex Cohen

Korach and Vince Cotroneo do their thing," Cohen remembers. "I just learned so much. I learned how to broadcast. I learned that I wanted to get back into broadcasting and I wanted that mic to be dangling in front of my face again." That led our broadcaster to Melbourne, Australia, where he took the mic back up for the Melbourne Aces. He'll tell you that, unfortunately, it was a year prior to Ronald Acuña's tenure in the Down Under. While Cohen learned a lot of the nuts and bolts again in Oakland, listening to a pair of incredible major league broadcasters, he was instilled with an incredibly important lesson during his summer in Australia: above all else, you have to know your audience and how you can best relate to and entertain the people who are listening.

"Calling baseball in Australia is really unique. People like baseball out there, but it's not the most popular sport out there, it's like the 10th most popular sport," Cohen explains. "So, I get out there and the first day, I'm calling a 6–4–3 double play and after the broadcast, they're like, 'What's a 6–4–3 double play?'" Cohen freaked out initially, but then realized that he had to break it down at a more simplistic level so that the casual fan could understand what's going on.

"I really think that helped me to understand that not every listener is like me. There are other people too, and it's our job to help the listener understand and to relay the information to them." After the 2014 season abroad, Cohen earned a fresh start to bring him to where he is today. He came back stateside and broadcast for a season for the Idaho Falls Chukers, the Royals' rookie ball affiliate in the Pioneer League, then went to the Midwest League for a pair of years in Bowling Green, Kentucky, to work for the Hot Rods before making his way to the Iowa Cubs in November of 2017.

While the Philadelphia native's journey may seem like a long and winding road that took many twists and turns before he made it to where he is today, his early idols were much closer to home. The Philadelphia sports scene is full of ravenous, passionate fans and it only makes sense that the broadcasters who covered those sports for a long time were extremely talented and passionate individuals. In that sense, Cohen didn't have to do anything crazy to get a taste of good commentary behind the mic, and the two individuals that he grew up idolizing were none other than Merrill Reese and Harry Kalas, who broadcast for the Eagles and Phillies, respectively. Reese is best-known for his signature "It's gooooood!" call during made field goals and is the longest-tenured active NFL play-by-play broadcaster. He started with the Phillies in 1977 following a stint in the navy after graduating from

Play-by-Play from the Minors

Temple University. Kalas's career was born in the same era. The Ford C. Frick Award winner played for the Astros in the '60s and began calling games for the Phillies in 1971, and did so until his death in 2009. He had a propensity for the big moments, which almost strictly contradicted his mellow style outside of those moments. The Chicago native broadcast six no-hitters, six National League Championship Series and three World Series, including one in the fall before his death. He was best-known for his "That's way outta here!" call that he used on monumental homers and to punctuate Mike Schmidt's 500th career blast in 1987.

"We would turn on the television on mute and just listen to them [on the radio]," Alex explains. "Harry was the soundtrack to my summer and Merrill was the soundtrack to my fall." Both broadcasters were so much more than just entertainment for Cohen; these two defined his childhood. "Merrill was the guy during Sundays doing chores, he was the person who would get me into trouble, because I was listening to him rather than doing the work. Then Harry was the guy that I stayed up past my bedtime to listen to. It was every day for Harry and for Merrill it was every Sunday, those were my guys growing up."

Although Cohen says that he wishes he had the voice of Kalas, and the ability to imitate about three decades of smoking and whiskey, one thing that is much more controllable that he has adopted from his baseball hero was the genuine happiness that you can hear through the speakers of the one-time player and longtime broadcaster every time the players took the green grass on the field. "The pure professional joy that he had. Broadcasting with a smile on your face, which is something that you can imagine Harry doing. I try to do that in my own broadcasts," Cohen says.

We all wish to have untampered amounts of joy each time we sling on a headset to speak on air, but the reality is that everyone has bad days. Maybe it's the four tarp pulls as the sun keeps peeking through dark rainclouds for a break in the action that interrupt your day. Maybe you're feeling under the weather yourself or you had a long night with little sleep to prepare you for a long day. Whatever the case, in Oakland, Cohen learned the most important lesson he has learned while broadcasting, and it's the same lesson that made him idolize Kalas as a young kid.

"Vince Cotroneo gave the best piece of advice that I've ever gotten. Even if you're not having a good day or if you're tired or if your team has lost eight straight, go into every game and every inning with a smile

12. Alex Cohen

on your face. If you're smiling, the fans will be smiling. It's that trickle-down that creates your entire broadcast," Cohen explains. And plus, what's not to love about working in Minor League Baseball?

Part of the fun of the industry that can put a smile on anyone's face—even if you aren't a fan of the sport—are the wonky promotions that run rampant through the system. You have to go back to 2013, Cohen's first season in Huntsville, to find the most memorable promotion that he's seen. While most wacky promotions can bring a smile to your face, this one may have added a bit more stress to Cohen's day than it was worth. The Huntsville Stars wanted to go all out for their 2013 Independence Day Celebration, so they decided to hold a Second Amendment Night at Joe Davis Stadium. The promotion was supposed to encompass one of the liberties granted by the Bill of Rights, written more than 230 years ago by the United States' founding fathers. While the intention came from a sense of nationalism, the front office selected one of our nation's most polarizing political hot topics. The promotion did have a sponsor, Larry's Pistol & Pawn shop, with two locations in Alabama. The Huntsville location has a glass front with two neon revolvers facing each other outlined in red; above the two revolvers glows a blue neon "Larry's" marking the name. Their website in 2022 showed a picture of the owner, labeled "Larry appreciates your support of the 2nd amendment," on the front page. As far as Larry's involvement in the Huntsville Stars' Independence Day Celebration is concerned, the team announced that they would raffle off a Ruger American with a scope, a Ruger 22/45 MKIII and a Ruger 10/22 TD. If fans won the raffle, they would receive a gift certificate to pick up the weapon legally at the store. In addition to the raffle of three guns, members of the National Rifle Association would get free admission to that night's game.

The year 2013 was a different time for communication between broadcasters and the front office. Today, most buses have Wi-Fi on them and if not, mobile data can get email out from your phone so that you can stay in touch. Cohen did have a phone on him, though, so when the front office thought of the promotion and found a sponsor who wanted to push along the idea with some financial backing, the broadcaster received a warning call.

"I was heading from Jacksonville to Birmingham and I get a call from my general manager [Buck Rogers] saying, 'Hey, we're about to put out a press release. I know you're not going to be able to do it, but you can read it when you get back,'" Cohen remembers. "I ask, 'What's the press release?' and without hesitating, Rogers goes, 'It's a Second

Amendment Night at the ballpark.'" Cohen was shocked and had to ask again what was going on before Rogers reassured him that they were indeed having a Second Amendment Night at the ballpark. It didn't take long after his team released the promotion that Cohen started receiving emails. It's important to note that as the media relations contact, Cohen was receiving all the requests from different sources of media, but he was still on the bus and wouldn't see any of the emails for a pretty good chunk of time.

"I was just receiving email, after email, after email. From Huntsville media, from Nashville media outlets, from Deadspin, from ESPN, from protesters, from people who were for it and people who were against it," Cohen rattles the list off the top of his head rhythmically. As you can imagine, things got twisted and exaggerated quickly online, and the narrative of what was happening at the ballpark for Second Amendment Night was getting warped. Numerous national media outlets were writing scathing articles and sending profane emails to Cohen (who still couldn't answer any emails, as he was riding a bus to Birmingham). Things got so out of control that the front office needed to take action. "By the time I actually got to Birmingham, we ended up having to cancel the night. For a release that I didn't write, it ended up making for a very interesting 24–48 hours. I still get a few texts and emails each year of people asking if I remember some emails or articles from the event."

Yeah, that ended up being a pretty crazy night for Cohen and the Stars, but the broadcaster likes to lean into the fun and the promotions. At one of Cohen's later stops, in Bowling Green, Kentucky, the team used to donate jerseys to charity auctions each year. In 2017, they one-upped it, hosting their first ever Slime Fest. During the July 21 game vs. the Burlington Bees, the Hot Rods set up a table with each front office member's picture and a cup taped on top where fans could place money. The money was donated to the Norton Children's Hospital and the team announced that the top two-earning members would be slimed on the field following the game. Not only did Cohen participate in the contest, but he made it his mission to win the whole thing and sit on a tarp following the game as a bucket of green slime was poured on his head.

"Essentially, I used the entire three-hour radio broadcast as my infomercial," Cohen explains. "'If you want to see me get eviscerated after the game, completely embarrassed to have this concoction of slime poured on me that I have no idea what it is, you can donate to the Norton Children's Hospital here.' Well, I ended up tying our marketing director for the most money raised, and we both got slimed on the field after the game." That's what Minor League Baseball does best, finding creative ways to raise money. Cohen continues, "There are cancer research charities done everywhere in the world—and it's all for a great cause, but Minor League Baseball finds a way to make it interesting. I've shaved my head for cancer awareness, I've gotten slimed on the field, but it's about finding the creative ways to engage fans." In that Friday night game, 3,058 fans got to watch the Hot Rods win 9–7, and then the cheering continued for Alex as he was slimed on the field.

Good marketers can get fans to come to the park for a specific promotion that has garnered the interest of the general public, but at the core of Minor League Baseball, there's not quite anything that can beat out top prospects doing their thing while waiting for their chance at The Show. Even some of the best promotional nights piggyback off these big names doing well. Just think about one of the best giveaways a team can have: bobbleheads. The success of that giveaway is completely dependent upon the baseball player that is featured. In over 10 years in Minor League Baseball across all different levels, Cohen has had the opportunity to see a lot of players who deserve to be on a bobblehead. When thinking back, Cohen believes it would almost be easier to go year by year to pick some of the top players he's seen in the minors rather than just picking one out of the barrel to stand above the rest. There is a year that stands out above the rest for him: 2017.

In 2017, Alex was working with the Bowling Green Hot Rods, and their first trip of the year was against the Lansing Lugnuts, who were affiliated with the Toronto Blue Jays at the time. He remembers the hype around Bo Bichette. Bichette was a legacy player. His father, Dante, played 14 years in the majors and held a .299 average across 6,381 games, with the bulk of his career coming in Colorado as the franchise got off the ground in 1993. There was even more hype surrounding the younger Bichette because he was selected in the second round (66th overall) by Toronto in the 2016 MLB draft and he came out to a scorching start in the 2017 season. Prior to Bowling Green's trip to Lansing, the shortstop was mashing .400, scoring 11 runs in as many games while driving in another eight RBI.

"I remember he came up and he started off 0–2 with two strikeouts, and I thought, 'He must just be an A-ball hitter, he's not worth the hype'—whatever," Cohen remembers. The rest of that series, he went 4–11 with two doubles and five runs scored to propel the Lugnuts to a three-game series victory. "Then I was like, 'Okay. Shame on me.' But Bo Bichette and Vladimir Guerrero Jr. on the same team at the A-ball level was the most insane thing I've ever seen in my life. As the 3–4 hitters, they just obliterated pitches, pitcher's dreams, you name it—they did it." What some people may forget about that season in the Midwest League, as Jesse Goldberg-Strassler told us earlier when remembering the home run derby, is that Fernando Tatís, Jr., was playing for the Fort Wayne TinCaps as a 17-year-old. Like Bichette and Guerrero, he was a legacy player whose father had a ton of success in the majors, but just like those two, Tatís was bound to pave his own path, and 2017 was the year that a lot of fans who were watching in the heart of America at small A-ball stadiums were going to find out about this next generation of talent that was about to breach the majors.

Even for a wunderkind, there is bound to be a series of adjustments that have to be made as they transcend the various levels of play. For Tatís, the biggest adjustment of his baseball career came in A-ball. The shortstop hit .192 across his first 19 games in Fort Wayne. The TinCaps saw the Bowling Green Hot Rods at the start of April for four games and Tatís went 0–7 and had five strikeouts in his first two games. He finished the series 3–15 (.200) with no extra-base hits. The two teams would meet again later in the season. On August 11–13 when Fort Wayne visited Bowling Green, Tatís was hitting .270 entering the series. He had just come off a July where he had six homers, five triples and 19 RBI in 26 games, and Cohen was eager to see the young player again.

"I swear, he had a 5.0 WAR [wins above replacement] that series! He hit home runs, triples, diving plays, stolen bases. He did everything you could imagine on a baseball diamond," Cohen retells. "It was just like, 'Holy shit! This kid is incredible.' I was thinking, 'You traded *him* for James Shields? What did you do?'" The broadcaster is, of course, referring to the fact that the White Sox had signed Tatís Jr. as a 16-year-old and then, less than two years later, in the midst of a race for the 2016 AL Central title, traded the young phenom and Triple-A starter Erik Johnson to San Diego in exchange for the 34-year-old Shields, who Chicago hoped would complement their mix of southpaw starters Chris Sale, Carlos Rodón and José Quintana and lead them to a pennant. At the time, it was the Royals and White Sox competing for the division crown, but at the end of the season, the Indians would win the pennant, finishing eight games in front of second-place Detroit, 81–81 Kansas City and 78–84 Chicago, which fell apart after a 23–10 start to their campaign. The White Sox were willing to take that bet, though. They traded away a great player to chase that great moment, something that a franchise would love to be able to accomplish once a decade. The year prior to

12. Alex Cohen

that, the Royals won their first World Series in 40 years, and the White Sox were trying to keep the trophy in the division. Great moments come in more than just the form of championships, though. For Cohen, one of the biggest reliefs to him was the first of two no-hitters in the 2021 campaign.

To set the moment, one has to remember that while there was a 60-game Major League Baseball season in 2020, the minors were completely shut out. Players stayed home, stayed at spring training facilities and worked out or tried to find a way to practice without a full field of professional ballplayers. Most minor league employees were furloughed and many people were left to wonder if massive throngs of people would ever meet again within the confines of stadia for sporting events, concerts, beer festivals or any other gatherings while the wheels of government tried to formulate a response to the respiratory virus that would take as many people out of harm's way as possible. A host of the small community that populates the front offices in Minor League Baseball across the country opted to change career paths and head to different fields of work. Meanwhile, those who remained longed for the opportunity to entertain fans once more.

The moment for Cohen would come sooner than he could have imagined. He remembers the date, the number of pitchers used and the number of strikeouts as the Indianapolis Indians visited the Iowa Cubs on May 9, 2021,the first Sunday game of the season at Principal Park in Des Moines, Iowa. "After 600 some-odd days without baseball to be able to get life back at the park and to have the opportunity to call a no-hitter in the first series of the year.... That was something special," Cohen indulges. The game began with major league journeyman Shelby Miller on the mound. The Texas–born righty started his professional career with the Quad Cities River Bandits in 2009 and made his major league debut just three seasons later with the Saint Louis Cardinals. After bouncing up and down for a while, Miller found himself in Triple-A with the Cubs in 2021 and there, he spun three hitless innings, fanning five and walking one before passing the ball to the bullpen. Thirty-year-old Tommy Nance was up next. A career bullpen arm, the 6'6" pitcher would go the next three frames, matching Miller's line before the next reliever would enter. At this point, Iowa grabbed a one-run lead. Funnily enough, it was from Nance batting in the home half of the sixth, lifting a sacrifice fly to score Andrew Romine that broke the scoreless tie, eventually earning himself a win and paving the way for the final two pitchers to close out the contest. Southpaw Brad Wieck offered a

179

pair of hitless innings, ringing up five of the six hitters he faced before handing the ball to Ryan Meisinger, who closed out the game to earn his first of three saves that season.

It was a special moment, to be sure, fueled by a lot of players who would never dream of seeing their name on a top prospect list. Shelby Miller was the lone pitcher in that game to be lauded as a top-tier prospect. In 2012, after the Cardinals selected him in the first round of the draft, he was ranked the fifth-best prospect in all of Minor League Baseball, according to MiLB.com. By 2021, though, Miller had long since evaporated from those lists in various baseball publications. Those role players and guys who aren't labeled as future stars can sometimes have major impacts on teams, though. One of those guys has actually spent some significant time with the Iowa Cubs and was there while this chapter was being written in 2022. Dixon Machado has had his cup of coffee. He has spent part of four seasons in the majors—all of which were with the Detroit Tigers from 2015 to 2018. The Venezuelan played in 172 games and is a Swiss army knife, able to be slotted in anywhere on the infield in a pinch. His minor league journey began in 2009 and he had an international detour for a few years before coming back to the minors, where he found a home with the Iowa Cubs until the trade deadline (July 31, 2022) when the Cubs traded him to the San Francisco Giants for RHP Raynel Espinal, who never played a game in the Cubs system before being released and signed by Cincinnati. Machado is now in the Houston Astros system, playing for the Sugar Land Space Cowboys.

"He was a key part to the I–Cubs' 2019 Northern Division PCL championship before going to Korea for two years and now he's back in our clubhouse," Cohen says. "This is a guy who goes fishing with the pitchers, he eats dinner with the hitters and he'll come in and have a drink with the coaches. He's one of those guys. He interacts with everybody from the clubhouse attendant to the batboy to the broadcaster. He'll find some way, somehow, to relate to you and that's what makes him just a total team guy." Not only is he a great guy off the field who can bring the locker room together, but Cohen relays that he can really do a bit of everything. "He gets on base, he hits with runners in scoring position, he can hit anywhere in the lineup. He just sticks out in my mind as the guy who encompasses the minor league in the baseball game."

Machado's crowning achievement with the Iowa Cubs so far, though, was a walk-off homer against the New Orleans Baby Cakes in Iowa's second home game of the 2019 season, on April 11. The righty was slotted in the eight-hole and after New Orleans tied the game 4–4 in the top of the ninth, he came up with one out in the bottom of the inning. Righty Tommy Eveld, 6'5", was on the hill and tossed a 2–1 fastball over the heart of the plate that Machado crushed over the right-field bleachers. First-pitch temperature at 12:08 p.m. was 46 degrees in Des Moines. "It was like 40 degrees. He hit a home run over the left-field wall, over the skyboxes and into the parking lot. In a game that cold, I wouldn't think a ball would leave the infield, let alone leave the stadium and go into the parking lot, so I thought that was pretty impressive." Every year you have one or two guys who are just great clubhouse guys and keep the entire team loose. Most of the time, they are also the guys who do mountains of work in the community and who engage with the front office and the fan base. Machado is definitely one of those guys, but one 2022 Iowa Cubs player put a bit of a twist on how he inspired those around him to be better.

Narciso Crook was the first guy to the field every day. He was typically the last guy to go home at night, too. He's gotten his cup of coffee. He made his major league debut on June 30, 2022, and the Rowan College product went 1–8 at the dish before going back to Iowa. The outfielder always volunteered when there was an opportunity to do an appearance in the community or if a player needed to sign autographs prior to or following a game. He wouldn't just automatically sign autographs for fans, though. He made them earn the autograph. "He'll actually talk to the kids and he'll tell them that they won't get the autograph for free," Cohen explains. "He'll tell them that they need to go outside and do something nice for somebody else when [they] leave the ballpark. The kids are usually like, 'What?' and he'll say, 'You just need to do something nice—like make your mom dinner. Do the dishes. Just do something nice for someone else. If you can promise me you'll do that, I'll give you my autograph.' Whether the kids actually do it or not is irrelevant. It's the fact that he's making the kids think about doing something positive."

Crook makes the same impression everywhere he goes. On Iowa's second trip to Louisville in 2022, Cohen can remember the Bats' general manager joking that the Cubs could leave Crook in Louisville, because he'd love to have him on their team with the way that he had interacted with the fans, the ushers and members of his front office staff during his visit a few weeks prior. An example of how Crook relates to different staffers in a positive light is how he worked with Iowa's deaf photographer. "Narciso is learning sign language to try to communicate with him, and I think that that is really cool," Cohen says. "It's all basic stuff, but you can see Dylan, our deaf photographer, teach him different basic sign language prior to and after some games. It's just cool to see." Going that extra mile to learn how to communicate with a member of a team's game day staff is why, whether Crook goes on to have an amazing career or not, he will be remembered by so many people in Des Moines for a long time.

Cohen has traveled a lot in his career. Sure, it's one thing to mention all the home-to-home traveling he's done as he has broadcast games in Australia, the Southern League, the Pioneer League, the Midwest League, the Pacific Coast League and now the International League, but the day-to-day travel one accrues over the course of a career in baseball that spans over a decade also means that you spend a lot of time on buses and airplanes. So much so, that Cohen has carved out his own little spot in the St. Louis Airport that he uses for layovers. "It's right underneath the Starbucks. There's a bench I sleep at," Cohen tells me. "I know that area. I go there all the time. I've brought visiting broadcasters and players there, and they sleep there as well." But trips can sometimes take unexpected turns that don't include a few-hours-long power nap on a bench outside Starbucks. In August 2016, the Bowling Hot Rods were in the midst of a playoff race with five games remaining where they would take a trip from western Kentucky to northeast Ohio to take on the Lake County Captains.

At 3:30 in the morning, the bus halted on the side of the road, and it would not move again for quite some time. "We kept calling the bus company. At 4:30, 5:30, 6:30 in the morning. Eventually, the sun started to rise, so we got to watch the sun rise on the side of the road in Ohio," Cohen remembers. "Now it's completely bright outside and finally at 8 o'clock, whenever the bus company opens, somebody answers and is able to get help to us." The Hot Rods were playing a doubleheader that day. They finally got to their hotel at 11 a.m., headed to the stadium at 1 p.m., swept the Captains through a five-game series, and, on the final game in Lake County, won the division to clinch the playoffs. Of all the unlikely things that Cohen can think of from that trip, the one that really pops out is major league All-Star Brandon Lowe and him watching that sunrise from the side of the road in southern Ohio, just saying to each other that they never would have thought they would be right there in that moment. "Now he's in the big leagues and probably doesn't have to deal with that as frequently as we do in the minors," Cohen says.

Not all road trips end in delays, and every broadcaster has one or two trips that they really look forward to when they see it on the schedule prior to the start of the season. In 2022, that city for Cohen was Buffalo. The broadcaster knew he would spend six consecutive nights in upstate New York, so he set a goal of going to a different wings' place each night and writing a review of the wings. Cohen ended up having wings six days in a row, and he published his rankings of the establishments he tried on Twitter.

"I felt like the dude from *Super Size Me*. I thought that I was going to puke by the end of it," Cohen says. "It was well worth it, though. It was definitely a lot of fun." The Philadelphia native actually sampled only five wings' places because he went to Gabriel's Gate twice. The different restaurants in Buffalo he tried in order of his ranking are: Gabriel's Gate, Eddie Brady's, Duff's, Anchor Bar and Bada Bing. Gabriel's Gate started serving wings in the historic Allentown district about 50 years ago, according to their website. The restaurant embraces its history, with fireplaces inside, stone and hardwood accessories and pew-like booths where families can enjoy the delicious food. Cohen's description of the medium and barbecue wings he ordered is: "Meat tender to perfection, not overbearing amount of sauce, and medium was perfect amount of hot. Skin crisp but not burnt. Medium better than BBQ. Best wings I've ever had. Ranking 9.4/10."

The wings of Gabriel's Gate were good enough that Cohen considers the restaurant as one of the best of his on-the-road dining spots. There's one more restaurant that has served him some incredible food. In 2013, he drove with some friends to Jackson, Tennessee, on the final road trip of the season. They had a three-and-a-half-hour drive to Jackson from Huntsville, Alabama, and before they got to their destination, they stopped at Diddy's BBQ. "My friends looked up this place on Yelp that was in the middle of nowhere. It was this little shack that had Kool-Aid on tap, but it had the absolute best BBQ I've ever had," Cohen explains. "It literally looked like an old rundown house that had a very large kitchen in the back. It was incredible. It was Kool-Aid on tap, fried baloney sandwiches and an all-you-can-eat rib plate for $6.99 in the absolute middle of nowhere."

Cohen has a lot of hesitation when picking a favorite restaurant. There are so many good restaurants he's visited; he has a theme for each city he visits and he likes to revel in each place's specialty. But when thinking about the one moment in baseball history that he would like to have broadcast, that doesn't require any time. Without taking a breath, he goes into his explanation: "The 2008 World Series Champion Philadelphia Phillies' Brad Lidge strikeout with Carlos Ruiz catching.

Play-by-Play from the Minors

I would call that because I'm a Phillies fan and I would duplicate the Harry Kalas call calling them the world champions of baseball, and then I would pause for a minute and a half." That's the passion that Cohen brings to the game. Staying true to his roots, he'd call one of the most iconic moments of Phillies history, and he'd give the fans an opportunity to make the biggest impact, celebrating for the first time in almost 30 years.

13

Emma Tiedemann

Currently with the Portland Sea Dogs
Previously with the Lexington Legends, St. Paul Saints,
Medford Rogues and Mat-Su Miners

The broadcasting community isn't very large. Many of the people in this book are connected through a wealth of shared experiences. Every time a group of broadcasters meets, there's typically a pow-wow of conversations about top players seen, changes to the industry and web formatting that bonds all of us together or funny travel stories that everyone can relate to. Emma Tiedemann is one of the elite broadcasters in Minor League Baseball, as she's a part of an even smaller community within the broadcasting community. In 2022, there were only three women broadcasting in MiLB. Tiedemann is one of the original four women broadcasters, hired by the Lexington Legends for their 2018 campaign. She was the first-ever South Atlantic League female broadcaster, and she and Kirsten Karbach were the only female lead broadcasters in Minor League Baseball at the start of the 2018 season, according to an article written by Benjamin Hill in March of 2018. For Tiedemann, the path to baseball was carved out very early.

The group of women broadcasters is extraordinarily tight-knit. They didn't have the chance to all meet in person until the Legends decided to hold a panel in February of 2020. "It really helped solidify the group because until then, I had never met Jillian Gearin or Maura Sheridan. I had seen Kirsten Karbach a few times at Winter Meetings and met Melanie Newman in passing once in Dallas, so this led to all these awesome women meeting in one place. It's led to multiple group chats and Snapchat groups and has created such a strong group for us. We talk just about every day now," Tiedemann explains. "We're really the only people who can completely understand what we're all going for, not just as broadcasters, but also as women in a very male-dominated industry."

185

Part of a family of baseball royalty, Emma Tiedemann broke through as one of the first four women broadcasters in Minor League Baseball and has established herself as an elite talent in Portland, Maine (photograph courtesy Emma Tiedemann).

Seeing Kirsten do it helped Tiedemann believe that she could be successful as a broadcaster in baseball, so these panels and different moments that help recognize the incredible female talent throughout the minor leagues is important in paving the way for more women and girls to grow up and believe in themselves. Tiedemann especially feels that this is true now that she's in Portland, where she works with a female manager and a female athletic trainer. "For the first time in my career, I have women that I travel with. Because, up until this point, it was just me and a bunch of dudes who would travel the country together," Tiedemann says. "It's cool that girls can go to Sea Dogs games and see that there's a woman in the broadcast booth, but there's also a woman on the field and there's also a woman athletic trainer taking care of the guys too, so [they think,] 'I can do any of that.'"

One of the gratifying moments for Tiedemann after the gates open

13. Emma Tiedemann

is that a handful of parents bring their young daughters to the booth to have them meet her. "When that happens, I think it's the coolest thing ever. One of the great things about Minor League Baseball is our accessibility. In Portland, you can walk to my window and talk to me," Tiedemann glows. "When people bring their daughters up, I put a headset on them and introduce them to my producers to show them what it's like when you talk and hear yourself in the headset. I show them everything to spark their interest." Tiedemann enjoys being that inspiration, and a big reason why is because, for most of her life, she had someone very close to her inspire her to take the steps to get to where she is today.

The Texas native's *tutu*, which is Hawaiian for grandpa, is Bill Mercer, who by the time Emma was around was retired from broadcasting and was teaching at the University of North Texas. He was also filling in, broadcasting some games with Mike Capps for the Midland Rock-Hounds and working a bit with the Frisco RoughRiders. When he was younger, though, Mercer broadcast for the Texas Rangers, Chicago White Sox and even the Dallas Cowboys. His experience went beyond just the sporting world, as he was a news reporter who covered the John F. Kennedy assassination in 1963. Many of Mercer's stories can be found in his book *Play-by-Play: Tales from a Sports Broadcasting Insider*, which was published in 2007. Mercer both directly and indirectly was able to influence the beginning of Emma's career. The exact starting point came at age 15 for Tiedemann. When attending a women's basketball game at the University of Texas at Dallas, her tutu happened to have an extra headset with him and allowed his granddaughter to put the equipment on. "I just fell in love with play-by-play at that moment," Tiedemann remembers. "From that moment on, that's all I ever wanted to do, so when I went to the University of Missouri, I made it my goal to get to network one day."

To do that, her goal was to get better at baseball. It led her to Wikipedia, where she looked up every collegiate summer league in the country. She found the general manager in those leagues and emailed them with her resume and information to apply to become their broadcaster so she could gain some experience in baseball. "Only two responded. One was in Alaska and they offered me a job. I kept in touch with the other general manager that responded during that 2014 season, and later ended up accepting a job with them in 2015." Tiedemann explains how she started her career with the Mat-Su Miners and the Medford Rogues in Alaska and Oregon, respectively. She also confirms that she needed to continue to push for her dream. "Just working in those

Play-by-Play from the Minors

day-to-day baseball offices was a phenomenal experience," Tiedemann remembers. "Calling a game every single night and seeing how a team develops over the course of a season. Just the whole package made me fall in love with working in baseball."

When Emma was young, she would go to minor league games, attending Frisco RoughRiders and Round Rock Express games when her tutu was filling in for those teams. When Emma was finally old enough to drive, she became her tutu's driver to all the games and she would hang out in the press box and take in everything around her. One day, she got a bit more than she bargained for in Frisco. "I left the press box early in the game to get a drink of water and none other than Nolan Ryan is sitting there with his grandson watching the Rangers game," Emma remembers. "I thought, 'Oh my God! That's Nolan Ryan!' But I had to keep my composure." As a 16-year-old, meeting one of your childhood heroes is one thing, but then getting to hear that childhood hero analyze the game and talk about current players on your favorite team is something that is next-level cool. "I was sitting in the presence of Nolan *freaking* Ryan and they're talking about the Texas Rangers, my major league team. It was one of the coolest experiences and it still sticks with me to this day because you never know what could happen at a minor league game."

Tiedemann still needed to take another step to make it to that level after working collegiate summer league baseball, but it didn't take long for her to check the next box off the list. She found a job with the St. Paul Saints, who, at the time, were a part of the independent American Association, working under Sean Aronson, which prepared her to move to affiliated ball with the Lexington Legends. After attending baseball's Winter Meetings at Disney Springs, near Orlando, Florida, and interviewing with Lexington's front office staffers three times over the course of four days, Tiedemann was able to leave one of America's vacation capitals with the job of her dreams, holding one of baseball's affiliated broadcaster jobs. "I got the job over the course of those three days at Winter Meetings, and it was really a whirlwind of a process," Tiedemann recalls. She spent a pair of seasons in Lexington before interviewing and receiving her job with the Portland Sea Dogs.

She remembers finding out about the Sea Dogs opening from broadcaster Shawn Murnin and being in disbelief because Mike Antonellis had been in Portland for a long time, and it is one of the better MiLB markets to be in. Emma didn't know if she was ready for that opportunity, but her fiancé, Jesse, thought otherwise. "Jesse almost

188

physically pushed me to the computer and said, 'No, this is going to be great. You have to apply for this. They're a fantastic franchise and you have to at least put your name in the hat.'" Emma sent in her application and had a few interviews, and then the Sea Dogs flew her to Portland so she could see if she liked the town and ballpark before accepting the job.

Through that journey, Emma has grown a lot, and, like many broadcasters, says that sometimes it's difficult to believe how much your style changes over the course of a few years. One reason Emma was able to progress so quickly through the baseball world is the dedication of her tutu.

"He still listens to every game, whether it's baseball or it's the off-season and I'm doing basketball, he listens to everything. He used to stay up until three or four in the morning when I was in Alaska, critiquing my games," Tiedemann recalls. "He would send me these really long emails after every game so I could pick something each night to choose to work on, and it really has helped me grow and improve." The perspective her tutu instilled in her taught Tiedemann one of the greatest lessons she has learned while working in baseball: there's always something new you can work on.

"You can have the best inning you've ever had, and you can listen back and think, 'Well, maybe I could have done this better,' or 'I said he had two hits, but it was really his third,' but there's always room to improve what you're doing," Tiedemann explains. That attitude of never being satisfied and constantly striving for the best is a big reason why Tiedemann has been able to climb the ranks as quickly as she has.

Tiedemann grew up listening to more than just her tutu, though. She remembers Eric Nadel, the Ford C. Frick Award winner and Texas Rangers broadcaster, being the soundtrack of summer as she and her friends would sit by the pool. You can still hear some of Nadel in Tiedemann's broadcasts. "For Eric, it's his delivery that I really like. You can tell by the tone of his voice what's going on in the game. It's also the changes of his vocabulary. He's been doing it for decades with Texas, but every broadcast is unique for him."

While Emma has traveled in Alaska, the Pacific Northwest, and along the Eastern Seaboard, she says that after taking a look around, Portland, Maine, became one of her favorite cities in America.

"I got to experience Portland in the midst of a global pandemic where a baseball season was canceled, but was fortunate enough to be a part of a front office staff where the ownership group decided to keep everyone on staff," Tiedemann explains. "I got to see the city come back from all that and fall in love with this little city. We are one of the smallest markets in Double-A, but we already have double-digit sellouts this year, and just to see the dedication of the fans to this sport and to the Boston Red Sox has made me fall in love with Portland, Maine." Proximity and timing certainly had some influence on Maine stealing Tiedemann's heart, but the old-school New England feel is hard to get away from. Seemingly coming from another generation, Portland holds to its tradition, as there are very few chain restaurants and stores in the city. Nearly everything is locally owned, of which Tiedemann is a big fan. One of her favorite places to go is Portland Lobster Co., which is in the Old Port district—right on the Fore River. The restaurant brands itself as "the place where locals go" and their lobster roll has won various awards, including the Best of Portland Poll every year since 2015. "When you're in the Old Port, you can start at Portland Lobster Co. and just adventure down the different streets with the cobblestones. It's just such a fun New England town that's right on the ocean," Tiedemann says.

For her, the beauty of Portland, Maine, is about more than just the local bites to eat, though. Her go-to adventure on an off day is to pack a book and drive 15 minutes to Scarborough Beach State Park. "It's me and it's a whole bunch of grandparents reading books on the beach typically," Tiedemann laughs. "There's a food truck that stops by occasionally and it's cool that we're all just quietly reading our books and looking out over the ocean on our Mondays together. It's a pretty cool experience."

While her favorite foods and sights may be in her current hometown, Tiedemann really enjoys the historic experience of going to Reading. History is a mainstay for the Pennsylvania town, which first hosted baseball in the early 1900s. That history is honored at FirstEnergy Stadium where you can see the traces of the longest active affiliation in Minor League Baseball—where it has has come from and where it has ventured to. The Reading Fightin Phils are about an hour away from the Philadelphia Phillies, which they've been attached to since 1967, when the Phillies became their parent club. It isn't just its history that makes Reading an attractive place to go to a minor league game, though. Tiedemann knows a lot about the crowd and fan experiences that are a part of going to games at Reading. The ballpark has a small capacity for a Double-A stadium, so every night the yard is packed with fans. It all

13. Emma Tiedemann

starts before the game. "I always like to pay attention to the pre-game festivities because there's always so much going on," Tiedemann says. "It feels like they always have 20 to 30 first pitches, but they always start on time. It's really fun to experience."

One of the unique aspects of going to a game in Reading is the Crazy Hot Dog Vendor. A member of the front office dresses in a wig with a paper cap and a red-and-white striped vest with a button-down shirt underneath and ... well ... he's riding an ostrich. It all started with the team's graphic designer, Matt Jackson, who donned the costume for nearly a decade, according to a Paul Caputo article on SportsLogos.net, but eventually he retired from the part and now the Crazy Hot Dog Vendor is a new person. Despite the influx of people wearing the costume, fans remain enthralled with the tradition and it is a regionally famous part of going to Reading games. There are now fan sections that show up, also dressed as the ostrich-riding person, waiting for him to come out and sling free hot dogs in between innings. "He comes out in an inflatable ostrich and throws hot dogs to the crowd. They have T-shirts of him, he's on the video board a bunch, he's awesome," Tiedemann says. "They actually have post-game live music and drinks and I've gotten to meet him. It's a good time."

Reading is known for its baseball history; the roots of the game began not far from FirstEnergy Stadium. But Tiedemann's minor league roots took shape in the red dirt of Lexington, Kentucky, and, in her tenure with the Lexington Legends, the Kansas City Royals made an impact on that city that will never be forgotten. In 2018–19 the Legends (now the Counter Clocks) won back-to-back South Atlantic League championships in their last two seasons in affiliated baseball. During those two seasons, the Royals had 17 future major leaguers make their way through Whitaker Bank Ballpark (now Counter Clocks Field), and there are likely more to be coming in the near future as Kansas City continues its rebuild beyond the 2022 season. If Tiedemann had to pick which of the two teams she thought was better than the other, she would side with the 2018 squad, because of the number of guys who have gotten called up to The Show from that team already and the impact that they have had for the Royals and for other teams.

"Nick Pratto, MJ Melendez, Carlos Hernández and Sebastián Rivero, you name it and they did it. It was a pretty epic season and it ended with a championship," Tiedemann remembers. If she were to pick the greatest moment she's witnessed, though, she points to how the 2019 team ended their season. "I guess you could say the 2018 championship was a little tamer than the 2019 one with the walk-off in the 13th inning, but the 2018 Lexington Legends was a pretty special team."

Tiedemann knew that the 2018 Lexington Legends were dominant, but it took until the playoffs for her to realize just how special that team was. It was in the Legends' first series that season vs. the Rome Braves, where the Legends swept Rome two games to nothing. In the first game of the series, Lexington won 3–1 at home before busing down to Georgia for a pivotal Game 2. Daniel Lynch hopped on the rubber and twirled four scoreless frames before handing the ball off to Daniel Duarte, who spun three one-hit innings before allowing the bullpen to close out a 6–0 shutout to advance to the championship.

"I was following the game in Lexington, and I remember being so impressed that we were having success against a team that we didn't know if we were going to win [against] or not," Tiedemann recalls. "After seeing us have that type of success in the first round, it was at that point that I knew that we had it in the bag."

That 2018 team was absolutely dominant, but the championship moment that Tiedemann had the opportunity to call in 2019 was something that can't be compared to anything else that she's experienced in her career thus far. The Legends once again skipped through the first round of the South Atlantic League playoffs with relative ease before they met up with the Hickory Crawdads for the championship series. After winning the first two games at L.P. Frans Stadium 6–4 and 7–0, it was time for the Legends to come home to try to win the series. They dropped Game 4 by a score of 5–1 and had one last opportunity to win a championship in front of their home fans after winning it on the road in 2018. Game 4 of the championship series took place on Friday, September 13, at Whitaker Bank Ballpark, and it turned out to be one of the most epic pitcher's duels of the 2019 season.

Legends starter Zach Haake went six no-hit innings before getting pulled for the bullpen. It took Lexington until the home half of the sixth to get on the board. With Jeison Guzmán on second, Nathan Eaton was able to lace a single to right to put Lexington in front, 1–0. Hickory would answer promptly in the top of the seventh as Pedro González smashed a solo homer to right center to tie the game. Both bullpens picked up right where the starters left off, and the two teams had to go to extra innings. Neither team was able to plate a run in the 10th, 11th and 12th innings, even with fatigue setting in and a moment looming larger than any in that game had played before. In the bottom of the 13th, on Friday the 13th, Eric Cole drew a walk to begin the frame. Then

13. Emma Tiedemann

Chris Hudgins and Eaton were unable to reach safely, creating a two-out opportunity for Reed Rohlman.

"Rohlman came up and hit that walk-off two-run home run to right field," Tiedemann recites. "I blacked out and then I said the word *dinger* in a championship call. It was pretty epic. Rohlman retired after that, and why not? He got to retire on a high note." The Clemson product had 15 career homers in the minors, and he ended his career with a towering blast to give Lexington their second championship in as many years, and their first at home. The only other championship Lexington had in the South Atlantic League came in 2001 when they were declared co-champions as the post-season was canceled in the wake of the September 11 terrorist attacks. The emotion was palpable, both for the fans and for our broadcaster. "It was surreal in the moment, because Rohlman clicked after having a rough night offensively, and you just knew the ball was gone off the bat," Tiedemann remembers. "It's not the same winning a championship on the road, because fans leave pretty quickly, so it was great getting to stay and celebrate in front of the fans."

That moment, and that iconic call, get to live on every time Tiedemann looks at her championship ring. The front office staff inscribed "Dinger" on the inside of her ring. "They did inscribe 'dinger' on the inside of the ring, because I did call it a walk-off dinger on the broadcast. It is immortalized on my championship ring," Tiedemann says. "I hinted at it, because people were getting inscriptions on theirs, so I joked and said, 'Maybe I should get "dinger" on mine,' and then they showed up and sure enough, it was there."

That 2018 Lexington Legends team had to face a real tough opponent when the Hagerstown Suns came to town. A young player in the Nationals system left his indelible mark on Minor League Baseball and all who crossed paths with him, rising from Class-A ball to the majors in one season. Juan Soto was cut from a different cloth than most minor leaguers, but the star spent more time with the Hagerstown Suns than any other MiLB team he played for that season, and Tiedemann can remember what happened when he visited Whitaker Bank Ballpark. "I was walking around with stat packs or game notes to take them to the clubhouse and I just remember thinking, 'Wow. That sounds different.' And lo and behold, it was Juan Soto in the cages. Then a few weeks later, he was a big leaguer."

A few years later, Soto was bargaining to sign one of the largest contracts in MLB history because of the impact he had on the game prior to his 24th birthday. Soto broke through to the majors as a 19-year-old

193

and clubbed over 118 homers while slashing .291/.427/.537. In the first five years of his career, he finished top five in MVP voting twice and second in Rookie of the Year voting in 2018. Needless to say, Soto has fulfilled the prophecies of many people who watched him transcend Minor League Baseball during the 2018 season.

Not all guys end up signing mega-deals and becoming blockbuster headliners, but there are some behind-the-scenes players who are incredibly important to the team's success at the end of the year. While in Indy ball with the St. Paul Saints, Emma ran into a 6'4" right-handed pitcher, Mark Hamburger, who she says is as unique as his name. In 2017, Hamburger got the opportunity to pitch for his hometown team after the Texas Rangers gave him a cup of coffee in 2011. When he went back down to AAA for a few years before trying to extend his career in the American Association, Hamburger was sure not to be one of the bitter veterans who sometimes plague a clubhouse. The Minnesotan drove an old station wagon and rode a longboard around the ballpark, so you could always tell when he was coming through the tunnel or around the concourse.

"He was just a really fun guy to be around. He was an absolute fan favorite and he was lights out on the mound," Tiedemann remembers. "He was in a lot of our videos, and our videos were wacky in Saint Paul, so you had to be a character to be in them, but Mark was definitely one of those guys." That longboard is something she'll always remember, though. "I just remember walking from the parking lot to the stadium through the tunnel, and he would high-five you while riding his longboard across. I'll never forget that." Hamburger had a great season that year, but would move on to the Australian Baseball League and hop around independent baseball until 2018, when he played his final season professionally.

One guy who Tiedemann would love to see make his major league debut is Ryan Fitzgerald. In 2018, Fitzgerald was signed as a free agent out of the Gary SouthShore RailCats and has slowly climbed his way up the ladder of the Red Sox farm. In 2021, he found himself in Portland. In 95 games, he hit .271 and added a career-high (at the time) 13 homers and 49 RBI in a breakout season for the former Creighton Bluejay. "He went from a guy who was playing in independent baseball, where you play to win, to going to Minor League Baseball, where it's more about developing guys, and it was really exciting to watch him because every day he would play like he would live or die on that game," Tiedemann explains. He did all that while moving from being an everyday shortstop to playing shortstop, second base and a few games in the outfield or first base. "He was never supposed to be the guy, but now he has put himself in the discussion of maybe getting called up. He went to major league spring training ..., hit a bunch of home runs and is now a fan favorite in Boston." That type of gritty play is contagious and has really pushed Tiedemann to follow along with the utility player even while he's up in Triple-A with Worcester. In 2023, Fitzgerald is still a step away from getting called up and has drawn the intrigue of Red Sox bloggers, but despite significant success in his last few seasons, he has not been added to the 40-man roster and was passed up for a promotion earlier this season by Enmanuel Valdez, who was called up to replace an injured Yu Chang.

Not every aspect of working in Minor League Baseball is as glamorous as championships and seeing players realize their potential and succeed at the next level. Sometimes you sign up to work for a summer league team and they change leagues, so you end up spending a large portion of your summer riding a bus. That was the case for Tiedemann when she worked for the Medford Rogues. A lot of the teams that the Rogues played were down in California, which isn't a short trip away from Oregon. On one trip, the team realized that as they were heading southbound, the bus was getting progressively hotter. They eventually found out that the air conditioning on the bus was no longer functioning.

"It was probably 95 to 100 degrees on the bus, and we're still driving down to Chico. We're dying on the bus because it's so hot, and out of nowhere, I feel a big gust of air," Tiedemann reminisces. "So I look back, and the players have busted out the emergency exit on the roof, they have their shirts off and they are taking turns sticking their head out of the roof so that they can get a breath of fresh air." Unfortunately for Tiedemann and the Rogues, the terrible ride was only the beginning. As is the case for most collegiate summer league teams, after they made it to their destination, they would play their game and head immediately back home. When the team finished playing their contest, they were ready to load up the bus, only to find out that now the bus had entirely broken down. The team decided to make the most of the time that they had to wait for a new bus to come along, so they decided to play football in the outfield while they waited for a new bus to pick them up.

Tiedemann became the quarterback of that temporary team. "For a lot of those players, that's when they found out that I'm from Texas, so I can throw a football. So, they would go out and run routes while I would throw the ball to them. It definitely taught me who played football in high school and who didn't," Tiedemann explains. "I'm sure the coaches were watching and just hoping that no one would take a bad route to the ball and hurt themselves," she adds, laughing about the experience. They played with the stadium lights on until midnight, tossing the ball around and having a good time, and Tiedemann said her biggest goal was just to live in the moment.

At the end of the day, that's what a baseball game is about. Broadcasters talk about the moment a ball leaves the park or smacks into a catcher's mitt for the final out, and we use the moments in between the action to tell stories about different moments in players' lives or critical moments in a team's history. Thinking back, if there were one moment in baseball history that Tiedemann could call herself, she'd mirror the goal that many broadcasters have: to call a World Series. The World Series that Emma would want to inject herself into is one that had a lot of passionate fans waiting on it. She would broadcast the Cubs breaking their 108-year curse at Progressive Field in 2016. She would want to call the Michael Martínez groundout to Kris Bryant in the bottom of the 10th inning to seal the deal and end the drought. She would most want to pause to capture the polarizing reaction that the fans at Progressive Field had as cheers from the Chicagoans who had traveled burst through the crowd mic.

One reason Tiedemann sees the significance and the passion of that fan base, and what the moment that ended the Billy Goat Curse meant to so many people, is that in 2022 she had the opportunity to visit Cooperstown on an off day for the Sea Dogs. While walking through the halls of the museum, she stopped at the exhibit honoring the 2016 World Series champions, and naturally, there were some Cubs fans who were also there as the museum replayed critical moments from the last game on a screen. "I was with some people from Chicago and they all got a little emotional as the final play looped through with the call about them ending their drought," says Tiedemann. Who knows, maybe one day fans will be hearing one of Tiedemann's calls in the Hall of Fame. She's already broken some barriers and climbed her way into the conversation about All-Star broadcasters in Minor League Baseball.

Index

Index

Printed in the USA
CPSIA information can be obtained
at www.ICGtesting.com
LVHW050244161023
761156LV00006B/912